Baedeker

D0785426

Dresden

www.baedeker.com

Verlag Karl Baedeker

SIGHTSEEING HIGHLIGHTS ★ ★

Dresden's princes were impassioned art lovers. They collected beautiful and valuable things that give the city its distinctive character: the Altstadt is packed with ancient splendour and unique cultural treasures.

★★ Brühlsche Terrasse
Promenaders enjoy the view of Elbe and Neustadt, and a cup of coffee, on the »balcony of Europe«! ▶ page 162

★★ Frauenkirche
People from all over the world made rebuilding possible. ▶ page 178

★★ Galerie Neue Meister
From the Romantics via »Die Brücke« artists to Baselitz, Penck and Richter. ▶ page 185

★★ Gemäldegalerie Alte Meister
With the great names of European painting, one of the finest collections of paintings in the world draws in visitors. ▶ page 189

★★ Großsedlitz Baroque garden
One of Saxony's most perfect gardens, thanks to the sculptures and *Still Music*. ▶ page 201

★★ Hofkirche
This Baroque church has Permoser's Rococo pulpit, a Silbermann organ and Wettin burial crypt. ▶ page 203

★★ Meissen
The »cradle of Saxony« with a historic Altstadt, Albrechtsburg, cathedral and the famous porcelain factory. ▶ page 216

★★ Moritzburg
Set among ponds, with 300-year-old leather wall-hangings and the Feather Room. ▶ page 226

Alte Meister picture gallery
Raphael's Sistine Madonna

Meissen porcelain factory
See porcelain being painted in the w

✶✶ Pillnitz
Light elegance and serenity on the Elbe – the Wettin summer residence inspired by China, and home to Europe's oldest camellia. ▶ page 237

✶✶ Sächsische Schweiz
The Romantics' picture-book landscape, charming little towns like Pirna, Wehlen and Bad Schandau, bizarre cliffs and woods – a paradise for hikers and climbers. ▶ page 249

✶✶ Bastei in Rathen
Fantastic viewpoint high above the Elbe! Nearby is the open-air rock theatre.
▶ page 255

✶✶ Schloss
Former Wettin residence, now home to art and science. From the Hausmannturm there is a wonderful view of the Altstadt.
▶ page 260

✶✶ Grünes Gewölbe
Europe's most splendid museum of jewels and treasures in the Schloss – one of the gems includes the largest green diamond in the world. ▶ page 265

✶✶ Semper Opera
World-famous, with a grand tradition: the brilliant performances and beautiful building are a treat for ear and eye.
▶ page 267

✶✶ Theaterplatz
Dresden's most beautiful square is surrounded by magnificent buildings: Schloss, Hofkirche, Zwinger and Semper Opera. ▶ page 271

✶✶ Zwinger
World-famous masterpiece of Baroque architecture and sculpture, with one of the most important porcelain collections in the world, and a valuable collection of splendid weaponry in the armoury.
▶ page 277

Schloss Moritzburg
A jewel surrounded by water

Semper Opera
Musical delight

BAEDEKER'S BEST TIPS

Knowing a city's highlights is important for a successful stay, but it gets really exciting when you know a bit more than most others: so read Baedeker's best tips!

◼ Historic view
How did Dresden look in 1756? The panorama shows you. ▶ **page 41**

◼ Jazz, Jazz, Jazz
Brilliant musicians to carry you away!
▶ **page 128**

◼ Igeltour
Unconventional themed tours somewhat off the tourist trail. ▶ **page 129**

◼ Wenzel's hearty fare
Do you like Bohemian dumplings, beer and pancakes? ▶ **page 145**

Schloss Wackerbarth
Taste wine and sekt in the state vineyard

Villa Marie
A wonderful place to relax directly beneath the Blaues Wunder bridge

Yenidze
Once a tobacco company – now a fairytale venue

Dresden, city of music
▶ page 52

BACKGROUND

PRACTICALITIES

Pearl figure in the Grünes Gewölbe
► page 266

SIGHTS FROM A to Z

TOURS

From the Kunstakademie »Fama« trumpets Dresden's fame out over the city roofs.

Background

DRESDEN HAS AN EXCEPTIONAL MUSICAL TRADITION – HERE IN THE ZWINGER COURTYARD, FOR EXAMPLE, WHERE THE KREUZCHOR, THE PHILHARMONIC ORCHESTRA AND THE DRESDEN SYMPHONY ORCHESTRA ARE PERFORMING.

BAROQUE AND HI-TECH

»Dresden enjoys a magnificent and noble setting amidst hills along the river Elbe; they keep their distance, as if too much in awe to come any closer«, wrote Heinrich von Kleist.

The Elbe winds around the centre of Dresden like half a figure-of-eight, with the Neustadt (New Town) on the right bank and Altstadt (Old Town) on the left. Canaletto captured the picturesque quality of historic Dresden, which resembles an architectural composition painted onto the landscape. The renown of the Saxon court, its scenic setting, its buildings and art collections, music and artistic life roused keen expectations in all who came here, and they were seldom disappointed. Dresden's princes were so addicted to art and art collecting that they gathered items from all over the world which can still be admired today: exquisite porcelain and famous paintings. The most important museums in Dresden are the Gemäldegalerie Alte Meister (Old Masters picture gallery), the Grünes Gewölbe (Green Vault), and the porcelain collection. They are the bedrock of the world reputation of state collections that comprise eleven museums in total.

Silhouette
The Elbe seems to have been created solely to reflect the Altstadt buildings.

Dresden's citizens are proud to have maintained the classical traditions of the Saxon court even during the GDR years – the art collections, the famous choirs and orchestras, and the opera. With its Staatskapelle and Philharmonie, Dresden has two world-famous orchestras, and the Semper Opera is one of the most popular opera houses in the world, giving some 300 performances every year. Yet Dresden's reputation as city of culture does not rely exclusively on the past; it also has a wide-ranging theatre scene that delights in experimentation!

Dresden's Memory

»Pain and fear have a long memory«, as Erich Kästner recalled in *Als ich ein kleiner Junge war* (When I Was a Little Boy), writing of the bombing that reduced Dresden to rubble and ashes on the night of 13 February 1945. This inferno is still an open wound affecting every de-

Music in stone
In the Zwinger the sculpted figures and décor of the Nymphenbad seem to flow out of the stone – everything is in flux, like the fountains.

Stallions on parade
Superb horses are on show every September at the stallion parade in Schloss Moritzburg.

Cultural highlights live
The Semper Opera's famous ensemble ensures that most performances are sold out, like this one of Verdi's Don Carlos.

Dresden's promenade
The Brühlsche Terrasse, named after Count Brühl, offers a good view of Neustadt and the river with its paddle-steamers.

Exquisite porcelain
August the Strong gave the Prussians 600 of his cavalrymen in exchange for 151 Chinese »dragoon« vases, on show in the porcelain collection.

Côte de Sax
A little sand, a few deck chairs and a couple of palm trees transform the Elbe bank in summer into the Côte de Sax, with view of the Altstadt panorama.

bate about the future of the city centre. Many people still base plans for the future on the pre-World War II Dresden, which was one of the richest cities in Germany, and one of the loveliest in Europe. Under Augustus the Strong and his son Friedrich August II in the 18th century Dresden became a much-admired Baroque jewel, and some people still like to celebrate everything that harks back to the Baroque era. Usually there is a discernible wish not to tamper with any vestige of former splendours that were saved after the deluge of bombs – and to reconstruct as much of the historic glory as possible. Not everything can rise from the ashes, but the rebuilding of what is vital to the citizens of Dresden, the beloved heart of the city and the famous »Canaletto view« of the Altstadt, culminated in the completion of the new Frauenkirche. Outside the Altstadt, where Dresden's citizens react less strongly to change, there have been opportunities for contemporary architecture, as in the transparent Sächsischer Landtag (Saxon Parliament), the minimalist stone cube of the Neue Synagoge (New Synagogue) and the Gläserne Manufaktur (Factory of Glass).

Appeal to the Senses

Traditional splendour on one side of the river and the sensual delights of Neustadt pub life and gastronomy on the other, preservation of Baroque treasures on one hand and development of technology on the other: during the GDR era the city was already an important scientific and hi-tech centre. The Dresden region is in the vanguard of micro-electronics: after German reunification the regional capital was able to attract Europe's most up-to-date chip manufacturers and research organizations such as the Max Planck Institute, which now make Dresden one of Germany's leading biotechnology centres. Dresden has everything: a fine cityscape, unique cultural treasures and, all around, beautiful scenery that is among the best of any large German city. Cycle along the Elbe valley, since 2004 a Unesco World Heritage site, and enjoy a good view from the water meadows of the castles, mansions and villas on the hills along the river. There is a paddle steamer to Pillnitz, and the »Lössnitzdackel« (Lössnitz dachshund) train carries visitors to the hunting grounds of Schloss Moritzburg. Just outside Dresden is the porcelain manufacturing town of Meissen, and it is not far to the wonderfully romantic cliffs of the Sächsische Schweiz (Saxon Switzerland). Plenty of good reasons for a trip to Dresden ...

National park
The Königstein fortress commands a view of the picture-book landscape of the Sächsische Schweiz (Saxon Switzerland).

Facts

Here is a quick survey of what you need to know about one of the most popular German cities, some of the consequences of post-1989 restructuring, and why the Elbe valley around Dresden is referred to as »Silicon Saxony«.

Population · Economy

Population

Dresden has a population of 507,500, still considerably below its **Population density** highest mark of 649,250 in 1933, but more than the total of 454,250 at the end of World War II. This figure had risen to 521,000 by 1981, but fell again after German unification to 476,600 in 1990, as residents who saw no good employment propects left the city. Since then, however, the population of Dresden has been growing again. The period of most rapid increase was during the industrialization of the years 1885 to 1916, when it rose from 246,000 to 528,000.

Dresden is an episcopal seat both of the Lutheran Church and of the ◄ Religion Roman Catholic Church. Only one-quarter of Dresden's citizens have any religious affiliation: 17.5% belong to the Lutheran Church, 4.7% to the Roman Catholic Church, and 1.5% to the Jewish faith or other religions.

Economy

Dresden's emergence as an **industrial city** began in the first half of **Development** the 19th century and took it to fourth place in Germany by the end of the century, as measured by the number of people employed in industry.

Dresden's reputation as an industrial centre was based on light engineering, precision mechanics, optics and electro-technology. The city maintained this profile after 1945, with a strong focus on collaboration with research establishments. Shortly after German reunification 38% of the city's workforce were employed in manufacturing, predominantly by Robotron (computers, electronic components), Pentacon (cameras, optical equipment), Nagema (food-processing and packaging machinery), air-conditioning and cooling technology, electrical engineering, Germed pharmaceuticals and the Dresden aviation works. Economic and currency union with the west, and separation from Comecon in the east, meant that these companies lost their markets almost entirely. For individuals, restructuring after unification meant above all anxiety about jobs, or actual unemployment.

Although the new beginning was difficult for Dresden's economy, today it may be deemed to have succeeded: since 1990 the number of businesses has trebled to more than 40,000.

Today Dresden has more than 750 companies with 20 or more employees. Most have to do with electronics, information and communications technology, electro-technology, engineering, plant con- **Industry**

← *Peter Kulka designed the new Saxon parliament building, the first such building in the East German states.*

Facts and Figures Dresden

© Baedeker

Dresden •
Germany

Capital of the Free State of Saxony

Lage
▶ latitude 51° 02′ north
▶ longitude 13° 44′ east

Area
▶ area of city: 328.5 sq km/127 sq mi
of which 37% is built up
62% green spaces

By comparison
▶ 4th-largest city in Germany by area
after Berlin, Hamburg, Cologne

Government
▶ 10 city districts
▶ seat of state parliament and prime
minister of Saxony

Population
▶ total population 507,500
population density 1528 persons per sq
km/3961 per sq mi

By comparison
▶ 13th-largest city in Germany by population

Economy
▶ centre of the upper Elbe valley con-
urbation (between Riesa and Czech
border) employment
▶ 72.1% services, trade, transport, public
sector
13.9% manufacturing
10.9 construction
1.7% energy
1.3% agriculture, forestry
▶ rate of unemployment (2007):
13.7%, the lowest in any city of the
former GDR, but with a disproportion-
ately large number of women (45%)
▶ average annual income per head:
€ 14,837
▶ tourism: 9.8 million visitors per year
(6th place in Germany after Berlin,
Munich, Hamburg, Frankfurt, Cologne)

*Dresden's city arms show the Meissen
lion and Landsberg pales, the oldest
ruler's emblem of the House of Wettin.*

struction, environmental technology, photo/optics/fine mechanics, pharmaceuticals and cosmetics, printing and publishing, foodstuffs and luxury articles, and building materials. In line with earlier tradition, **micro-electronics** is firmly established in Dresden once more, making the city one of the most highly regarded German hi-tech centres. Infineon has an ultra-modern factory for 16-megabite chips; the American company Advanced Micro Devices (AMD) has one chip factory, and another is under construction. This makes Dresden Europe's second-largest centre in this field, surpassed only by Grenoble; the Dresden region is a world leader among micro-electronic centres, and has been dubbed **»Silicon Saxony«**. 22,000 people in and around Dresden are employed in the semiconductor industry. Further well-known Dresden firms are ABB Energy Construction Dresden, the leading East German cable producer, Asta Medica (formerly Arzneimittelwerke Dresden), the largest pharmaceutical producer in the former GDR, Gruner & Jahr, which operates one of the most modern printing works in Europe, Philip Morris, which has taken over the Vereinigte Zigarettenfabriken and produces the popular East German brands F 6 and Karo, German Aerospace Airbus and AEG Starkstromanlagen (high-voltage power plants). There is also some production of cameras, at a relatively modest level, by Kamerawerke Dresden (formerly Pentacon). Volkswagen AG does something very special on the edge of the Grosser Garten: in the Gläserne Manufaktur (Factory of Glass) VW's top model, the Phaeton, is assembled by hand.

Dresden City Districts and Outlying Districts

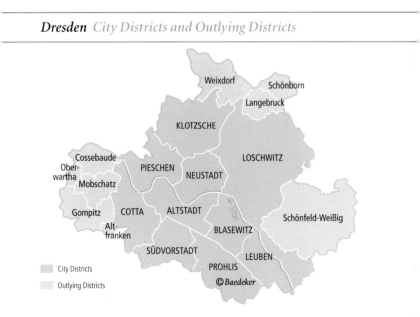

Weixdorf · Schönborn · Langebruck · KLOTZSCHE · Cossebaude · Ober-wartha · LOSCHWITZ · PIESCHEN · Mobschatz · NEUSTADT · Gompitz · COTTA · ALTSTADT · Schönfeld-Weißig · Alt-franken · BLASEWITZ · SÜDVORSTADT · LEUBEN · PROHLIS

City Districts
Outlying Districts
©Baedeker

Since the end of World War II Dresden has excelled in forging close **Science and** links between industry and science : research is undertaken in no less **research** than nine Fraunhofer institutes, four Leibniz institutes and three Max Planck institutes, and at the Technical University, especially in the fields of cell biology, genetics, medicine and pharmacology.
There are also technology, bio-innovation and centres for business start-ups. The emphasis is on technology-orientated research (material sciences, surface refinement, information and communications technology). Dresden now has the broadest and most powerful research capability in the east of Germany. For this reason the Stifterverband für die deutsche Wissenschaft (Sponsorship Association for German Science) chose Dresden as the »City of Science 2006«.

Although the city's importance as an economic and scientific centre **Tourism** is growing, tourism is still the largest employer. Dresden is one of the prime destinations for German city tourism. 9.8 million visitors come to Dresden every year, two thirds of them as day-trippers from the former West Germany. 1.5 million per year come from abroad, with Americans topping the list, followed by the Swiss, Japanese and British.

← *The VW Phaeton is fitted on the maple floor of the Gläserne Manufaktur, flooded with light.*

City History

Under Augustus the Strong Dresden became a princely residence of European significance. Napoleon proclaimed it the capital of the Kingdom of Saxony. It grew to be a major city, was destroyed on 13 February 1945, was rebuilt, experienced the Socialist years and German reunification. In 2006 Dresden looked back on 800 years of history.

Slav Settlement
and German Conquest

c600	Slav settlement
10th century	German conquest by King Heinrich I
1206	»Dresdene« first mentioned
1292	Town charter granted
1403	Altendresden, now Neustadt, granted town charter

In the 10th century King Heinrich I subjugated the Slavs, who had settled in the Elbe valley around the year 600, and built a castle in Meissen, from which to convert the land east of the Elbe to Christianity. The Wettin dynasty began in 1089 with Heinrich von Eilenburg, Margrave of Meissen, and ruled for more than 800 years.. **Wettin dynasty**

The area that is now the city of Dresden was in the middle of the district of Nisan, which fell to the province of Meissen in 1144. The first mention of »Nisani«, a port on the banks of the Elbe, in 1147 predates the foundation of the actual city of Dresden. From the mid-12th century St Mary's Church, later the Frauenkirche, stood in the centre of this settlement. In the mid-13th century the margraves built a castle on the Taschenberg hill, not far from the church. Close by, the Elbe meets the road from the main citadel of Meissen via Pirna to Bohemia, and the important Frankish road from Nuremberg via the silver mining centre of Freiberg to Cracow. There was initially a ford across the river, and from the mid-12th century a wooden bridge. A stone bridge, one of the earliest on record in the region, is mentioned in 1287.

The first document referring to **»Dresdene«** dates from 1206; a document of 1216 refers to Dresden as a »town«. In 1234 the Kreuzkapelle was added to the Church of St Nicholas (built c1170), in order to house a relic of the Cross; from the 14th century the church was therefore called Kreuzkirche (Church of the Cross). In 1292 Dresden was granted its town charter. After 1382 Margrave Wilhelm I began to extend the castle to create a royal residence; the original building of c1230 stood on what is still the palace precinct. At the end of the 14th century Dresden, with its outlying districts and Altendresden (Neustadt), had approx. 5,000 inhabitants. The town's municipal regulations, the »Dresdner Willkür«, date from before 1400. The Right of Staple granted in 1455 for merchandise and the Elbe trade promoted the town's development by stipulating that all

← *View of the Great Court in the Schloss, reconstructed in Renaissance style in recent years* shipping should stop to offer its goods for sale in Dresden. Altendresden, the present-day Neustadt on the right bank of the Elbe, is first documented in 1350 and had its own municipal regulations from 1403.

Residence of the Wettin Dynasty

1485	Leipzig Partition
1539	Introduction of the Reformation

Leipzig partition Elector Ernst of the House of Wettin and his brother Albrecht, Margrave of Meissen, resided permanently in the city from 1464 and had the small **castle** extended on a lavish scale to make it into a palace, on the site where the Schloss exists today. With the Leipzig Partition of the Wettin possessions of 1485 – the brothers Ernst and Albrecht divided Saxony between them – Dresden became the residence of the Albertine line. The court encouraged crafts and trade.

The great fire of 1491 destroyed half the city. When the fortifications were rebuilt from 1520 to 1529, the village around the Frauenkirche

Earliest view of the city of Dresden: engraving by Heinrich van Cleef (1565)

was drawn into the city. Up to that time the settlement around the Frauenkirche, which was originally Sorbian (i.e. a Slav community), and the German city of Dresden, encircled by city walls from 1299, had existed alongside one another. Nevertheless, throughout the Middle Ages, the Frauenkirche was Dresden's main parish church. The principal economic activity during this time was cloth-making and the cloth trade.

Although **Martin Luther** preached in Dresden's castle chapel as early as 1518, Duke Georg der Bärtige (George the Bearded) was able to suppress all attempts at church reform during his reign, 1500–39. It was his successor, Duke Heinrich der Fromme (Henry the Pious) who brought the Reformation into the duchy, and thereby into Dresden, in 1539.

Reformation

As a result of the Reformation the monasteries were dissolved; their possessions were taken over by the councils of Dresden and Altendresden (Neustadt).

> **? DID YOU KNOW ...?**
>
> ■ ... that Saxon is the model for the standard form of the German language? Luther's translation of the Bible, and in consequence the greater part of the modern written language, is based on a form of German used in Saxony for official purposes. Luther used this form as it incorporated written linguistic forms which were widely known.

In 1547 Duke Moritz (ruled 1541–53) obtained **the status of Elector** for the Albertine rulers of Saxony. His reign marked the beginning of Electoral Saxony's rise to become one of the leading German states in political, economic, urban planning and cultural terms. In 1549 he placed Dresden and Altendresden under joint municipal regulations. Through the Treaty of Passau of 1552 Saxony became the leading Protestant state in Germany, and Dresden its Protestant metropolis.

During the Renaissance architecture flowered in Dresden: the old city walls were pulled down, city gates were erected, new streets were made, Neumarkt was created as a second large city square, and the Schloss (palace) was extended and re-shaped.

Renaissance architecture

Elector Augustus (ruled 1553–86) established the **Kunstkammer (art cabinet)** – the earliest in the Holy Roman Empire, except for the one in Vienna – on the top floor of the Schloss in 1560, thereby establishing the nucleus of Dresden's present-day art collections. Dresden escaped damage during the Thirty Years' War, but in 1685 a fire in Altendresden destroyed 331 of 390 dwellings. The building plan developed after this event formed the basis for the renewal of Altendresden under Augustus the Strong in the late 17th and early 18th century. It was called the »Neue Stadt bey Dresden«, later simplified to **Neustadt** (New Town), whereupon the part of the city on the left bank became known as the Altstadt (Old Town).

17th century

Fürstenzug: *Saxony's rulers on the 102m/*
Procession of *335ft porcelain frieze along the*
Princes *Langer Gang (Long Passage) at*
the Schloss (reign in brackets)

Otto the Rich
(1156–90), Margrave
of Meissen, promoter
of silver mining

Heralds and
standard
bearers

Konrad the Great
(1123–56), from 1125
uncontested Margrave
of Meissen

Albrecht the
Proud
(1190–95),
Margrave of
Meissen

The Age of Augustus the Strong

1694–1733	Rule of Augustus the Strong; building of the Zwinger, Hofkirche and Frauenkirche, Schloss Moritzburg and Schloss Pillnitz
1697	Augustus the Strong becomes king of Poland
1706	Peace of Altranstädt: crown of Poland relinquished
1709	Invention of the first European hard-paste porcelain
1760	Bombardment of Altstadt during the Seven Years' War

Augustus the Strong In 1694 Augustus the Strong (Prince Elector Friedrich August I) began his period of absolute rule, which lasted until 1733. After his conversion to Roman Catholicism in 1697 he gained the crown of Poland (as Augustus II), which made Dresden a **royal court** of European importance. However, Augustus the Strong was not able to keep the Polish crown for long: he lost it at the beginning of the Great Northern War (1700–21) through the Peace of Altranstädt in 1706. Nevertheless, during the next five decades the city achieved world renown as a city of art. Baroque Dresden owes its fame to a culture of lavish festivals, magnificent architecture, opera and music, valuable art collections and manufacturing. After Ehrenfried Walter von Tschirnhaus and Johann Friedrich Böttger produced the first **Meissen porcelain** ▶ white **hard-paste porcelain** in Europe in 1709, porcelain manufacture was established in Dresden in 1710 and moved the same year to the Albrechtsburg in Meissen.

Dietrich the Hard-Pressed (1197–1221), Margrave of Meissen, compelled to fight against Heinrich VI and his brother Albrecht

Friedrich the Bitten (1307–23), Margrave of Meissen, bitten in the cheek by his mother in pain at parting

Heinrich the Illustrious (1221–88), who loved magnificence, spent the last 20 years of his life in Dresden.

Albrecht II the Dissolute (1288–1307), Margrave of Meissen, no favourite with the family

Friedrich II the Solemn (1324–49), Margrave of Meissen

The development of handicrafts and manufacture was closely linked to the needs of the court.

In 1719 the great 2000-seat Zwinger opera house was opened in celebration of the marriage of Elector Friedrich August II to the daughter of the Habsburg emperor, Archduchess Maria Josepha of Austria. Further remarkable buildings were completed under Augustus the Strong: in the Altstadt the Taschenberg Palais, the Zwinger, Kreuzkirche (Church of the Cross), Kurländer Palais, Hofkirche (Court Church) and the new **Frauenkirche (Church of Our Lady)**, the culmination of Protestant Baroque ecclesiastical architecture; in the Neustadt the Japanisches Palais, the Dreikönigskirche (Church of the Three Kings) and Königstrasse; and in the surrounding areas the palaces Schloss Pillnitz and Schloss Moritzburg.

On the death of Augustus the Strong in 1733, Friedrich August II (from 1734 King Augustus III of Poland) succeeded him. The new ruler had a decided passion for art treasures. His close confidant Count Heinrich von Brühl became general director of the art collections. The count rose to become prime minister and had various buildings constructed on the Elbe side of the Schloss and its gardens, the so-called Brühlsche Terrasse.

The Seven Years' War began in 1756. Dresden was besieged by the Prussians, and on 19 and 20 September 1760 the artillery of the Prussian king **Friedrich II** pounded Dresden's Altstadt and destroyed one-third of the city centre. At the end of the Seven Years' War Saxony, which was on the losing side, was politically insignificant and had to pay large sums to Prussia in reparation. Nevertheless, it recovered relatively quickly from the consequences of the war.

Seven Years' War

Friedrich the Quarrelsome (1381–1428), from 1423 Duke and Elector of Saxony

Friedrich II the Gentle (1428–64), Elector of Saxony

Friedrich III the Severe (1349–81)

Ernst and Albrecht the Stout-Hearted, 1464–85 joint rulers; 1485 division into Ernestine and Albertine lines, Albrecht was Duke of Saxony in Dresden until 1500

Kingdom of Saxony

1806	Saxony becomes a monarchy
1813	Imprisonment of the king, general governorship
1830	First Saxon constitution
1849	3–9 May: May rising in Dresden
1918	9 November: abdication of the king
	Free State of Saxony established
1923	29 October: Communist-Socialist coalition government overthrown

Monarchy established

Saxony became a monarchy in 1806 after joining the Rhine Confederation, and continued to be an ally of Napoleon until the confederation was dissolved in 1813 after the Battle of Leipzig and the Saxon king was taken prisoner. The **Congress of Vienna** in 1815 condemned Saxony to yield two-thirds of its territory to Prussia, with a resulting loss of political significance. The Russian prince Repnin-Volkonsky came to Dresden as governor-general of Saxony. A representative of the Enlightenment, he opened the Grosser Garten to the public and granted free access to the royal art collections. The 19th century brought an upsurge of trade, industry and science. In 1815 the Academy of Surgery and Medicine was founded, in 1828 the Technische Bildungsanstalt (precursor of the Technical University).

Johann the Steadfast (1525–32), Ernestine, Elector of Saxony, head of the Schmalkaldian Federation

Georg the Bearded (1500–39), Albertine, Duke of Saxony in Dresden

Moritz (1541–53), Albertine, from 1547 re-appointed Elector of Saxony in gratitude for his fight against the Schmalkaldian Federation

Christian I (1586–91), Elector of Saxony

Friedrich III the Wise (1486–1525), Ernestine, Elector of Saxony, promoter of the Reformation

Johann Friedrich the Magnanimous (1532–47), Ernestine, lost the title of Elector.

Heinrich the Pious (1539–41), Albertine, Duke of Saxony, converted to the Reformation.

August (1553–86), Elector of Saxony, founder of Dresden art collections

In 1830 popular pressure necessitated civic reforms and the acceptance of a first **constitution** in Saxony, which transferred the royal collections to state ownership in 1831.

The political upheavals of the bourgeois democratic revolution of 1848–49 reached Dresden rather late: the May uprising from 3 to 9 May 1849 was harshly crushed by Saxon and Prussian military forces. **Gottfried Semper** and Richard Wagner had to flee because of their part in the May uprising.

1849: Dresden's May uprising

The mid-19th century was a time of change not only in political life but also in the economy and in urban building: in 1837 the Saxon-Bohemian Steamship Company was founded, and at the same time **Johann Andreas Schubert** constructed the first German steam engine, *Saxonia*. Two years later the first rail link between Dresden and Leipzig was completed, and in 1851 the first train ran from Dresden to Prague. In mid-century Gottfried Semper's most important buildings were erected in Dresden: the Hasenberg Synagogue, the Hoftheater (the first Semper Opera) on Theaterplatz, which opened with Weber's *Der Freischütz*, and the Semper Gallery in the Zwinger. Prager Strasse was created in 1851, and developed into the city's most elegant and lively shopping street. The late 19th century saw the building of the second Semper Opera, after the first had burnt down in 1869, and of the Albertinum, the Kunstakademie (Art Academy) and the Sekundogenitur (a gallery belonging traditionally to the second-born prince). In Loschwitz vineyards were razed after the disastrous infestation with phylloxera, which created space for

Modern times

◄ Urban development

Johann Georg I (1611–56), Elector of Saxony, opportunist in 30 Years' War

Johan Georg III (1680–91), Elector of Saxony, helped defencd of Vienna against the Turks.

Friedrich August I (Augustus the Strong, 1694–1733), Elector of Saxony, from 1697 king of Poland as Augustus II, brought Baroque splendour to Dresden.

Friedrich Christian (1763), Elector of Saxony

Christian II (1591–1611), Elector of Saxony

Johann Georg II (1656–80), Elector of Saxony, initiated absolutist court regime in Dresden.

Johann Georg IV (1691–94), Elector of Saxony

Friedrich August II (1733–63), Elector of Saxony and, as Augustus III, King of Poland

Friedrich August III the Just (1763–1827), king from 1806, supported Napoleon in 1813

Industriali-zation   the building of villas. From the mid-19th century, industry was increasingly dominant in Dresden's economy. Eugen von Boch and Alfred Villeroy founded the Dresden firm **Villeroy & Boch**, which became one of the most important producers of ceramics in Germany. Europe's largest producer of sewing-machines at that time was Clemens Müller; in the Löbtau factory, glass was produced on an industrial scale for the first time anywhere. New branches of industry were tobacco, the chemicals and pharmaceuticals, precision mechanics and optical equipment, food products and luxury articles; the last-named included the first German chocolate factory, opened by Jordan & Timaeus (founded 1823), the inventors of milk chocolate. Among the other companies to be opened were the first German cigarette factory, Laferme (by 1880 there were 21 cigarette factories in Dresden), the pharmaceutical company Heyden, the sewing-machine and (subsequently) typewriter factory Seidel & Naumann, and the Lingner Works, whose product Odol was the world's first mouth-rinse.

Dresden becomes a large city   Dresden's growth to become a large city was accompanied by development of the transport system; several bridges across the Elbe were constructed, for instance the **Blaues Wunder** (Blue Miracle, 1893). The same year saw the appearance of electric trams in the city; the Elbe harbour was built and the large rail stations in both Altstadt and Neustadt were re-shaped. The main rail station, opened in 1897, was considered ultra-modern and was a model for the whole of Germany. In 1900 the much-admired Loschwitz **cable car**, the first of its kind in the world, went into operation. By the turn of the century Dresden's population had increased to half a million thanks to the incorporation of outlying areas.

Anton the Benev-
olent (1827–36),
King of Saxony,
first constitutional
monarch

Johann (1854–73),
King of Saxony,
translated Dante
under pseudonym
»Philaletes«.

Georg
(1902–04),
King of Saxony

Nobles, soldiers, scholars and artists,
including the draughtsman and
painter Ludwig Richter (1803–84)

Friedrich August II
(1836–1854), King
of Saxony

Albert
(1873–1902),
King of Saxony

Saxony's last king, Friedrich August III
(1904–18), is not portrayed: he was still
a child when the Procession of Princes
was made.

In the course of the November revolution, on 9 November 1918, the Saxon government and king had to abdicate. The king's farewell words were reportedly »Get on with it on your own!« That was the end of Dresden as royal seat; Saxony was renamed a **free state**.

1918: November revolution

On 1 November 1920 the constitution of the Free State of Saxony was passed. The government was formed by left-wing Social Democrats under Erich Zeigner on 21 March 1923, and on 10 October in the same year they united with the Communists. On 29 October the coalition government of KPD (German Communist Party) and SPD (Socialist Party of Germany) was deposed by the Berlin government with help from the army, and its members were arrested.

Constitution of the Free State of Saxony

From the Third Reich to 1945

1938	9–10 November: Semper`s synagogue burnt down
1945	13–14 February: destruction by Allied bombing
	8 May: entry of the Red Army

As in the whole of Germany, opponents of the National Socialist (Nazi) regime were persecuted from 1933: Otto Dix and Viktor Klemperer lost their teaching posts, Fritz Busch was dragged from his conductor's rostrum and Wilhelm Külz, the democratically elected mayor, was sacked. Nazis burnt books on Wettin Square; in the »Reichskristallnacht« of 9–10 November 1938 the Semper Synagogue was burnt down.

Dresden under National Socialism

The Herculean figure of the »golden Rathaus man«, created by Richard Guhr, is 4.9m/16ft tall, and survived the fire storm of 1945 undamaged! The figure wears a wreath in the form of fortifications and extends his right hand in blessing over the city, while his left hand empties a cornucopia.

THE DESTRUCTION OF DRESDEN

After the destruction of Dresden in 1945 the city was nothing but a landscape of ruins. There is still speculation today about the motives behind the air raid so close to the end of the war.

On the afternoon of 13 February 1945, 245 Royal Air Force Lancaster bombers left their base and headed for the centre of Saxony's capital city, which until then had suffered little damage. After the advance aircraft

»Any who no longer knew tears, learnt to weep again at the destruction of Dresden«. (Gerhart Hauptmann)

had marked their targets shortly after 10pm, the bombers dropped a total of 2659 tons of bombs – tens of thousands of explosives followed by 650,000 firebombs, which caused an unprecedented **firestorm** with tempe-

ratures of more than 800 °C/1500°F. A few hours later, in the night before Ash Wednesday, 311 B17 bombers of the US Air Force appeared over Dresden and dropped a further 711 tons of bombs. The work of destruction was completed the same day by 210 B17 bombers, with another 461 tons of bombs pouring down on the dying city. During these three days the Allied forces were hardly troubled at all by German **anti-aircraft measures**. The approaching bombers employed successful confusion tactics, so that only half-a-dozen fighters stationed at the nearby

314636. Dresden
Blick vom Rathausturm
auf die zerstörte Innere
Stadt

Klotzsche airfield took off a few minutes before the first bombs were dropped, and flew initially in the direction of what they mistakenly presumed to be the targets, without engaging with the enemy in the Dresden area. One solitary German plane appeared over Dresden – a messenger aircraft. Only one of the 771 attacking bombers was lost. The heavy anti-aircraft guns, and most of the light defences (except what was needed for security of the fighter airfield), had been moved to the Ruhr area in January 1945 in order to protect its mines and power stations.

When the inferno ended ...

... 15 sq km/6 sq mi of Dresden's inner city had been razed to the ground. The famous »Florence on the Elbe« no longer existed. The **number of the dead** is still not known today, since the city was crammed full of refugees from East Prussia and Silesia. Estimates range from 30,000 to over 100,000. Mass graves were quickly dug, but were insufficient to bury the dead: in order to prevent contagious disease, the corpses were burnt on Altmarkt on steel frameworks made from tramlines. Speculation continues today regarding the **motives** for the air attack, which British air marshal Sir Arthur Harris had suggested to prime minister Churchill – retaliation for Coventry, demonstration of the Royal Air Force's capability, solidarity with the approaching Soviet troops: ultimately, nobody knows. The fact is that there was no attack on the barracks or depot close to Neustadt, or on Klotzsche airfield, and even when Germany capitulated, the Red Army had not yet reached Dresden.

1945   At the beginning of 1945 Dresden had suffered less war damage than any other major German city. The inferno came from 13 to 15 February 1945, when **Dresden was destroyed by British and American bombers**: for three days and nights the city was on fire. At least 35,000 people were killed in attacks which had no military purpose; amongst the dead were many of the tens of thousands who had fled to Dresden in order to escape the advancing Soviet army. About 15 sq km/6 sq mi of the inner city with its cultural monuments were reduced to rubble and ashes.

Post-war period   On 8 May 1945, the day of the capitulation of the German army, the Red Army entered Dresden. Two days later the provisional city administration took over under Rudolf Friedrichs (SPD/Socialist) as mayor. In July a Saxon state administration was appointed by the Soviet military administration. In the same month the city's cultural life began again with the Interim Theatre's opening performance of Lessing's *Nathan the Wise* in the concert hall. The Dresden Philharmonie and the Kreuzchor gave their first concerts. In November a census put the population at 454,249 (as compared with 642,143 in 1933, the highest number of inhabitants in the city's history). Only a few Jews survived the Third Reich in Dresden. In January 1946 the city council was able to present the »great plan for rebuilding Dresden« at a public meeting.

Dresden under Socialism

1949	7 October: founding of the GDR
1952	Dresden becomes regional capital
1956	750th jubilee

In April 1946 Saxony's KPD (Communist Party) and SPD (Socialist Party) were united as the SED (Socialist Unity Party). Municipal elections took place in September of that year.

On 7 October 1949 the GDR was founded and in November the Soviet military administration transferred administrative responsibility for Dresden to the city council. Saxony's state government was dissolved in July 1952 and the cities of Dresden, Chemnitz (Karl Marx City) and Leipzig were named regional capitals.

17 June 1953   10,000 people demonstrated on Dresden's Postplatz, as elsewhere, on 17 June 1953. On the orders of the Soviet garrison commander the SED declared a state of emergency, and the **demonstration** was violently crushed by the arrival of Soviet tanks.

On the occasion of the 750th jubilee in 1956 the picture gallery in the Semper Building re-opened with paintings returned by the Soviet

Union one year earlier. At the same time the Transport Museum in the Johanneum opened its doors. In 1958 the Grünes Gewölbe (Green Vault) and the collections of copper engravings, coins, porcelain, armoury and sculpture returned from the Soviet Union.

The first historic edifice to be rebuilt was the **Zwinger**, in 1963. Two   **Rebuilding**
years later building work began around Prager Strasse. In 1969 the Kulturpalast (Culture Palace) and Fernsehturm (TV Tower) opened. New residential building had previously been concentrated in the city centre, but in the 1970s it moved to the outskirts of the town; large new prefabricated high-rise estates were constructed.
On the 40th anniversary of the destruction of Dresden, 13 February 1985, the festive re-opening of the Semper Opera was held with a performance of Carl Maria von Weber's *Der Freischütz*. One year later the foundation stone was laid for the rebuilding of the Schloss.

1989 to the Present Day

1989	Autumn: political change in the GDR
1990	May: first free local elections
	On 14 October Dresden becomes Saxony's state capital
1994	Rebuilding of the Frauenkirche begins
2002	August: severe flooding

On 4 October 1989 a special train with GDR citizens who had taken   **Change**
refuge in the Prague embassy of the Federal Republic passed through Dresden on its way to the West. At the main rail station there were violent confrontations between police and people wanting to leave the country. In the weeks that followed, dramatic events took place on Prager Strasse, Pirnaischerplatz and Fetscherplatz, and at the station, precipitating the political change that ensued in the GDR.
In four Dresden churches, including the Kreuzkirche (Church of the Cross) and Hofkirche (Court Church), there were non-religious meetings of citizens united in opposition to the GDR state leadership. In the state theatre, actors read out resolutions after the performances, and informed the audience of developments in other parts of the GDR. Through initial dialogue, enormous demonstrations, and the initiative taken by a democratically appointed citizens' committee, the Gruppe der 20 (Group of 20), the starting signal for peaceful **revolution** was given in Dresden.
On 19 December 1989 Chancellor Kohl of the Federal Republic and Prime Minister Modrow of the GDR addressed the inhabitants of Dresden. Kohl's Christian Democratic Union won the first free local

Dresden's inhabitants demonstrate for a united Germany in 1989.

elections in May 1990, and also gained an absolute majority in the state parliament. On 14 October the state of Saxony was restored, with Dresden as its capital.

Today

Economy ▶

During the first years after reunification, numerous highly regarded traditional businesses fell victim to the process of economic restructuring. Yet some traditional branches of the economy did survive, notably the pharmaceutical and tobacco industries. As a prime location for **electronics**, with well qualified professionals, Dresden was quick to attract international companies: in 1995 the Siemens chip factory (now Infineon) opened, the most important industrial start-up after the change. Although Dresden's unemployment rate is lower than in the other states of the former GDR, lack of employment prospects mean that the city still loses people who seek work in western Germany and abroad.

Restoration of the city ▶

In the years In the years 1991 to 1998 alone, Dresden invested the equivalent of €150 million in restoring the city. Significant amounts were invested in the neglected buildings of rundown areas: Königstrasse in Neustadt became the grand shopping street. In October 1991 the Hausmannturm in the Schloss was rebuilt; this was followed by the beginning of reconstruction of the Frauenkirche in 1994, and of Altmarkt three years later. Around the turn of the millennium, the new buildings for the state parliament, synagogue and Factory of Glass won international acclaim.

August 2002 saw the »flood of the century«: the river Weisseritz overflowed into the city centre and the level of the Elbe rose to a historic high of 9.4m/33ft. The railway lines linking Dresden with Leipzig, Chemnitz, Prague and the Erzgebirge were washed away and it took more than a year for some parts to be restored. In Saxony more than €2 billion were spent on relief for flood victims, restoration of the public infrastructure and repair of flood damage. By the end of 2004 all the essential repairs had been paid for and reconstruction completed. Since 2004 the Elbe valley, from Schloss Übigau in the northwest to Schloss Pillnitz in the southeast, has been designated a **UNESCO world heritage site**, highly commended for the harmonious blend of Dresden's Altstadt with the gentle curves of the Elbe and the water meadows by the river. Extensive meadows, historic village centres, fine parks, magnificent palaces and steeply sloping vineyards contribute to a unique harmony between city architecture and the natural river valley.

In August 2004 the exterior of the Frauenkirche was completed, two years earlier than planned, and on Reformation Day, 30 October 2005, the church was solemnly dedicated. Thus in 2006 Dresden was able to celebrate **800 years of history** with the city silhouette complete – though somewhat darkened by a dispute over the planned Waldschlösschen bridge, which jeopardizes the Elbe valley's status as a World Heritage site.

◄ 2002: flood disaster

◄ 2006: 800th jubilee

Arts and Culture

What gives Dresden its reputation as a city of arts and music? What are the characteristics of Dresden Baroque? How did the Expressionist artists of »Die Brücke« create a stir? What gave rise to the first German garden city in Hellerau? Which treasures are housed in the city's museums and art collections?

The Middle Ages

First came the settlement of **»Nisani«**, a port on the bank of the Elbe documented for the first time in 1174. In the middle of this settlement, from the mid-12th century, stood the Romanesque basilica of St Mary, the later Frauenkirche (Church of Our Lady). At this time there was also a Romanesque citadel on the Taschenberg. Not far from these two edifices, around which settlements grew, a third was built: the small citadel on the site of today's Schloss. Here, in the lower part of the Hausmannturm, are Dresden's oldest medieval remains, dating from c1400. Around 1500 Dresden had significant Gothic churches: the re-modelled Frauenkirche, the Church of St Nicholas (predecessor of the Kreuzkirche) and a Franciscan church. The last-named became the Protestant Hofkirche (Court Church), and from 1602 was called the Sophienkirche . This was the only one to retain its medieval form right through to the 20th century, and it survived the bombs of 1945, albeit as a ruin. Not until 1962–63 was it demolished, on the orders of Walther Ulbricht, leader of the GDR. Early 16th-century console busts from its penitential chapel have been preserved in Dresden's Stadtmuseum (city museum). They are Dresden's earliest surviving pieces of sculpture, and show the influence of the Parler style from Prague. Overall, Dresden's cityscape was not particularly impressive in the early 16th century: a proverbial verse of 1520 praises Leipzig, Freiberg, Chemnitz and Annaberg, but makes no mention at all of Dresden.

◄ Hausmannturm

◄ Sophienkirche

Renaissance

The partition of Saxony in 1485 brought political advancement to Dresden; Duke Albrecht resided permanently in the city from this time on. Under Duke Moritz, who in 1547 gained the title of Elector (i.e. one of the German rulers who elected the emperor), Dresden developed into a European centre of arts and culture.

Dresden becomes a ducal seat

In the Renaissance the appearance of the city changed fundamentally: the old city walls were pulled down, new city gates were built, new streets such as Moritzstrasse were created, and Neumarkt, a second large square, was laid out. In the second half of the 16th century the Moritzbau, Turnierhof (jousting yard), Pretiosensaal (treasury), Schlosskapelle and Stallhof (stable yard) with Lange Galerie were built, as well as the Zeughaus (armoury) with Geschützgiesserei (ordnance foundry), the Jägerhof (huntsmen's court) and the Ge-

Renaissance architecture

← *Detail from Balthasar Permoser's pulpit (1722) in the Hofkirche*

Detail of the Dresden »Dance of Death«: a blind old man is led by a usurer and a boy, Death follows with his scythe.

Moritz Monument ▶
wandhaus (cloth hall) on Neumarkt. Dresden's first monument, the Moritz Monument of 1553, also dates back to the Renaissance; since 1896 it has stood beside the Jungfernbastei, opposite Carolabrücke (bridge).

Ducal residence
Between 1530 and 1535 Duke Georg had the Schloss (palace) extended and decorated. The 12m/40ft sandstone relief made for the old Georgentor (gate) with the ***Dresden Dance of Death*** is now in the Dreikönigskirche. In 1548–56 Elector Moritz extended the Schloss on a magnificent four-winged plan, the first of this kind in Renaissance Germany. For the first time Italian artists were employed in Dresden, and they painted the inner courtyard façades in black and grey using sgraffito technique. Other parts of the Schloss, stairway towers and entrance portals display high-quality Renaissance architecture and sculpture. The Riesensaal (Great Hall), with interior design typical of the Renaissance, will be recreated in its historical form when the Schloss is restored, starting with the exterior.

Kunstkammer
In 1560 the Kunstkammer (art cabinet) was established on the top floor of the Schloss. It was the second in the Holy Roman Empire, preceded only by Vienna. This laid the foundation for Dresden's reputation as city of the arts. In 1587 the inventory already listed 10,000 items, which subsequently found their way to the armoury, the

sculpture collection, the picture galleries, the graphics collection and the Grünes Gewölbe (Green Vault), and especially to the Mathematischer-Physikalischer Salon.

Painting

Dresden did not have its own tradition of painting until after 1500. In the Stadtmuseum there is a panel painting of 1529, the *Ten Commandments* by Hans der Maler (Hans the Painter), which came from the Kreuzkirche. However, the Renaissance paintings by Lucas Cranach, Albrecht Dürer and Hans Holbein, which give the Gemäldegalerie Alte Meister (Old Masters) its international standing, attest the history of collecting in Dresden, rather than its own tradition of painting, as they did not arrive in the electors' collection until after 1700. Court painting in Saxony did not begin until the Baroque era: Augustus the Strong and his son Friedrich August II were not only collectors, but also patrons of art.

The Augustan Age

Dresden Baroque

The electors' love of ostentation meant that the Baroque style spread rapidly: in 1676 the Grosser Garten was laid out, modelled on French landscape architecture. Within it lies the **Grosses Palais** of 1683 by Johann Georg Starcke, the earliest Baroque building in Saxony.

The reign of Elector Friedrich August I, known as Augustus the Strong (ruled 1696–1733), and his son Friedrich August II (ruled 1733–63; from 1734 King Augustus III of Poland) is described as the »Augustan Age«. Dresden became a gathering point for artists and a centre of the arts. The city's fame was not only founded on outstanding architectural achievements and art collections, some of them unique in the world; at the same time music, theatre, literature, painting, sculpture and craft-

> **❗ Baedeker TIP**
>
> **Historic view**
>
> What did Dresden look like in the Baroque period? To find out, go to the Panometer at Dresden-Rieck. It is a 105m/345ft long and 27m/89ft-high 360° panoramic painting in an old gasometer, showing Dresden in exact detail as it looked in 1756 (Gasanstaltstr. 8b, Tue–Fri 9am–7pm, Sat and Sun 10am–8pm; S-Bahn S1 and S2 to Dresden-Rieck, tram 1 and 2 to Liebstädter Str.).

work blossomed. Even if many of the Baroque buildings were destroyed for ever by the bombs of 1945 and the rebuilding of the city under Socialist auspices, yet the city's museums and collections still have a rich Baroque heritage. The flowering of culture is attested by the founding in 1705 of the Malerakademie (Painters' Academy, from 1764 renamed Kunstakademie), and the invention of the first white hard-paste porcelain in Europe by Ehrenfried Walther von

Tschirnhaus and Johann Friedrich Böttger in 1709, followed one year later by the establishment of porcelain manufacture. The outstanding Grünes Gewölbe (Green Vault) was set up in 1721–24 as the world's newest specialist museum, the Zwinger housed several collections, and the collection of antiquities was founded with the purchase of the Chigi und Albani collections. To this day the ***Sistine Madonna*** by Raphael, purchased in 1753, is acknowledged to be the outstanding item of the collections.

Architecture From the beginning of the 18th century the city attained its full beauty, with Pöppelmann's chief work, the Zwinger, a gem of Baroque architecture. Further buildings included the Catholic Hofkirche (Court Church), the Kreuzkirche, the Frauenkirche, the Dreikönigskirche and numerous palaces; grand streets were created, such as Königstrasse in the Neustadt. Dresden's urban planning began with the appointment of Matthäus Daniel Pöppelmann as head of the newly founded state building office in 1718. Plans for all civic buildings had to be submitted to him before construction started. Pöppelmann re-modelled Schloss Moritzburg, while the Japanisches Palais and Schloss Pillnitz are the continent's first large-scale instances of architectural chinoiserie.

George Bähr's Frauenkirche, 1726–43, represents the apogee of Protestant church building in the Baroque era.

*Dinglinger/
Permoser:
»Moor with
Emerald Slab«
(1724)*

The turn of the 17th to the 18th century produced outstanding works, particularly in **sculpture**: Balthasar Permoser adorned the Zwinger and Grosser Garten with sculptures of expressive vitality; his ivory carvings are unsurpassed.

Johann Melchior Dinglinger brought the goldsmith's art to perfection with his sumptuous *Court at Delhi on the Occasion of the Birthday of the Grand Mogul Aureng-Zeb*. Some of the most beautiful and original treasures in the Grünes Gewölbe were made by him.

Painting Painting of the Baroque era from Dresden is hardly less splendid, although it is often overshadowed in the Gemäldegalerie Alte Meister by Italian, Dutch, French and Spanish masterpieces. Anton Raphael Mengs, a leading figure among German neo-classical painters in Rome, often worked in Dresden as well; the altar painting in the Hofkirche is by him. Johannes Alexander Thiele, court painter of Augustus III, was the founder of Saxon landscape painting. His student Christian Wilhelm Ernst Dietrich, much admired as an infant prodigy, was appointed court painter by Augustus the Strong, and is considered a master of late Baroque art; he continued the tradition of Saxon landscape painting, which attained great importance in the 19th century. Bernardo Bellotto, known as Canaletto, was court painter under Augustus III from 1748 to 1766. His art advanced towards realistic portrayal of landscape, as is evident in the precise topography and depiction of his views of Baroque Dresden.

19th Century

Anton Graff, who displayed neoclassical tendencies, was appointed professor of portrait painting in 1798. His portraits are characterized by naturalness, subtle grasp of the subject and warm colouring. He marks the beginning of Dresden's early Romantic era, which gained international significance. Painting displayed the new Romantic sensibility that was grounded in poetry, a combination unknown in European art up to that time. Graff belonged to the highly educated aristocratic and bourgeois circle that also included the writers Ludwig Tieck, Friedrich Schlegel, Novalis, Heinrich von Kleist, Theodor Körner and E.T.A. Hoffmann, painters such as the major Romantic masters Philipp Otto Runge and **Caspar David Friedrich**, Saxony's most important late Romantic painter Adrian Ludwig Richter, the physician and painter Carl Gustav Carus and Johann Christian Klengel. They all inspired, and were inspired by, one another.

Early Romantic era in Dresden

Gottfried Semper created his first great building, the Semper Gallery in the Zwinger, where the Old Masters are housed today. Theaterplatz beside it is one of the loveliest squares in Germany.

Architecture

In 1832 the sculptor **Ernst Rietschel** was appointed professor at the Kunstakademie. He made the head of the monument to Luther by the Frauenkirche, the statues of Schiller and Goethe by the Semper Opera and the memorial to Carl Maria von Weber by the Semper Gallery. Rietschel was one of the founders of Dresden's 19th-century school of sculpture. His student Johannes Schilling commemorated him on the Brühlsche Terrasse, where Schilling's *Four Seasons* and the memorial to Semper also stand. The equestrian statue of King Johann on Theaterplatz and the panther quadriga on the Semper Opera are also by Schilling.

Sculpture

From 1900 to the Third Reich

Dresden owed its prosperity and its **urban development** during the second half of the 19th century largely to the industrial revolution. The development of transport led to the growth of the first industrial areas, especially along Leipziger Strasse (**Villeroy & Boch**) and Blumenstrasse. The Waldschlösschen brewery on Bautzner Strasse was one of the earliest factory buildings. The building plans of 1863 and 1874 were blueprints for urban development which separated industrial areas from residential areas and banned chimneys entirely from the inner city. These were disguised as minaret in the tobacco firm Yenidze, or as Baroque cupolas, for instance in the Ostragehege slaughterhouse. Whole new city districts grew up quasi overnight from the mid-19th century. The city centre was beautified with grand civic buildings on Prager Strasse, the town hall, the ministries on the north bank of the Elbe, the state court of justice on Sachsenplatz, the Albertinum on the Brühlsche Terrasse, and the Kunstakademie and Semper Opera on Theaterplatz.

The most elaborate residential architecture in the city has survived in the **district of Blasewitz**. Numerous **villas** reflect the diversity in style and also the cosmopolitan taste of their owners: traditional Saxon and southern German country house style, Swiss houses, Italian and French villas, southern English cottages and floral art nouveau. The years between 1905 and 1914 under the city's chief architect, Hans Erlwein, were important. It was his job to convert Dresden into a major city. Erlwein provided technology and utilities; he built the gasworks in Reick, a slaughterhouse, schools, administrative buildings and dwellings. He built the warehouse known today as the Erlweinspeicher entirely of concrete, the first building of this kind in Dresden. During his period of office the first German garden city, **Hellerau** (▶ Baedeker Special p.46), was built in 1908 in collaboration with the Deutsche Werkstätten. Heinrich Tessenow's plans for the garden city were widely acclaimed.

▶ »Erlwein Era«

Painting Impressionism and art nouveau dominated the art scene around 1900. **Robert Sterl**, the main Impressionist in Dresden, liked to paint people working in the Elbe sandstone quarries. He also painted portraits from the world of music and landscapes inspired by his journey to Russia.

The association of Expressionist artists known as »Die Brücke« (The Bridge) was founded in Dresden in 1905; it marked the beginning of German modern art and had a decisive influence on the development of European art. Its founders were Karl Schmidt-Rottluff, Ernst Ludwig Kirchner, Erich Heckel and Fritz Bleyl. They were anti-academic, critical of traditional painting, and provocatively dismissive of bourgeois values: their spontaneous and untamed formal language with powerful two-dimensionality and the intoxication of pure, undiluted colours was intended to shock and dispensed with inner feel-

▶ »Die Brücke«

»Die Brücke« painters Mueller, Kirchner, Heckel and Schmidt-Rottluff (Kirchner, 1925)

ing. Their main themes were human figures and landscapes, reflecting their sense of nature as pure abundance of life – free from conventions that stifled zest for living.

After World War I Dresden continued to be the most important centre of Expressionist art in Germany: in 1919 Oskar Kokoschka was appointed professor at the Dresden Kunstakademie, the first painter to gain such a position. His views of Dresden date from the early 1920s. In the same year the painter and graphic artist Conrad Felixmüller and Otto Dix founded the **Dresden Secession** group of artists. Both taught at the Kunstakademie.

Inter-war period

Lea and Hans Grundig joined with other Dresden painters in 1929 to form the Association of Revolutionary Artists, with Communist leanings. Members of this group created works of social criticism.

HELLERAU GARDEN CITY

Germany's first garden city was founded in Hellerau in 1908. The international garden city movement started in England at the end of the 19th century. It was initiated as an alternative to industrialized towns with their slums and associated social problems. The garden city as an urban project for social reform strove to express the harmony of a society designed to be of benefit to all, an aim which the design of residential areas and buildings was intended to reflect.

Hellerau Garden City, on the northern outskirts of Dresden, was conceived and financed by Karl Schmidt, a furniture manufacturer with a keen interest in social policy. He was a pioneer of modern furniture production, the first to make affordable individual and mass-produced furniture in a simple and sober style. In 1907 he moved his **Deutsche Werkstätten** (German Workshops) to Hellerau, intending to create a total work of art »from sofa cushions to urban architecture«, and he appointed Richard Riemerschmid to oversee the whole design. An important feature was the separation of factory, infrastructure and dwelling areas.

1910 saw the appearance first of the functional factory buildings of the Deutsche Werkstätten, followed by terraced housing and individually de-

Festspielhaus (theatre) in Hellerau, built by Heinrich Tessenow in 1910–12

signed dwellings for Werkstätten employees, which anticipate early Bauhaus ideas in their simple architecture with no historical frills. Roads lined with gardens curve through the residential area, following the natural contours of the landscape. During the first 30 years of the 20th century Hellerau offered the **three-fold harmony** of Deutsche Werkstätten (to work in), houses (to live in) and the Festspielhaus (a theatre for art and culture).

The Hellerau Myth

The garden city has two centres: first, the market as focal point of daily life with residential buildings designed by **Riemerschmid**, and second, the Festspielhaus as the residents' cultural centre. It was built in 1910–12 by **Heinrich Tessenow**, like Riemerschmid one of the leading architects of the Werkbund movement, and its monumental simplicity secured it a place in architectural history.

In it, music pedagogue Émile Jaques-Dalcroze from Geneva opened his educational institution for rhythmic gymnastics in 1912. One of his students, **Mary Wigman** (► Famous people, p.65), brought fame to Hellerau as the cradle of expressive modern dance. With its Festspielhaus Hellerau was renowned at the beginning of the 20th century not only for urban planning, but also as a social centre of civic renewal and reform, aiming to bring all the arts together with a common end, extended to all classes of society.

Right up to the 1920s Hellerau attracted progressive artists and writers: Paul Claudel, George Bernard Shaw, Upton Sinclair, Frank Wedekind and students of Sergei Diaghilev's Russian Ballet visited the garden city. Anna Pavlova danced in the Festspielhaus and Max Reinhardt staged his first theatre productions here. When the Nazis took power,

Mary Wigman – dancer, choreographer and dance teacher – dancing in c1930

Hellerau sank into a kind of slumber. In 1937 the Festspielhaus complex was converted into barracks, which was used by the Russian army after the war and until the collapse of the German Democratic Republic in 1989.

Rebirth

After almost a century – restoration work ended in 2005 – Hellerau is once more on the way to becoming a place for the **avant-garde**. The European Centre for the Arts in Hellerau is working on the Festspielhaus site to re-awaken the myth of Hellerau, with music, theatre, dance, art and architecture as its artistic pillars. In recent years several different organizations have come together under one roof, building on strong local traditions: Dresden's Centre for Contemporary Music, the Russian and German Derevo experimental dance theatre, the organizers of Tanzherbst (Dancing Autumn) and the Hellerau Rhythmics Institute. Since 2005 the Festspielhaus has also been the home of choreographer **William Forsythe's** ballet company.

The Festspielhaus events calendar (tel. 24 46 20; www.KunstForumHellerau.de) includes readings, performances and concerts. There is a conducted tour of the Festspielhaus on Sundays at 2pm (tel. 883 37 00). The visitor information office at Markt 2 (bookings under tel. 888 18 01) offers a guided tour through the Deutsche Werkstätten and to the Festspielhaus (11am–1pm, Sundays April–Sept). The Hellerau Werkstätten (Moritzburger Weg 67) have remained true to their furniture-manufacturing tradition: specializing nowadays in high quality individual interiors, they have furnished, for instance, Dresden's town hall, the Semper Opera, the New Synagogue and Saxony's parliament building.

During the Third Reich all cultural diversity perished in Dresden. Important artists and teachers like Otto Dix were dismissed, went into exile or were murdered in concentration camps.

Third Reich

The exhibition *Spiegelbild des Verfalls in der Kunst* (Mirror of Degeneracy in Art) of September 1933 defamed works of progressive artists as »degenerate«. The city and university rapidly fell in line with Nazi policies and procedures. There was little opposition. The most important personality in Dresden's anti-Fascist resistance was the Jewish literary scholar **Viktor Klemperer**. Forbidden to teach by the Nazis, in 1947 he wrote his book *Lingua Tertii Imperii* (Language of the Third Reich), a linguistic and sociological exposure of the Nazi era in Dresden.

Since 1945

Almost as painful a process as the destruction of Dresden was its reconstruction. Those who opposed the development of the new »Socialist metropolis«, such as the director of urban planning Rummrich and the conservation officer Bachmann, quickly lost their posts and their influence; in 1949 a start was made on large-scale clearance of the ruins. Much valuable architecture which could have been rebuilt was demolished, including the Altes Rathaus (old town hall), the Neustadt town hall, Albert Theatre, Narrenhäusel (»little madhouse«), Fernheizwerk (district heating plant), Hotel Bellevue and burgher houses in the Altstadt, the Sophienkirche and 17 further churches.

Rebuilding

Among those rebuilt were the Zwinger, Schauspielhaus (playhouse), Kreuzkirche, Hofkirche and public buildings such as the Sekundogenitur gallery, Gewandhaus (cloth hall), Japanisches Palais, Blockhaus and Stallhof (stable yard), the Neustadt ministries on the Elbe, the police headquarters, the new town hall and the Semper Opera.

In the 1950s new buildings went up in the centre around Altmarkt (old market place), initially in historicist style. Building in the 1960s was characterized by chilly, monotonous anonymity: prefabricated high-rise estates were put up first in the centre, then increasingly in the 1970s on the outskirts of the city.

Modern architecture

After German unification reconstruction and restoration went ahead at top speed, with a lot of conventional architecture but more recently also with spectacular contemporary works. The transparent parliament building and the deconstructivist UFA cinema complex are remarkable; distinctly innovative new work includes the multiform Gläserne Manufaktur (Factory of Glass), the minimalist stone cube of the **Neue Synagoge (New Synagogue)**, and also the Sächsi-

Contemporary architecture

Up to date: the reading room in the Sächsische Landesbibliothek

sche Landesbibliothek (Saxon State Library, state and university library), which consists of two travertine-covered cubes with a glass-roofed subterranean reading room.

Rebuilding of the Frauenkirche An idea conceived in the minds of Dresden citizens and artists led by the trumpet virtuoso Ludwig Güttler was the rebuilding of the Frauenkirche, financed by donations from all over the world. It was dedicated on 30 October 2005, and completed the restoration of the »Canaletto view«, the famous Dresden silhouette.

Sculpture After the founding of the GDR on 7 October 1949, social realism on Soviet lines, depicting workers and history, was declared compulsory for all branches of art. Polemics were directed against modern art; the East German art scene became isolated. Important artists of the post-war era include the constructivist Hermann Glöckner and graphic artist Joseph Hegenbarth, one of the outstanding book illustrators of the present time, who interpreted fairy tales and legends in pen and brush work and watercolours. The painter, draughtsman and sculptor **A.R. Penck** (true name: Ralf Winkler) was never officially recognized as an artist in the GDR; he became known only after he moved to the West in 1980. His expressive, narrow matchstick-type figures reflect the human condition, the perception of German history, and memory and time as process.

A famous native of Dresden is the artist Gerhard Richter (►Galerie Neue Meister).

City of Music

»Give thanks for your good fortune, blessed Saxony,
For God preserves the throne of your king.
Joyful land,
Thank heaven and kiss the hand
That augments your prosperity day by day
And keeps watch over your citizens.«

These are the words of Johann Sebastian Bach in Cantata 215, celebrating Saxony's ruling house in music, specifically Augustus II, Elector of Saxony and King of Poland. Under his rule and that of his father, Augustus the Strong, Dresden's musical life was at its zenith.

Kreuzchor

Boys sang in the Kreuzkirche as long ago as 1300; a first schoolmaster is attested in that year. An invoice of 1370 also lists a »magister scholae« and an organist. From this time on the Kreuzchor is mentioned regularly; it was one of the first boys' choirs in the world, and became one of the most famous. According to his instructions, Johannes Baumann, appointed as first cantor in 1540, was expected to sing with his choir and provide accompaniment above all for »Christian German hymns from the hymn book of Dr Luther«. The Kreuzchor achieved its greatest distinction under cantors Christoph Neander and Michael Lohr. They gave the first performances of religious compositions by **Heinrich Schütz**, who was active at court in Dresden in their time. From 1651 the Kreuzkirche cantors were also responsible for church music in the Frauenkirche and Sophienkirche. However, one of the most famous pupils at the school, Richard Wagner, did not manage to become an active singer in his schooldays, from 1822 to 1827. In the 20th century the choir of 140 nine to thirteen-year-old boys undertook many tours and became famous throughout the world.

Religious music

From Hofkapelle to Staatskapelle

Dresden's Staatskapelle (state orchestra) originated as a choir: in 1548 Elector Moritz signed the foundation charter for the Dresden court singers; initially their task was to perform the liturgy in the palace chapel, but soon they were required to provide secular music as well. The ensemble that was then called Hofkapelle (court orchestra) and is now the Staatskapelle is thus the oldest orchestra in the world.

Court singers

Instrumentalists are attested in 1555, and in 1568 Kapellmeister Antonio Scandelli initiated the close contact that was sustained for centuries between Dresden's Hofkapelle and the Italian musical tradition.

One of the most famous boys' choirs in the world: the Kreuzchor

Heinrich Schütz A milestone in Dresden's music and theatrical culture was the appointment of Heinrich Schütz as court cantor in 1615 by Elector Johann Georg I. Schütz worked in Dresden for 56 years, until his death. He wrote the first German opera, ***Daphne*** (first performed in 1627 in Torgau), but composed mostly religious music.

Italian period In 1641 another orchestra was founded, the Elector's Kapelle, headed by Giovanni Andrea Bontempi, Dresden's first castrato.
In 1666 the two orchestras were combined and were firmly in Italian hands until Elector Johann Georg III dismissed all the Italians.

Opera orchestra: From 1664 the court orchestra was regularly used for opera. This
over 300 years was particularly important for the lavish court entertainments that
old took place first in the Stallhof, and later in the Zwinger and Schloss Pillnitz.

Hofkapelle and Opera

City of opera In 1664 Dresden's first opera house opened on the Taschenberg, in one of the earliest theatre buildings in Germany. This was the beginning of Dresden's reputation for opera. As was the fashion at the time, most performances were Italian opera. Dresden opera reached a pinnacle with **Johann Adolf Hasse**. In 1731 he took over as director of the Hofkapelle, and the new Zwinger opera house opened with his

Cleofilde on 13 September 1731. When Dresden came under Prussian fire in 1760 he was obliged to witness the burning of musical treasures, including all the secular works of Heinrich Schütz. Hasse's most important musical contemporary was the Czech Jan Dismas Zelenka, who was regarded as an outstanding Baroque master. He was in Dresden from 1710, and in 1735 was appointed composer for church music. The composer Johann Georg Pisendel contributed greatly to the reputation of the orchestra in his own time, so that it was described by Rousseau as the »most perfect and best formed ensemble« in Europe. Pisendel's famous teacher **Antonio Vivaldi** wrote demanding concertos especially »per l'orchestra di Dresda«.

> **!**   *Baedeker* TIP
>
> **Sandstone and Music**
>
> Each year between March and November the Festival Sandstein und Musik organizes outstanding performances in Dresden and in the palaces, castles, gardens and churches of the Sächsische Schweiz and the eastern Erzgebirge. No-one should fail to take the rare opportunity to listen to vocal and instrumental music with a sandstone quarry as a backdrop (tel. 0 35 01-44 65 72).

Georg Philipp Telemann, Johann Friedrich Fasch, Johann Gottlieb Graun and Christoph Willibald Gluck were great names in 18th-century music whose activities with the Hofkapelle left their mark on the golden age of music in Dresden.

Carl Maria von Weber

E.T.A. Hoffmann directed the Dresden opera in 1813–14 and promoted German opera in particular. Carl Maria von Weber, employed in Dresden from 1817 as Hofkapellmeister, wrote his German national opera here: his *Freischütz*, first performed in 1821 in Berlin, was a resounding success in Dresden six months later.

From Richard Wagner to Fritz Busch

In 1841 the first Semper Opera opened on what is now Theaterplatz. Two years later Richard Wagner was employed here, and he immediately described the Staatskapelle in glowing terms as a »magic harp«. *Rienzi*, *The Flying Dutchman* and *Tannhäuser* had their premieres on this stage. Following a fire which destroyed the first Semper Opera, a second one was built in 1878, again by Gottfried Semper. From 1901 onwards, the public enjoyed a total of nine premieres of operas by Richard Strauss under the baton of Ernst von Schuch and Fritz Busch, including *Salome*, *Elektra* and *Der Rosenkavalier*. Strauss regarded the Semper Opera as an »eldorado for premieres«. It also saw the first performances in Germany of Puccini's *Tosca*. The Hoftheater (Court Theatre) and Hofkapelle (Court Orchestra) were re-named Sächsisches Staatstheater and Staatskapelle in 1919, when Saxony ceased to be a monarchy.

◄ Richard Strauss

Destruction and rebuilding

The bombs of 1945 destroyed all the theatres. The Staatskapelle and opera ensemble used the Schauspielhaus, rebuilt in 1948, until the re-opening of the Semper Opera in 1985.

Civic Music Culture

Dresden Konservatorium
As the middle classes strove for higher things in the 19th century, a civic music culture developed. In 1854 Dresden's Tonkünstlerverein (Musicians' Association) was founded, with the aim of cultivating and performing instrumental music »of all periods, including the most recent«. Two years later the Dresden Konservatorium was founded, which in 1952 became the Hochschule für Musik, named after Carl Maria von Weber. Many famous composers came to Dresden to perform their works, including Nicolo Paganini, Hector Berlioz, Franz Liszt and Robert Schumann.

Dresden Philharmonie
1870 marked the birth of the Gewerbehausorchester; in 1915 it became the Dresdner Philharmonisches Orchester, and from 1924 was known as the Dresdner Philharmonie, under which name it has gained a brilliant reputation in recent times on its tours in Germany and abroad.

DZzM
The Dresdner Zentrum für zeitgenössische Musik (DZzM, Dresden Centre for Contemporary Music) also enjoys an international reputation. Since 1986 it has organized popular **contemporary music days** each autumn.

Concert in Schloss Rammenau, part of the »Sandstone and Music« festival

Since 1997 the Dresdner Sinfoniker (Dresden Symphony Orchestra) have staged adventurous musical programmes: it is the first symphony orchestra in Europe that is devoted exclusively to a repertoire of contemporary music, including world premieres,. The ensemble is made up of members of well-known European orchestras who meet several times a year to rehearse their wide-ranging concert programme.

Dresdner Sinfoniker

Since 1978 the Dresden music festival in the two weeks around Whitsuntide has become a famous international occasion, bringing classical music stars to the Elbe. Staatskapelle, Philharmonie and Kreuzchor always participate in the festival, and the audience can rely on high-quality performances.

Dresden music festival

Famous People

What does Dresden owe to the rule of Augustus the Strong? What was the link between the Venetian painter Bernardo Bellotto, better known as Canaletto, and the electors' city? How did Erich Kästner relate to his home town? What did Heinrich Schütz, Richard Wagner and Carl Maria von Weber contribute to Dresden's legendary reputation as city of music?

Augustus the Strong
Elector Friedrich August I,
Augustus II as King of Poland (1670–1733)

After his elder brother died without issue aged 26, Friedrich August came to power in 1694, at the age of 24. After converting to the Catholic faith he was able to gain the Polish crown with the help of immense bribes; he lost it during the Northern War in 1706, and regained it with Russian help in 1709. Yet his ambition to turn Poland into a hereditary monarchy was not fulfilled. Under his rule the magnificent Dresden court became a European centre of culture and the arts, largely financed by tax burdens repeatedly imposed on the people. Augustus the Strong died in 1733 in Warsaw and was buried in Cracow Cathedral. His heart, however, lies in the crypt in Dresden's Hofkirche.

George Bähr (1666–1738)

George Bähr, architect of Protestant churches in Saxony, came from **Architect** the Erzgebirge region. Trained as a carpenter, he was appointed official master carpenter in 1705. In 1722 he was commissioned to build the new **Frauenkirche**, which from 1726 became one of the most important Baroque buildings in Europe. Bähr did not live to see the completion of his greatest architectural achievement in 1743. A few months after his death the great controversy over the dome of the Frauenkirche came to an end; it was completed according to his plans and became Dresden's emblem.

Bernardo Bellotto,
known as Canaletto (1721–80)

The painter and copper engraver Bernardo Bellotto, better known as **Painter** Canaletto, was born in Venice; his early works were views of various Italian cities.

← *»I don't want to dance nicely and prettily!« was the motto of Gret Palucca, who founded a school of modern dance in Dresden in 1925.*

In 1747 he accepted an invitation from Friedrich August II (Augustus III), who appointed him court painter one year later, and for whom Canaletto painted pictures of Dresden, Warsaw, Pirna and the Königstein fortress in landscape settings. Canaletto's paintings and engravings are among the most valuable in Dresden's art collections. His landscapes are notable for his sophisticated technique, and they mark a great step forward in the development of realistic depiction of landscape. Canaletto's topographically exact city views make it possible to appreciate the beauty of Dresden as a consummate Baroque city and the unique quality of its buildings.

Johann Friedrich Böttger (1682–1719)

Producer of porcelain

From 1702 Augustus the Strong put Böttger, a native of Schleiz, under close guard in Königstein fortress, where he was given the task of making gold. When these alchemical experiments failed, the king ordered him from 1707 to take part in attempts to make porcelain in the vaults of the Jungfernbastei, now the Brühlsche Terrasse, under the supervision of the scientist Ehrenfried Walther von Tschirnhaus.

Ehrenfried Walther von Tschirnhaus (1651–1708) ►

Von Tschirnhaus, born in Kieslingswalde near Görlitz, had fired the first piece of hard-paste porcelain as early as 1694 with a double-lens firing apparatus. Böttger witnessed von Tschirnhaus's ultimate success, after much experimentation, in finding materials from which it was indeed possible to form vessels and fire porcelain.

On 15 January 1708 the recipe for porcelain was finally written down; von Tschirnhaus and Böttger succeeded in making **the first European hard-paste porcelain**. Yet only on 28 March 1709, five months after von Tschirnhaus's death, did Böttger report to Augustus the Strong the discovery of the »white gold«. Böttger alone became famous for it, improved the glaze and the porcelain mass, and put the discovery into production in the Meissen porcelain factory, founded in 1710. In 1714 Böttger was conditionally set free, but re-arrested on suspicion of betraying the secrets of Meissen porcelain production. He died – sick and blind – in 1719.

Carl Gustav Carus (1789–1869)

Universal talent

Carus, born in Leipzig, was knowledgeable in many fields. From 1814 he lived in Dresden, where he practised as royal physician from 1827 and published seminal works on gynaecology, anatomy and physiology.

As a natural philosopher and psychologist he recognized the importance of the unconscious and its expression in dreams and the emotional world, and was one of the first to investigate comparative psychology. Under the influence of his friend C.D. Friedrich he turned his attention to Romantic painting and in 1815–24 wrote *Nine Letters regarding Landscape Painting*. The university hospitals at Dresden's Technical University are named after him.

Anna Constanze, Countess of Cosel (1680–1765)

At the age of 25 the daughter of a Danish officer became mistress of Augustus the Strong. In 1707 he made her Countess of Cosel. For nine years the **»Saxon Pompadour«** kept the Dresden court on their toes; she got Augustus to give her Schloss Pillnitz and build Taschenberg Palais as a love nest. When Augustus tired of her and cast his eye on the Polish countess Maria Dönhoff, she refused to give up her position. Thereupon Augustus banished her from Dresden and she fled to Prussian territory. From there she demanded the fulfilment of a promise of marriage and the recognition of their three children as heirs. Augustus, however, came to an arrangement with Friedrich Wilhelm I of Prussia: the countess was exchanged for a number of Prussian prisoners and imprisoned in 1716 in Stolpen Castle, where she died after 49 lonely years.

Otto Dix (1891–1969)

Dix, a painter and graphic artist, was born in Gera in Thuringia. **Painter** After his return from World War I he studied at the Kunstakademie (Academy of Art) in Dresden, and was one of the founders of the »Dresden Secession«. After four years in Düsseldorf and Berlin he returned to Dresden in 1927; he was appointed professor at the Kunstakademie, until the Nazis dismissed him in 1933 and defamed his art as »degenerate«. His social criticism and realism relentlessly analyzed forms of human existence and decadence. His themes were prostitution, war, big cities and religion. His major works, the triptych *War* (Galerie Neue Meister) and the *Big City* triptych were painted in Dresden.

Caspar David Friedrich (1774–1840)

The most important German Romantic painter lived in Dresden **Painter** from 1798 until his death. Friedrich painted landscapes and discovered the mountainous area known as Sächsische Schweiz (Saxon Switzerland) as a source of motifs. He saw in art an »intermediary between nature and mankind«, a possibility of portraying conditions of the human soul that appear in his paintings as autumnal mood, twilight, moonshine or mist. His *Mountain Cross* of 1808, now exhibited in the Galerie Neue Meister, was a pioneer work for Romantic painting; the Alte Nationalgalerie in Berlin has an outstanding collection of his work.

Rudolf Harbig (1913–44)

Runner Harbig was born in Dresden, and became a cartwright and later a casual worker and gas-meter reader for the Dresden City Works; after a long period of unemployment he became a professional soldier. In 1934 he was discovered as runner in a competition, went on to win a bronze medal in the 4 x 400m relay at the Olympic Games of 1936, was German champion seven times, and European middle-distance champion twice; he broke six world records. Today Dresden's Rudolf Harbig Stadium bears the name of this German running prodigy.

Erich Kästner (1899–1974)

Writer The writer Erich Kästner, born in Dresden's Neustadt, wrote ironic and sarcastic volumes of verse that railed against petit-bourgeois morality and militarism, such as *Herz auf Taille* (Heart on Waist). He was also a successful author of novels and fantasies for children and

young people, of which *Emil and the Detectives* is one of the best known. Kästner's language was marked by trenchant humour and perspicuity in regard to the world of his time. After World War II he settled in Munich, where he died in 1974. In Dresden there is an Erich Kästner Museum; a street, a square and a café are named after him. In his recollections of childhood, *Als ich ein kleiner Junge war* (When I Was a Little Boy) he wrote: »If [...] I know not only what is bad and ugly, but also what is beautiful, then I owe this gift to the good fortune of having been born in Dresden. I didn't have to learn what is beautiful from books. [...] I could breathe in beauty as foresters' children breathe in woodland air«.

Ernst Ludwig Kirchner (1880–1938)

Painter Kirchner, born in Aschaffenburg, was one of the leaders of German Expressionism. He is regarded as the most famous member of the »Die Brücke«, an association of artists which he co-founded in Dresden in 1905. The group rented an empty butcher's shop at Berliner Strasse 60, in the artisan and industrial district of Friedrichstadt, as a studio and dwelling. In Dresden Kirchner was interested mostly in city views and everyday street scenes, and in female nudes, painted for preference in the open air in the Moritzburg district. Anti-academic in orientation, his pictures broke with accustomed ways of seeing and the aesthetic conventions of the time: forms are reduced to a minimum, traditional perspective and proportions are abandoned, the intoxication of powerful, undiluted colours expresses subjective experience of the world. In 1911 Kirchner left Dresden. Denounced as a »degenerate artist« in 1937, he shot himself one year later.

Karl May (1842–1912)

Karl May, born the fifth of 14 children to a weaver's family in Hohenstein-Ernstthal, was initially a primary school teacher, and then scraped a living in dubious ways, which resulted in a spell in prison, before he began to write. From 1890 he was **one of the most-read German writers**, producing Western adventures that are still popular today. In April 1883 he moved to Dresden, and finally settled in 1896 in his Villa Shatterhand in Radebeul. His books were translated into 28 languages and sold in their millions, and have been dramatized for film, theatre and radio. At the time he was writing he knew most of the places he wrote about only from books, which makes his precise descriptions of the Wild West all the more astonishing. After achieving fame and fortune he made up for this to some extent by travelling. Plays based on his writings are performed at the Felsenbühne, a theatre in Rathen.

Johann Georg Palitzsch (1723–88)

A farmer throughout his life, Palitzsch, who was born in Dresden-Prohlis, was an active self-taught astronomer. In 1758 he succeeded in rediscovering Halley's Comet, and in 1782, independently of others, he discovered the periodic light variation of Algol in the Perseus constellation. The academies of Paris, London and St Petersburg elected him as a corresponding member. Palitzsch was also the first farmer to grow potatoes in the Elbe valley, and he installed the first lightning conductor on the Schloss in Dresden. The Palitzsch Museum in Prohlis commemorates his life (Prohliser Str. 34; Tue–Thu, Sun 1pm–5pm).

Astronomer

Gret Palucca (1902–93)

Gret Palucca's fame at home and abroad is founded on the expressive dance she developed, her legendary solo performances and her methods as a dance teacher. Born in Munich, she continued her studies from 1921 in Dresden with Mary Wigman, and became a member of Wigman's dance group.

The school of dance opened by Gret Palucca in 1925 was closed by the Nazis in 1939, and made into a state institute for professional stage dance training in 1949. Since 1993 it has been a dance academy, and for decades one of the most highly regarded training institutions in the world for classical and modern dance.

Balthasar Permoser (baptized 1651–1732)

Sculptor Balthasar Permoser came to Dresden as court sculptor in 1689 via Salzburg, Vienna, Venice, Rome and Florence. He gained great acclaim for his monumental Hercules figures in the Grosser Garten and for his accomplished ivory carving and small works of sculpture. Permoser's artistic capabilities range from the decorative to the expression of extreme emotion, from the most profound sorrow to the merriest joie-de-vivre. He was in charge of the sculpture workshop when the Zwinger was built, and in collaboration with Matthäus Daniel Pöppelmann fashioned the unique blend of sculptural art and architecture which makes the Zwinger one of Germany's greatest artistic and architectural achievements.

Matthäus Daniel Pöppelmann (1662–1736)

Architect The architect Matthäus Daniel Pöppelmann was born in Herford in Westphalia. After his years as apprentice and journeyman he entered Dresden's office of works in 1680, and in 1718 he was made chief architect.

Pöppelmann is **Dresden's most famous Baroque architect** and was one of the most important of his time by international standards. His versatile building activities ranged from burgher houses to churches and palaces in Dresden and the surrounding area. He drew up new plans for the Schloss; among his most significant works were the Taschenberg Palais, the Japanisches Palais, the Weinbergkirche (vineyard church) in Pillnitz, the palaces at Schloss Pillnitz, Schloss Moritzburg, the Dreikönigskirche (Church of the Three Kings), the Baroque Elbe bridge and the buildings in the Baroque garden at Großsedlitz. The Zwinger, built during his time as Augustus the Strong's chief architect, was his greatest achievement, and one of the most important examples of German late Baroque found anywhere.

Helmut Schön (1915–96)

Helmut Schön, »the tall one«, was one of the most successful trainers of the German national football team to date. From 1930 to 1945 he played for SC Dresden, then until 1950 for Dresden-Friedrichstadt and finally for Hertha BSC Berlin. Due to the war he had few opportunities as a national player, but he was all the more successful from 1964 as trainer of the West German team: runner-up in the 1966 world championship, third in 1970, European champions 1972, **world champions in 1974** und European runner-up in 1976. After his team was knocked out by Austria in the world championship of 1978 in Argentina, he hung up his famous peaked cap in disappointment and ended his career.

Johann Andreas Schubert (1808–70)

Engineer

The gifted engineer Johann Andreas Schubert was a university teacher, inventor, technical designer and businessman, and one of the pioneers of the industrial revolution in Germany. Originally from the Vogtland region, he was appointed at the age of 20 to the Königliche Technische Bildungsanstalt (Royal Technical Training Institution) in Dresden; he succeeded in establishing practical engineering as a main component in training. In 1836 he built Saxony's second-largest mechanical engineering factory in Dresden-Übigau. In 1836–37 the first Elbe passenger steamers were constructed from his plans, and in 1836–39 *Saxonia*, **the first German steam engine**. It ran on the Leipzig–Dresden route from the time of its opening in 1839, and was in service for 18 years; there is a model of the engine in Dresden's transport museum.

Heinrich Schütz / Henricus Sagittarius (1585–1672)

Composer

In 1609 Landgrave Moritz of Hessen sent Schütz, who was born in Köstritz, to Giovanni Gabrieli in Venice for three years, to complete his musical training. In 1617 he took up his post in Dresden as master of music at court, and kept this position for the rest of his life. Heinrich Schütz was the first to combine the new forms of 16th-century Italian music with German traditions of composing. He elevated German church music to new heights and made the Saxon court with its Hofkapelle into a centre of European renown for music. The »father of German music« composed **the first German opera**, *Daphne* (1627), of which, however, the score has not survived.

Gottfried Semper (1803–79)

Architect

Born in Hamburg, Gottfried Semper studied law, mathematics and architecture in Rome, Munich and Paris, and travelled subsequently

to France, Greece and Italy. In 1834 he was appointed professor of architecture and director of the school of building at the Kunstakademie in Dresden. In 1849 he had to flee Dresden because of his active participation in the May uprising. Important works by Semper in Dresden are the first Hoftheater (burnt down in 1869); the Villa Rosa (destroyed in 1945); the Synagogue (set alight and demolished in 1938) and the Semper Gallery. The second Hoftheater (Semper Opera) was built under the supervision of his son Manfred and destroyed in 1945. It was reconstructed, and re-opened in 1985.

Johann Gottfried Silbermann (1683–1753)

Organ builder Johann Gottfried Silbermann was born to a Saxon family of organ and piano makers in Kleinbobritzsch near Frauenstein, and was apprenticed to his brother Andreas in Strasbourg. He succeeded in building organs of unusual purity, clarity and resonance. In 1740 he invented the cembal d'amore, and made a significant contribution to the spread of the pianoforte by improving the mechanical hammers invented by Christofori. The organs in Dresden's old Hofkirche (1720), the Sophienkirche (1720–21) and the Frauenkirche (1730–36) were among the 50 built by J.G. Silbermann. His last and largest organ in the Hofkirche was the only one of his Dresden organs that escaped destruction. It was completed between 1750 and 1755 by his nephew Johann Daniel Silbermann and pupil Zacharias Hildebrandt.

Richard Wagner (1813–83)

Composer Richard Wagner was born in Leipzig and grew up in Dresden, where he attended the Kreuzschule until 1827. On completing his studies he was employed to run the orchestra and choir, then as director of music; in 1843 he was appointed **director of the Hofkapelle for life**. The first performances of *Rienzi* (1842), *The Flying Dutchman* (1843) and *Tannhäuser* (1845) were given in the first Semper Opera, and at the same time he wrote his epoch-making theoretical works. His participation in the May uprising of 1849 forced him to flee Dresden.

Carl Maria von Weber (1786–1826)

Composer Carl Maria von Weber was born in Eutin. His formative years in his father's travelling theatre troupe were a strong influence. After studies in Salzburg, Vienna and Darmstadt he was appointed musical director of the German Opera in Dresden in 1816. He is renowned as the creator of German Romantic national and popular opera, most famously in *Der Freischütz*, first performed in Berlin in 1821. His musical compositions and his passionate theoretical controversies, borne on the wave of patriotic enthusiasm generated by the wars of liberation, influenced Chopin, Liszt und Wagner. Carl Maria von Weber composed major parts of *Euryanthe*, *Oberon* and his *Invitation to the Dance* in Dresden. Shortly after the first performance of *Oberon* in 1826 the sickly Weber died in London. Today Dresden's school of music bears his name.

Mary Wigman (1886–1973)

Mary Wigman, a dancer, choreographer and teacher of expressive modern dance, was born in Hanover. In the years 1910–13 she studied at Émile Jaques-Dalcroze's school of dance in Dresden-Hellerau. In Dresden she achieved her first great successes. In 1920 she founded the Wigman School in the city, with branches in Munich, Berlin, Hamburg and New York, and in 1924 established the Wigman Group, of which her most famous student, Gret Palucca, was a member. After Mary Wigman's dance school was closed by the Nazis, she left Dresden and emigrated. From 1947 her choreography of works by Gluck, Orff and Stravinsky was acclaimed all over the world. Mary Wigman died in 1973 in West Berlin.

Dancer

Practicalities

WHERE ARE THE MOST BEST PLACES TO EAT? WHAT FESTIVALS, MUSIC AND THEATRE EVENTS ARE NOT TO BE MISSED? WHICH ARE THE BARS FOR NIGHT OWLS?

Accommodation

▶ RECOMMENDED HOTELS IN DRESDEN

▶ ① **etc. see plan p.96/97**
Without number: outside the area covered by plan.

▶ **Hotel bookings**
Dresden Werbung und Tourismus GmbH
www.dresden-tourist.de
Tel. 49 19 22 22, fax 495 12 76
▸ Information

▶ **Price categories**
The prices listed are average prices for double room with breakfast; actual costs may be higher or lower. The prices are therefore not a definitive indication of category. It is worth enquiring about group and weekend arrangements in many hotels, including the expensive ones.

Luxury: more than €160
Mid-range: €100–160
Budget: €50–100

! *Baedeker* TIP

Ice skating

Advent is the time of year when fans of winter sports get their skates out of the cupboard. Until late February hotel guests and everyone else can take a turn on the rink in the inner court of the Taschenberg-Palais. The snow bar provides inner warmth, and sometimes live music is played (hours, including hire of skates: Mon–Fri 4pm–10pm, Sat and Sun 11am–10pm).

LUXURY: MORE THAN €160;

▶ ① **Bülow Residenz Dresden**
Rähnitzgasse 19, D-01097 Dresden
www.buelow-residenz.de
Tel. 80 0 30, fax 800 31 00
59 beds. Rooms suitable for travellers with disabilities, Caroussel gourmet restaurant, conference room, car park; one of the loveliest hotels in the city in a comprehensively refurbished Baroque house in Neustadt. Keen competition for the really big top hotels, because it is decidedly cosier and more intimate.

▶ ② **Dresden Hilton**
An der Frauenkirche 5,
D-01067 Dresden, www.hilton.de
Tel. 86 4 20
522 beds. Rooms suitable for travellers with disabilities, congress centre, saloons, several restaurants, cafés, swimming pool, sauna, whirlpool, solarium, garage, car park; top hotel in Dresden Altstadt

▶ ③ **Kempinski Hotel Taschenberg Palais Dresden**
Am Taschenberg,
D-01067 Dresden
www.kempinski-dresden.de
Tel. 49 1 20, fax 491 28 12
400 beds. 25 suites, rooms suitable for travellers with disabilities, Intermezzo gourmet restaurant, bar, pool, sauna, fitness room – reside in grand style in the restored Taschenberg Palais

A fine address: Kempinski Hotel in the Taschenberg Palais

▶ ④ **Maritim Hotel Dresden**
Ostra-Ufer 2 / Devrientstr. 10-12,
D-01067 Dresden
www.maritim.de
Tel. 216-0 , fax 216-1000
328 beds. Rooms suitable for
travellers with disabilities, large
restaurant, swimming pool, well-
ness. The famous Erlwein Speicher
as hotel – something very special.

▶ ⑤ **Schloss Eckberg**
Bautzner Str. 134,
D-01099 Dresden
www.schloss-eckberg.de
Tel. 80 9 90, fax 809 91 99
34 beds. Restaurant, conference
room, sauna, car park; spend the
night in an Elbe palace, wonderfully situated above the Elbe,
idyllic park. There are rooms in
the Schloss, and also in the
Kavaliershaus, rather less expensive!

▶ ⑥ **Steigenberger
Hotel de Saxe**
Neumarkt 9
www.desaxe-dresden.
steigenberger.de
D-01067 Dresden
Tel. 43 86-0, fax 4386 888
178 rooms. Restaurant, spa, conference rooms. Newly opened, and
the only hotel in Dresden with a
view of the Frauenkirche – from
rooms in the front.

▶ ⑦ **The Radisson SAS
Gewandhaus Hotel Dresden**
Ringstr. 1, D-01067 Dresden
www.radissonsas.com
Tel. 49 4 90, fax 494 94 90
194 beds. Rooms suitable for
travellers with disabilities, conference rooms, swimming pool,
restaurant; luxury hotel behind
historic façade of Dresden tailors'
guild house completed in 1770

► ⑧ **The Westin Bellevue**
Grosse Meissner Str. 15,
D-01097 Dresden
www.westin-bellevue.com
Tel. 80 50, fax 805 16 09
654 beds. Rooms suitable for
travellers with disabilities, conference rooms, several restaurants
(incl. Canaletto), cafés, wine
tavern, hotel club, pool and night
bar, casino, fitness club with
special Kneipp-Kur section,
swimming pool, sauna, garage, car
park. This old-established top-
class hotel has rooms with the
»Canaletto view«!

MID-RANGE: €100–€160

► ⑨ **Am Blauen Wunder**
Loschwitzer Str. 48
D-01309 Dresden
www.hotel-am-blauen-wunder.de
Tel. 33 6 60, fax 336 62 99
76 beds. Restaurant, conference
room, sauna, car park

► ⑩ **Am Terrassenufer**
Terrassenufer 12,
D-01069 Dresden
www.hotel-terrassenufer.de
Tel. 440 95 00,
Fax 440 96 00
196 rooms. High-rise building
with restaurant and splendid view
of Altstadt, just a few minutes'
walk away

*Penck everywhere: those who like his
paintings will feel at home in the art'otel.*

► ⑪ **art'otel Dresden**
Ostra-Allee 33, D-01067 Dresden
www.artotel.de
Tel. 49 2 20, fax 492 27 77
174 rooms. Suitable for the disabled, restaurant, bar, conference
rooms, fitness room with view of
Altstadt, sauna. Special attraction
for art lovers: the hotel has a lot of
pictures by A. R. Penck.

► ⑫ **Artushof**
Fetscherstr. 30, D-01307 Dresden
www.artushof.de
Tel. 44 59 10, fax 44 59 11 29
24 rooms, some with tiled stove, a
few minutes' walk from Grosser
Garten; renovated in 2005

► ⑬ **Dorint Novotel Dresden**
Grunaer Str. 14, D-01069 Dresden
www.dorint.de
Tel. 49 1 50, fax 491 51 00
475 beds. Rooms suitable for
travellers with disabilities, restaurant, conference room, pool, sauna, fitness room, garage

► ⑭ **Elbflorenz**
Rosenstr. 36, D-01067 Dresden
www.hotel-elbflorenz.de
Tel. 86 4 00, fax 864 01 00
227 rooms. Rooms suitable for
travellers with disabilities, restaurant, conference room, car park;
modern hotel in World Trade
Centre

► ⑮ **Martha Hospiz**
Nieritzstr. 11, D-01097 Dresden
www.marthahospiz.
dresden.vch.de
Tel. 81 7 60, fax 817 62 22
85 beds. Rooms suitable for travellers with disabilities, restaurant,
conference room – good value for
money, pleasant alternative to
luxury hotels

▶ ⑯ **Pullman Newa Dresden**
St Petersburger Str. 34,
D-01069 Dresden
Tel. 48 14 1 09, fax 495 51 37
444 beds. Restaurant, conference
room, sauna, fitness room,
garage, car park and panorama
window

▶ ⑰ **Ringhotel Residenz
Alt Dresden**
Mobschatzer Str. 29,
D-01157 Dresden
www.residenz-alt-dresden.de
Tel. 42 8 10, fax 428 19 88
300 beds. Rooms for travellers
with disabilities, restaurant, conference room, sauna, fitness room,
car park, cycle hire

▶ ⑱ **Rothenburger Hof**
Rothenburger Str. 15,
D-01099 Dresden
Tel. 81 2 60, fax 812 6222
76 beds. Restaurant, car park,
pool, sauna, fitness room, cycle
hire

BUDGET: €50 – €100

▶ ⑲ **Alpha-Hotel**
Fritz-Reuter-Str. 21,
D-01097 Dresden
www.alphahotel-dresden.de
Tel. 80 9 50

160 beds. Rooms suitable for
disabled travellers, restaurant,
conference room, sauna, garage,
car park

▶ ⑳ **Ibis Hotel Bastei**
Tel. 485 63 05; 426 beds.

▶ **Ibis Hotel Königstein**
Tel. 48 56 66 62; 495 beds.

▶ **Ibis Hotel Lilienstein**
Tel. 48 56 66 63; 495 beds.
Three inexpensive large hotels on
Prager Strasse, all with restaurant,
suitable for travellers with disabil-
ities

▶ ㉑ **An der Rennbahn**
Winterbergstr. 96,
D-01237 Dresden
www.hotel-an-der-rennbahn-
dresden.de,
Tel. 21 25 00, fax 212 50 50
40 beds. Restaurant, conference
room, car park; pleasant, quiet
location with good restaurant
close to race-course

▶ ㉒ **Novalis garni**
Bärnsdorfer Str. 185,
D-01127 Dresden
Tel. 82 1 30, fax 821 31 80
104 beds. Car park, sauna

● HOTELS IN SURROUNDING AREAS

MEISSEN
▶ **Mercure Grand Hotel Meissen
(mid-range)**
Hafenstr. 27–31, D-01662 Meissen
Tel. (03 5 21) 72 2 50, 97 rooms.
Restaurant, car park; rooms with
view of Elbe and castle

▶ **Am Markt 6 (mid-range)**
Am Markt 6, D-01662 Meissen
Tel. (03 5 21) 41 0 70, fax 41 07 20
11 rooms and restaurant

▶ **Burgkeller (mid-range)**
Domplatz 11, D-01662 Meissen

Meißen's recently renovated marketplace with street cafés and the Hotel Am Markt 6

Tel. (03 5 21) 41400
10 rooms. Böttgerstube restaurant, in-house patisserie, wine bar

▶ **Elbdamm (budget)**
Siebeneichener Str. 44,
D-01662 Meissen
Tel. (03 5 21) 47 0 50, fax 47 05 10
18 rooms, car park

▶ **Goldener Löwe (mid-range)**
Heinrichsplatz 6
D-01662 Meissen
Tel. (03 5 21) 41 1 10, fax 411 14 44
36 rooms, restaurant, wine tavern

MORITZBURG

▶ **Churfürstliche Waldschänke (mid-range)**
Grosse Fasanenstr.,
D-01468 Moritzburg, www.chur-fuerstliche-waldschaenke.de
Tel. (03 52 07) 86 00, fax 86 0 93
61 beds. Restaurant (game, carp), conference rooms, cycle hire, fishing.

▶ **Eisenberger Hof (budget)**
Kötzschenbrodaer Str. 8,
D-01468 Moritzburg
www.hotel-eisenberger-hof.de
Tel. (03 52 07) 81 6 73, fax 81 6 84
20 rooms. Restaurant with wholesome home cooking, sauna, car park.

▶ **Landhaus (budget)**
Schlossallee 37
D-01468 Moritzburg
Tel. (03 52 07) 89 6 90,
fax 81 6 04
16 rooms, restaurant, car park

PILLNITZ

▶ **Schloss Hotel Dresden-Pillnitz (mid-range)**
August-Böckstiegel-Str. 10
D-01326 Dresden,
www.schlosshotel-pillnitz.de
Tel. 26 1 40, fax 261 44 00
89 beds. In Schloss Pillnitz gardens with Schloss café and acclaimed restaurant

RADEBEUL AND AROUND

► **Steigenberger Parkhotel (mid-range)**
Nizzastr. 55, D-01445 Radebeul
www.steigenberger.de
Tel. 83 2 10, fax 832 14 45
202 beds in hotel and 216 beds in nine villas, rooms suitable for travellers with disabilities, restaurants, conference room, swimming pool, computer golf, car park

► **Villa Sorgenfrei (mid-range)**
Augustusweg 48,
D-01445 Radebeul
Tel. 89 33 30, fax 830 45 22
28 beds. Decorated and furnished in Louis XVI style in restored, listed winery, restaurant with French cuisine, swimming pool, sauna, fitness room, park.

► **Waldhotel Weinböhla (mid-range)**
Forststr. 66, D-01689 Weinböhla
www.waldhotel-weinboehla.de
Tel. (03 52 43) 410, fax 32 8 40
114 rooms. New house in wine-growing village of Weinböhla, rooms suitable for travellers with disabilities, acclaimed restaurant (wine tasting), conference room, sauna, bowling, tennis courts, car park.

► **Zum Pfeiffer (budget)**
Pfeifferweg 1
D-01445 Radebeul
www.hotel-zum-pfeiffer.de
Tel. 83 98 70
12 rooms. Restaurant, above Radebeul vineyards

SÄCHSISCHE SCHWEIZ

► **Lindenhof (budget)**
Rudolf-Sendig-Str. 11
D-01814 Bad Schandau

www.bad-schandau.de
Tel. (03 50 22) 48 90, fax 48 9 12
76 beds. Central location between historic centre and well kept town park

► **Mittelndorfer Mühle (budget)**
Kirnitzschtalstr. 4
D-01814 Bad Schandau
www.mittelndorfer-muehle.de
Tel. (03 50 22) 58 50, fax 58 5 98
52 beds. Rooms suitable for travellers with disabilities, car park; peaceful location in wild, romantic Kirnitzsch valley and good base for walking

► **Parkhotel Bad Schandau (mid-range)**
Rudolf-Sendig-Str. 12,
D-01814 Bad Schandau
www.parkhotel-bad-schandau.de
Tel. (03 50 22) 520, fax 52 2 15
73 rooms, restaurant, sauna, fitness centre, car park

► **Lindenhof (budget)**
Gohrischer Str. 2
D-01824 Königstein
www.lindenhof-koenigstein.de
Tel. (03 50 21) 68 2 43, fax 66 2 14
65 beds, restaurant, car park

► **Panoramahotel Lilienstein (budget)**
Ebenheit 7, D-01824 Königstein
www.hotel-lilienstein.de
Tel. (03 50 22) 53 1 00
33 rooms, restaurant and good view of Lilienstein and fortress

► **Romantikhotel Deutsches Haus (budget)**
Niedere Burgstr. 1, D-01796 Pirna
www.romantikhotel-pirna.de
Tel. (03 5 01) 46 88 00, fax 46 88 20
78 beds. Marvellous Renaissance

burgher house in old town centre, with good restaurant and terrace, conference room, car park.

▶ **Pirna'scher Hof (budget)**
Am Markt 4, D-01796 Pirna
www.pirnascher-hof.de
Tel. (03 5 01) 44 3 80
33 beds, restaurant, conference room, car park

▶ **Berghotel Bastei (budget)**
D-01847 Lohmen/Bastei
www.bastei-berghotel.de
Tel. (03 50 24) 77 90
63 rooms, panorama restaurant, sauna, car park

▶ **Erbgericht (budget)**
Wehlener Weg 1

D-01824 Rathen
www.erbgericht-rathen.de
Tel. (03 50 24) 77 30, fax 77 33 77
65 beds, restaurant with good food, indoor pool, sauna, car park; situated above the Elbe

▶ **Hotel Amselgrundschlösschen (budget)**
Amselgrund 3, D-01824 Rathen
Tel. (03 50 24) 743 33
86 beds, sauna, swimming pool and massage

▶ **Strandhotel (mid-range)**
Markt 9
D-01829 Stadt Wehlen
www.strandhotel-wehlen.de
Tel. (03 50 24) 78 4 90
45 beds, restaurant, car park

▶ GUESTHOUSES AND ROOMS

▶ **Prices**
Guesthouse prices usually range from €40 to €75 for a double room with breakfast.

▶ **Private accommodation**
Dresden Werbung und Tourismus GmbH ▶ Information

▶ **Mitwohnzentrale (shared accommodation)**
Dr- Friedrich-Wolf-Str. 2
D-01097 Dresden
www.mitwohnzentrale.de
Tel. 19 4 30
Fax 802 25 09

RECOMMENDATIONS

▶ **Am Berg**
Berggasse 9
01109 Dresden (25 beds)
www.pension-am-berg.de
Tel. 88 48 60, fax 8848634

▶ **Lorenz**
Lindenplatz 1
D-01157 Dresden (8 beds)
Tel. 421 20 47, fax 427 56 70

▶ **Gästehaus Loschwitz**
Grundstr. 40
D-01326 Dresden (24 beds)
Tel. 268 77 85, fax 267 87 75

▶ **Ogon**
Burgwartstr. 10
D-01159 Dresden (7 beds)
Tel. 411 67 05, fax 411 67 57

▶ **Pension Andreas**
Mendelssohn-Allee 40
D-01309 Dresden-Blasewitz
www.pensionandreas.de (29 beds)
Tel. 31 57 70, fax 315 77 55

▶ **Villa Daheim**
Berthold-Haupt-Str. 141

D-01259 Dresden (10 beds)
Tel. and fax 201 35 13

► **Wölfnitz**
Altwölfnitz 5, D-01169 Dresden
Tel. 411 99 11, fax 411 99 12
25 beds. Hotel/guesthouse

► **Zu den Linden**
Plattleite 62, D-01324 Dresden
Tel. 268 24 85, fax 263 17 80
38 beds. Art nouveau villa, top
location in Weisser Hirsch district,
cycle hire

► **Zum alten Fährhaus**
Fährstr. 20, D-01279 Dresden
Tel. 257 18 42

12 beds, inexpensive food, nice
courtyard.

► **Zur alten Säge**
Dresden Str. 107
D-01326 Dresden
Tel. 261 84 20, fax 261 84 20
11 rooms, 10min walk to Schloss
Pillnitz.

► **Zur Königlichen Ausspanne**
Eugen-Dieterich-Str. 5
D-01326 Dresden
www.koeniglicheausspanne.de
Tel. 268 95 02, fax 268 95 18
8 rooms, in grand old house on
Elbe slope, cycle hire.

▶ YOUNG PEOPLE'S ACCOMMODATION

YOUTH HOSTEL

► **Youth hostel »Rudi Arndt«**
Hübnerstr. 11, D-01069 Dresden
www.djh-sachsen.de (75 beds)
Tel. 471 06 67, fax 472 89 59

HOSTELS

► **Die Boofe**
Hechtstr. 10, D-01097 Dresden
www.boofe.de, tel. 801 33 61
In Äussere Neustadt,
facilities for disabled travellers,
cycle hire, sauna, guided walks
Incidentally: »Boofen« is a Saxon
dialect word for sleeping in the
open air with natural protection,
or in a cave.
In the Sächsische Schweiz national
park there are approx. 50 such
sites.

► **Gästehaus Mezcalero**
Königsbrücker Str. 64,
D-01099 Dresden
www.mezcalero.de

Tel. 81 07 70
Centrally located in Neustadt,
Mexican-style rooms

► **Hostel Louise 20**
Louisenstr. 20, D-01099 Dresden
www.louise20.de
Tel. 889 48 94, fax 889 48 93
Directly above Planwirtschaft
tavern, in Neustadt

► **Hostel Mondpalast**
Louisenstr. 77, D-01099 Dresden
www.mondpalast.de
Tel. 563 40 50, fax 563 50 55
In the middle of Neustadt pub and
bar district, with cycle hire and
laundrette

► **Lollis Homestay**
Görlitzer Str. 34, D-01099 Dresden
www.lollishome.de
Tel. 810 84 58, fax 646 52 50
Right in the middle of Neustadt,
with fully equipped kitchen

⏵ CAMPING

IN DRESDEN

▶ **Campingplatz
am Freibad Mockritz**
Boderitzer Str. 30,
D-01217 Dresden
Tel. 471 52 50
Open all year

▶ **Campingplatz Wostra**
An der Wostra 13
D-01259 Dresden
Tel. 201 32 54
www.campingplatzwostra.de
Open April–Oct

AROUND MORITZBURG

▶ **Campingplatz Mittelteichbad**
Am Mittelteichbad
D-01468 Moritzburg
www.mittelteichbad.de
Tel. (03 52 07) 81 4 23
Open March–Oct

▶ **Campingplatz Boxdorf**
Am Oberen Waldteich,
D-01468 Boxdorf
Tel. (03 52 07) 81 4 29
Open April–Oct

IN SÄCHSISCHE SCHWEIZ

▶ **Camping und Pension
Ostrauer Mühle**
Ostrauer Mühle,
D-01814 Bad Schandau
www.ostrauer-muehle.de
Tel. (03 50 22) 42 7 42
Open Easter–Oct

▶ **Campingplatz Königstein**
Schandauer Str. 25e,
D-01824 Königstein
Tel. (03 50 21) 68 2 24
Open April–Oct

Arrival · Before the Journey

By air   There are flights from Dresden airport to about 50 destinations in
Europe and the Mediterranean region. The only direct connection
from an English-speaking destination is currently an Air Berlin flight
from London Gatwick. Dresden has regular connections to major international German airports such as Düsseldorf, Frankfurt, Hamburg
and Munich. Dresden-Klotzsche airport, 9km/5.5mi from the city
centre, is served by public transport. The S-Bahn line S2 (regional
and suburban railway) takes approx. 25min to reach the main train
station (Hauptbahnhof), stopping en route at Dresden Neustadt and
Dresden Mitte stations; a taxi to the city centre takes approx. 15min.
No. 77 bus departs in front of the terminal; change at Karl-Marx-
Strasse into tram no. 7 in the direction of Gorbitz in order to reach
Pirnaischer Platz in the city centre.

By rail   Dresden can be reached direct by rail from all large German cities,
and from east and southeast Europe (Warsaw, Prague, Budapest,
Vienna, Zurich).

⏵ ARRIVAL INFORMATION

AIRPORT AND FLIGHTS

▶ **Dresden-Klotzsche Airport**
Tel. 881 33 60
www.dresden-airport.de

▶ **Air Berlin**
Tel. in UK (0871) 50 00 737
www.airberlin.com

BUS

▶ **Eurolines**
Bookings online and in UK
through National Express
Tel. 087 05 80 80 80
www.eurolines.com and
www.nationalexpress.com

RAIL INFORMATION

▶ **Rail timetable**
Tel. (0800) 150 70 90

▶ **Deutsche Bahn
(German rail service)**
Tel. 11 8 61, www.bahn.de

▶ **Rail information**
Tel. (0190) 50 70 90

CRUISE SHIPS

▶ **Köln-Düsseldorfer
Deutsche Rheinschifffahrt AG**
Frankenwerft 35
D-50667 Köln
Tel. (0221) 208 83 18, fax 208 83 45
www.k-d.com

▶ **Peter Deilmann Reederei**
Am Holm 25
D-23730 Neustadt in Holstein
Tel. (04 5 61) 39 60, fax 82 07

Dresden has two important rail stations, the Hauptbahnhof (main rail station) and Dresden Neustadt. Not all long-distance trains stop at both! **Two important rail stations**

The **Hauptbahnhof** is at the southern end of Prager Strasse; it is Dresden's most important station for long-distance national and international travel, as well as for suburban travel. Tram stop: Hauptbahnhof (nos. 3, 7, 8, 10, 11)
Bahnhof Dresden Neustadt is in the northwest of Neustadt on Schlesischer Platz. Tram stop: Bahnhof Dresden-Neustadt (nos. 3, 6, 11).

The journey from London to Dresden via Magdeburg on a Eurolines international **bus** takes 21 hours. There is a regular bus service from several German cities to the bus station on the north side of the main rail station (Busbahnhof). Many travel agents offer affordable package trips by bus.

*Grand art nouveau painting
in Neustadt rail station*

By car From the south: Nuremberg – Hermsdorfer Kreuz – Chemnitz – Dresden (E 51/A 9 and E 40/A 4); alternatively, take E 441/A 72 from Autobahndreieck Bayerisches Vogtland via Plauen and Zwickau to Autobahndreieck Chemnitz (connecting to E 40/A 4).

From the west and northwest: Eisenach – Erfurt – Hermsdorfer Kreuz – Chemnitz – Dresden (E 40/A 4), exit Altstadt.

From the north: via Berlin (A 13/A 4/E 40), exit Hellerau for the centre.

From the east: via Görlitz (A 4/E 40) and Prague (A 17).

Further exits: Wilder Mann (for Neustadt), Neustadt (for Elbe Park, and Radebeul).

Up-to-date road travel information and road works schedule: www.dresden-info.fhg.de.

By ship An unusual way of approaching the Saxon capital is by ship: Elbe cruises lasting several days stop in Dresden.

Children in Dresden

Activities and museums for children Dresden and the surrounding areas are very suitable for family holidays, with plenty of activities for all. Fans of cowboys and Indians will be thrilled by the Karl May Museum in ▶Radebeul; just getting there on the narrow gauge Lössnitzdackel train is a treat. A paddlesteamer trip on the Elbe is good fun too; with bikes it's possible to go part of the way on the level Elbe cycle route. An afternoon in the ▶Grosser Garten is very pleasant; the park railway run by children (only the engine-driver is grown up) goes all the way to Carolasee lake, where you can take a boat trip or eat ice-cream in the Carolaschlösschen. The Grosser Garten also has the zoo and Sonnenhäusl puppet theatre.

No-one, children or grown-ups, will ever forget an outdoor theatre performance on the Felsenbühne in Rathen! And children who understand German will love the fairy-tale story-telling beneath the Oriental glass dome of ▶Yenidze.

If the weather isn't marvellous there are plenty of tempting museums, starting with the ▶German Hygiene Museum which is well presented, with lots of opportunities for hands-on participation. The Gläserne Frau (glass woman) is a special attraction, and there are plenty of events where children can play and join in the experiments.

! *Baedeker* TIP

Waldidylle (Forest Idyll)

is the apt name of an inn situated in the Uttewalder Grund, in the middle of the Sächsische Schweiz national park. It can be reached on foot from Marktplatz Stadt Wehlen via Wehlner and Uttewalder Grund. Plain, wholesome food is served on the terrace and indoors (reservations tel. (03 50 24) 79 8 46) and outside there is plenty of room to have fun.

A pleasure park is what you make of it.

Look at almost everything that runs, flies or floats in the Verkehrs-museum (Transport Museum) in the ▶Johanneum. The ▶Techni-sche Sammlungen (technical collections) cater for everyone with sci-entific interests. The Garnisonskirche in Outer ▶Neustadt has one of the greatest puppet theatre collections, with fantasy marionettes, hand-, rod- and stick-puppets from different countries, and support-ing figures; there are performances on the last Sunday in the month.

Electricity

The German mains grid generally supplies 230-volt electricity at 50Hz. Visitors who are not from mainland Europe are advised to take an **adapter**.

Emergency

▶ **Police**
Tel. 110

▶ **Fire Service**
Tel. 112

▶ **Ambulance, pharmacies**
▶ Health

▶ **Breakdown service**
▶ Transport

▶ **Loss of bankcards**
Emergency numbers ▶ Money

Entertainment

For long nights people usually make their way to the Neustadt bars, where the legendary jazz club Neue Tonne is located. The »Kneipensurfer« (bar map of Outer Neustadt) is displayed in most Neustadt bars and in hotels, and can be consulted on-line: www.kneipensurfer.de. Things have been happening in the Altstadt too, and you might be lucky in the bars around Weisse Gasse. There are many music clubs to choose from, and you are sure to discover a favourite beer garden for warm summer nights (►Food and Drink).

CLUBS, BARS AND CINEMAS

DANCING

► Arteum
Am Brauhaus 3
(in the Waldschlösschen vaults)
Tel. 563 65 55
Exclusive atmosphere

► Ballhaus Watzke
Kötzschenbrodaer Str. 1
(Pieschen)
Tel. 85 29 20
Ballroom with painted ceiling and chandeliers, terrace with Canaletto view of Altstadt

► Bärenzwinger
Brühlscher Garten (Altstadt)
Tel. 495 14 09
Student club in vaulted cellar beneath Brühlsche Terrasse

► Café Griessbach
Neunimptscher Str. 13
Tel. 402 20 99
Thu and Sat tea dance for middling generation

► Club Mensa
Reichenbachstr. 1
Tel. 462 26 20
Student club in university district

► Dance Factory
Bautzner Str. 118
(Neustadt, near Waldschlösschen)
Tel. 802 24 51
Occupies former Stasi quarters: two restaurants with Elbe view, games arcade, good choice of cocktails in Bar Warehouse

► Downtown
Katharinenstr. 11 (Neustadt)
Tel. 803 64 14
Fri: hits from Seventies and Eighties; Sat: black music, house, pop, indie

► El Paraiso
Louisenstr. 79 (Neustadt)
Tel. 802 07 72
Fri and Sat: salsa

► Fun Factory
Enderstr. 59 (Dresden-Seidnitz)
Tel. 250 77 44
Fun Disco, Lollipop dance café and Mäx rock disco

► Flower Power
Eschenstr. 11 (Outer Neustadt)
Tel. 804 98 14
Hiphop and techno für teens and twens

The belles-de-nuit meet in the Dance Factory and at other venues.

▶ **Gare de la Lune**
Pillnitzer Landstr. 148
(Wachwitz)
Tel. 267 85 54
Garden, restaurant, ballroom:
from tango to disco fox, and
concerts

▶ **Groove Station**
Katharinenstr. 11 – 13
(Neustadt)
Tel. 802 95 94
Rock scene – bottled beer and
good atmosphere, often live music

▶ **Industriegelände Strasse E**
Werner-Hartmann-Str. 2
Eight clubs offer a diverse range of
parties and concerts

▶ **Katy's Garage**
Corner of Alaunstr./Louisenstr.
(Neustadt), tel. 810 39 23
For all ages: Seventies, Eighties and
Nineties rock, funk, soul

▶ **Lofthouse**
Katharinenstr. 11 – 13 (Neustadt)
Tel. 810 39 23
Cult hits of Seventies, Eighties and
Nineties

▶ **Motown Club**
Petersburger Str. 9 (Altstadt)
Tel. 487 41 50
Black music

▶ **Nachtcantine**
Lohrmannstr. 19 (Reick)
Tel. 281 61 91
Wed: Independent; Czech disco

▶ **Parkhotel Blauer Salon**
Bautzner Landstr. 7
(Weisser Hirsch), tel. 804 25 71
Former hotel in Weisser Hirsch, a
grand district; Tue in winter, drop
in for after-work parties.

▶ **Saloppe**
Brockhausstr. 1

(Access via Bautzner Str.)
Tel. (0172) 353 25 86
Parties with Elbe view, May to
October, open-air stage and dance
space

▶ **Terminal 1 Airport Dresden**
Flughafenstrasse 100
(Flughafen Dresden)
House club with view of runway

BARS

▶ **Karl May Bar**
Taschenberg 3
(in Kempinski Hotel /
Taschenberg Palais)
Tel. 49 27 20
Jazz piano

▶ **Busmann's Brazil**
Kleine Brüdergasse 5
(close to Postplatz)
Tel. 862 12 00
View of Zwinger, good range of
food, extensive bar menu

▶ **Försters**
Weisse Gasse 5 (Altstadt)
Tel. 484 87 01
Restaurant, bar

▶ **Frank's Bar**
Alaunstr. 80 (Neustadt)
Tel. 802 67 27

▶ **Havanna Club**
Bautzner Str. 77 (Neustadt)
Tel. 802 42 54
See and be seen – cocktails and
Cuban beer

▶ **Jim Beam's Bar**
Alaunstr. 57 (Neustadt)
Tel. 804 20 00
Football – live, meeting-point
for Americans in Dresden

▶ **Mondfisch**
Louisenstr. 37 (Neustadt)
Tel. 804 41 83
Cocktail bar in submarine style

Frank's Bar: small bar with a big name – Frank Ulbricht mixes 200 drinks

HOT SPOTS

► **Aqua Lounge**
Louisenstr. 56 (Neustadt)
Tel. 810 61 16
Range of DJs at weekends; illumination and water displays, large aquarium with brightly coloured fish

► **B.liebig**
Liebigstr. 24 (Altstadt)
Tel. 471 87 59
Beer garden and cocktail bar

► **Blue Note**
Görlitzer Str. 2b (Neustadt)
Tel. 801 42 75
Persian rugs, dim lighting, stage with jazz, draught beer and Merrydown cider

► **Blumenau**
Louisenstr. 67 (Neustadt)
Tel. 802 65 02
Trendy, with changing menu and smart coffee creations – glass front opens in hot weather

► **Café Europa**
Königsbrücker Str. 68 (Neustadt)
Tel. 804 48 10
Open 24hrs,
opposite Kino Schauburg

► **Café 100**
Alaunstr. 100 (Neustadt)
Tel. 801 39 57
Excellent wine list

► **Café No. 3**
Weisse Gasse 3 (Altstadt)
Tel. 485 08 88
Trendy bistro in bar district close to Rathaus

► **Dr Schlüter**
Augsburger Str. 85 (Striesen)
Tel. 340 00 92
Hearty food; Tue, half-price cocktails

The glass front of Blumenau can be opened in hot weather

▶ **El Cubanito**
Corner of Sebnitzer Str./
Görlitzer Str. (Neustadt)
Tel. 804 78 70
Fresh cocktail Fruit Margarita is
just right to start things off;
regular Latin music

▶ **El Perro Borracho**
Alaunstr. 70 (Neustadt)
Tel. 83 93 00
Tapas and wine in the »Mad Dog«,
Kunsthofpassage

▶ **Hebedas**
Rothenburger Str. 30 (Neustadt)
Tel. 895 10 10
Cult corner bar/club

▶ **Kontinental**
Corner of Görlitzer Str./
Louisenstr. (Neustadt)
Tel. 801 35 31
Open daily 24hrs

▶ **Leonardo**
Rudolf-Leonhard-Str. 24
(Neustadt)
Ttel. 804 22 47
Nicest bar in Hecht district

▶ **Madness**
Louisenstr. 20 (Neustadt)
Tel. 899 61 35
For lovers of reggae, ska and
wicked beer concoctions

▶ **Marrakech**
Rothenburger Str. 16 (Neustadt)
Tel. 456 88 57
Moorish inspiration, improvised
music sessions

▶ **Maximus**
Maxstr. 5
Tel. 810 41 00
Cool rendezvous close to
Altstadt

▶ **New California**
Wallgässchen 4 (Neustadt)
Tel. 811 35 10
150 cocktails every day, special
steak and fingerfood menus

▶ **Paul Rackwitz
Schankwirtschaft**
Plauenscher Ring 33
Tel. 472 08 26
Traditional

▶ **Pinta – American Bar**
Louisenstr. 49 (Neustadt)
Tel. 802 66 12
Tiny espresso bar with
fabulous cocktails

▶ **Planwirtschaft**
Louisenstr. 20 (Neustadt)
Tel. 801 31 87
Classic

▶ **Raskolnikoff**
Böhmische Str. 3 (Neustadt)
Tel. 804 57 06
Café and beer garden with foun-
tain and wild herbs, ▶ Baedeker
Tip p. 235;

▶ **Red Rooster**
Rähnitzgasse 10 (Neustadt)
Tel. 272 18 50
Irish-English pub in
Neustadt with 100+
Scotch single malts

▶ **Scheunecafé**
Alaunstr. 36 – 40 (Neustadt)
Tel. 804 55 32
Popular, but rather in-between
atmosphere – mix between café,
beer garden and bar; inexpensive
Indian food

▶ **Zora**
Priessnitzstr. 12 (Neustadt)
Tel. 204 72 20

Idiosyncratic: in 1999 the UFA-Palast cinema won the German Architecture prize.

Cocktail bar opposite Travestie Theatre Carteblanche

CINEMAS

▶ **Casablanca**
Friedensstr. 23 (Neustadt)
Tel. 804 29 24

▶ **Thalia**
Görlitzer Str. 6
Tel. 652 47 05

▶ **Metropolis**
Am Brauhaus 8 (Neustadt)
Tel. 816 67 21

▶ **Programmkino Ost**
Schandauer Str. 73
Tel. 310 37 82
Reliably good programme all the time

▶ **Schauburg**
Königsbrücker Str. 55 (Neustadt)
Tel. 803 21 85
Three well renovated cinemas, with café

▶ **UFA-Palast**
Prager Str. 6 (Altstadt)
Bookings tel. 482 58 25

Etiquette and Customs

Germans in general favour straightforwardness, and are sometimes direct to the point of bluntness.

Straightforward

Germany is a heavily regulated country, and although in this respect the rest of the world may have been catching up in recent times, many people still remark on how Germans tend to follow rules to the letter and often display more deference to those in authority than other nationalities. It is an offence (albeit a minor one) for example

Rules and regulations

to step out into the road at a crossing if the pedestrian signal shows red – visitors may be surprised to see people patiently waiting for the lights to change when there is no vehicle in sight. There are sometimes disapproving looks for those who break this rule (not to mention a fine should a police officer spot the guilty party).

Efficiency versus bureaucracy

German efficiency is of course world renowned, and though it will be regularly encountered in banks, hotels, and even government offices, the visitor may at times also come across instances of clanking bureaucracy. Contrary to the expectations of some, this is not in fact a country where everything runs like clockwork. Public transport is generally punctual and reliable, but German trains often do not run on time.

No smoking

Smoking is now prohibited in all public buildings in Germany, including cafés, bars, restaurants and nightclubs. A smoking zone is permitted in pubs and restaurants if it is closed off from the other public areas, but smokers are only served in non-smoking areas. Individuals breaking this law are liable to a fine of 100 euros; a 2000 euro penalty applies to the proprietor of the offending establishment.

Tipping

In restaurants and cafés it is usual to tip about 10% of the amount on the bill. If you pay cash, tell the waiter the amount you wish to pay (normally a rounded up figure) as you hand over the money, or say »Stimmt so« if you don't expect any change at all. If you pay by cheque or credit card, leave the tip in cash on the table or on the plate provided. Taxi drivers, city guides, toilet attendants and room service personnel are also pleased to receive a tip.

History and patriotism

With Dresden people of the older generation it is wise to be sensitive about the subject of the Socialist rule of the German Democratic Republic: the question of spying and denunciation by the internal security service, Stasi, still causes controversy. Many Germans do not feel comfortable talking about the events of the Nazi period and the Second World War, which are regarded as a subject for serious discussion and private thought, and the unquestioning patriotism of some other countries is frowned upon by many. Unless you intend to engage in learned discourse, it is best to follow the famous advice – and not mention the war. In recent years, particularly since the football World Cup was held in Germany in 2006 in a happy, harmonious, flag-waving atmosphere, the German flag has been more in evidence than before, and some observers detect a change in the Germans' previously uneasy sense of their identity.

Greetings

The accepted way to greet somebody is to shake hands; men and women who know each other better will kiss each other on both cheeks, like in France; established friends, men included, will even hug one another.

Festivals, Holidays and Events

The Dresden tourist office (▶ Information) has information about what's on (tel. 49 19 21 00, www.dresden-tourist.de). The city magazines (▶ Newpapers and Periodicals) give cinema programmes and up-to-date tips. Tickets are available from ▶ Information or box offices (▶ Theatre/Concerts).

● INFORMATION ABOUT FESTIVALS AND HOLIDAYS

PUBLIC HOLIDAYS

1 Jan: New Year's Day
Good Friday
Easter Monday
1 May: Labour Day
Ascension Day
Whit Monday
3 Oct: Day of German Unity
31 Oct: Reformation Day
Day of Penance and Prayer
25–26 Dec: Christmas

EVENTS IN JANUARY

▶ **Semper Opera Ball**
At the Saxon State Opera since mid-January 2006, with top stars and the Staatskapelle orchestra (www.semperopernball.de)

IN FEBRUARY

▶ **Special concerts in the Kreuzkirche and Semper Opera**
In commemoration of the destruction of Dresden on 13–14 February 1945

▶ **Operetta Ball**
With Strauss Orchestra of the State Operetta

▶ **Elbe-Florentine Carnival**
Baroque theatre spectacular in Hotel Westin Bellevue

People like the Elbhangfest, and the festival procession always attracts a lot of visitors.

! *Baedeker* TIP

Dixie fever

Every year in May Dresden is gripped by Dixie fever. Since 1970 the Dixieland festival has developed into the largest of its kind in Europe; more than 200 musicians from dozens of countries, from the USA (New Orleans) to Bali, play at around 60 venues (tickets: tel. 486 66 66). The Prager Strasse jazz mile is outdoors, and free.

IN MARCH

▸ **Festival Sandstein und Musik**
The »Sandstone and Music Festival« from March to November consists of concerts in castles and palaces in Sächsische Schweiz (www.sandstein-musik.de)

EASTER

▸ **Passion music and Easter concerts**
In Kreuzkirche and Hofkirche

▸ **Richard Wagner's *Parsifal***
In the Semper Opera

IN APRIL

▸ **International animation and short-film festival**
Short-film festival in Metropolis cinema

IN MAY

▸ **Karl May Days in Radebeul**
Weekend after Ascension Day

▸ **Dampferparade (Steamer Parade)**
On 1 May historic paddle steamers go from Terrassenufer to Schloss Pillnitz and back.

▸ **Dresdner Musikfestspiele**
A major music festival: for two weeks from late May to early June top international artists perform live in palaces and gardens (www.musikfestspiele.com).

▸ **Open-air theatre at Felsenbühne Rathen**
Season: May to September (www.felsenbuehne-rathen.de)

IN JUNE

▸ **Zwingerserenaden**
June to September: the Zwinger serenades are classical music at 6.30pm in front of the Wallpavillon, in the Marmorsaal if it rains.

▸ **Elbhangfest**
Street festival on the Elbe from Blaues Wunder bridge to Schloss Pillnitz with dragon boat race by night (www.elbhangfest.de)

▸ **Bunte Republik Neustadt**
Alternative and unconventional festival in outer Neustadt, the »colourful republic«

IN JULY

▸ **Museum-Sommernacht**
Events in 40 museums

▸ **Schaubudensommer**
International travelling theatre

groups put up their tents in the Scheune garden (▶ Theatre · Concerts).

▶ Filmnächte (Film Nights)
Film nights on the Elbe: through to August on Königsufer, when the illuminated Altstadt silhouette is also visible. The highlight is the »night of short films« (www.film-naechte-am-elbufer.de).

IN AUGUST

▶ Stadtfest (City Festival)
Every year on the second-to-last weekend in August: medieval crafts and jousting knights in the Schloss, open-air classical music in front of the Semper Opera

▶ Moritzburg Festival
Renowned international chamber music festival with established as well as young artists from all over the world. It is known for its exceptional quality and repertoire.

IN SEPTEMBER

▶ Hengstparaden (Stallion Parades) in Moritzburg
An opportunity to see fine horses at close quarters.

▶ Töpfermarkt (Potters` Market)
On the first weekend in September up to 50 potters sell ceramics of all techniques and styles around Goldener Reiter.

IN OCTOBER

▶ Dresden Festival of Contemporary Music
Ten days of unusual concerts by international avant-garde composers (Dresdner Tage der zeitgenössischen Musik)

▶ Volksfest in Moritzburg
The ponds are usually fished on the last weekend in October

IN NOVEMBER

▶ Tanzherbst (Autumn Dance Festival)
Festival devoted to women's dance and choreography (www.tanz-herbst.de).

ℹ Best festivals

- Dixieland Festival
- Elbhangfest: street party from the Blaues Wunder to Schloss Pillnitz
- Film nights on the Elbe banks
- Open-air theatre at Felsenbühne Rathen
- Bunte Republik Neustadt

IN DECEMBER

▶ Striezelmarkt
Germany's oldest Christmas market on Altmarkt

▶ Stollenmarkt
This event is inspired by a festival once held by Augustus the Strong. A gigantic Stollen is transported to the Strietzel-markt on a horse-drawn cart and cut up there, accompanied by actors in historic costumes (8 December).

▶ Stallhof Advent Spectacular
The Middle Ages come to life in the Langer Gang in the Schloss; especially atmospheric in the evening.

▶ Advent music in the Kreuzkirche
Musical food for thought, far from the pre-Christmas bustle

Food and Drink

Saxon cooking Traditional Saxon food is based on the hearty fare of foresters, mountain dwellers, Elbe watermen and farmers, refined by Italian and French influences from the court of the rulers of Saxony.

Saxon Specialities

Salads and starters **Saxon potato salad** is prepared in many variations with different ingredients (vegetables, sliced sausage, fish, apple). The well-seasoned classic version has to include sausage, pickled gherkins, onions and mayonnaise.

Fresh black bread spread with dripping, and garnished with apple and marjoram, is called **Fettbemme**.

Soups Boiled, puréed potatoes are cooked with vegetables in bone-marrow stock, well seasoned with marjoram, topped with fried bacon cubes and onions – and that's **Saxon potato soup** (Sächsische Kartoffelsuppe). Usually served with bockwurst.

Meat **Dresden Sauerbraten** is a very popular Sunday roast. It is prepared from larded beef marinaded for 4–6 days in stock, vinegar, vegetables, onions, bay leaves, pimento and pepper corns. Then it is slowly braised – delicious with dumplings and red cabbage.

Eierschecke (pastry): »Unknown to the rest of the world, to the detriment of mankind!«

Krautwickel are braised roulades: white cabbage leaves filled with minced beef and smoked bacon cubes, served with boiled potatoes garnished with parsley.

Saxons love sweet things and they love coffee, accompanied by Saxon cake. According to Erich Kästner (▶Famous People) **Eierschecke** is »a Saxon cake, which has remained unknown to the rest of the world, to the detriment of mankind.« This bright yellow cake has layers of quark and a light-as-air filling with lots of egg white on a pastry base.

Sweetmeats

But the most famous Dresden speciality is **Christstollen** (▶Baedeker Special p.92). Every year around 1.5 million Stollen cakes are baked, of which half are despatched as Christmas greeting from Saxony – transport can cost twice as much as the cake itself, for Dresden Stollen is in demand in Asia, Australia and America as well as in Europe. The recipe is kept secret, and only Stollen from Dresden may be called »Dresden Stollen«.

Another popular dessert is **Quarkkeulchen**: a dough is made of boiled potatoes, quark, flower and sultanas, shaped and fried golden-brown on both sides, finished off with a sprinkling of sugar and cinnamon.

Drinks

If one of the best German **beers** is brewed in nearby Radeberg, Dresden itself produces Feldschlösschen beer and local specialities in the Waldschlösschen and Watzke brewhouses.

Vines were planted by monks on the slopes of the Elbe more than 800 years ago, and over the centu-

> ! **Baedeker** TIP
>
> **Radeberger Pilsner**
>
> The Radeberg Export Brewery in the brewing town of Radeberg (Dresdner Str. 2) is one of the most modern breweries in Germany. A tour through the maltings and brewery cellar shows how beer is made. Freshly tapped Radeberger Pilsner and Zwickelbier are served in the tasting room (appointments for brewery tours, weekdays by tel. (03 5 28) 45 48 80).

ries the vineyards grew into a huge industry. Saxon wine enjoyed a good reputation up to the 19th century. The disastrous phylloxera infestation of 1887 destroyed many vineyards, after which the disused land was made into orchards, or used for building villas. Since the 1920s pest-resistant varieties of grape have been grown: but even without infestation there is no guarantee of a good harvest in this area, since it is one of the most northerly wine-growing regions in Europe. The most sought-after wines come from Meissen (Kapitelberg, Domprobstberg, Rosengründchen), but the vineyards around Radebeul (Schloss Wackerbarth) and the royal Dresden vineyard at Pillnitz with outlying Wachwitz and Loschwitz also produce good wine. The most important varieties of grape are Gutedel, Müller-Thurgau, Riesling and Traminer. A local speciality is Meissner Schieler, mixed from red and white grapes.

GENUINE ONLY WITH THE SEAL

Every year at Christmas time there is no doubt about what to eat in Dresden – naturally, Dresden Christstollen. Starting in autumn, this wonderful cake – actually rich marzipan rather than cake, according to the New Dresden Cooking, Baking and Household Book of 1805 – is mixed, kneaded, rolled and put in the oven.

The rolled form of the stollen is supposed to symbolize the Christ Child swaddled and laid in the manger. It is first mentioned, as »Strozel« to be eaten during the season of fasting, in documents preserved in the Dresden city archive dating back to 1486. Historians of baking put its origins as early as 1400. In accordance with church dogma, up until the end of the 15th century stollen was allowed to be made only of flour, yeast, a little oil and water. Then, in 1491, the pope was persuaded by the electors Ernst and Albrecht of Saxony to lift the ban on butter, in order to make the stollen more palatable. In another document of 1530 Christstollen is mentioned, which proves that the cake must have been popular hundreds of years ago. In 1727 Augustus the Strong was offered his first portion of Christstollen by Dresden's bakers. He enjoyed it – thanks to the Turks – with coffee, an excellent combination. In the late 19th century stollen made it across the Atlantic, in hand-soldered tins, and landed on the tables of North and South America, where it is still very popular. Not even the shortage of genuine ingredients in the GDR could detract significantly from the quality of the stollen. Shortly after Christmas,

Busy hands: 1.5 million Dresden Christstollen baked every year.

inventive bakers who wanted to use candied lemon and orange peel, rather than the standard extract of green tomatoes, set about organizing the next year's supplies. Housewives with relatives in the west got the necessary ingredients included in approved food parcels.

Recipe for a Four-Pound Stollen

Enough theory. How do you bake a Dresden Christstollen? Optimistically Baedeker's editor wrote to the Dresden Bakers' Association and promptly received a recipe (for six four-pound cakes!):

4000g white flour
1600g butter
500g butter dripping
600g crystal sugar
750g grated sweet almonds
250g grated bitter almonds
600g candied lemon peel
3000g sultanas
1000g milk
250g yeast
50g salt
100g lemon peel
10g spice
300g rum
1g vanilla pod

Unfortunately the bakers' letter ends here, so how is all that to be mixed, how long does it need in the oven, and what tips could they give? That will remain the Dresden bakers' secret. To guard against product pirates, the bakers have got together to form an association, and now the wrapping on each stollen is sealed – only with the authentic seal may the cake be called »Dresden Christstollen«.

Restaurants, Beer Gardens and Cafés

Restaurants in the Altstadt (Old Town) are concentrated mostly in and around Theaterplatz, Neumarkt and Altmarkt, and in Weisse Gasse. Inner Neustadt (New Town) has a mix of old, traditional and new establishments on Hauptstrasse, Königstrasse and Rähnitzgasse; Outer Neustadt also has a good mix, including international restaurants, between Alaunstrasse, Louisenstrasse and Görlitzer Strasse. Dresden also has a good range of cafés and beer gardens, and don't overlook the suburbs and surrounding areas, where some very good restaurants make a trip out of the city worthwhile.

▶ RECOMMENDED RESTAURANTS IN DRESDEN

▸ ① **etc. see plan p.96/97**
Without number: not on plan

▸ **Prices**
Expensive: more than €25
Moderate: €15–25
Inexpensive: €8–15

GERMAN / SAXON

▸ ① **Pulverturm (inexpensive)**
An der Frauenkirche 12a
Tel. 26 26 00
Hearty fare in the Coselpalais vaulted cellar next to the Frauenkirche – and jugglers, conjurors and musicians.

i Fine dining

- Pattis gourmet restaurant (French cuisine with a Saxon touch)
- Caroussel (French)
- Kahnaletto (Italian)
- Am Glacis (French Caribbean)
- Restaurant Schloss Eckberg (French cuisine with an international flavour)
- Ogura (Japanese)
- Villa Marie (Italian)
- Fischhaus Alberthafen (fish dishes)
- Wenzel – Prager Bierstuben (Bohemian)
- El Perro Borracho (Spanish)

▸ ② **Alte Meister (moderate)**
Theaterplatz 1a
Tel. 481 04 26
The best gourmet restaurant in the inner Altstadt (in the Alte Meister gallery!), and at midday well affordable even on an average budget.

▸ ③ **Bei Muttern (inexpensive)**
Schönfelder Str. 2, tel. 802 85 37
The name (»mother's place«) says it all – it's cosy here.

▸ ④ **BrennNessel (inexpensive)**
Schützengasse 18, tel. 494 33 19
Vegetarian restaurant and bar in a house dating from 1650 – one of the oldest in the city centre.

▸ ⑤ **Chiaveri (expensive)**
Bernhard-von-Lindenau-Platz 2
(in the Saxon parliament building)
Tel. 496 03 99
Saxon and Italian food,
terrace overlooking the Elbe

▸ ⑥ **Fischhaus Alberthafen (moderate)**
Magdeburger Str. 58, tel. 498 21 10
Fish restaurant with harbour atmosphere

»Chiaveri« in the Saxon parliament building offers a great view of Elbe and Altstadt

▶ ⑦ **Fischhaus (moderate)**
Don't be misled! The Dresden Fischhaus is not a fish restaurant, nor does it have anything to do with Fischhaus Alberthafen. Rather, it is one of Dresden's oldest hostelries and offers a combination of traditional Saxon and modern cuisine. Nice beer garden.

▶ ⑧ **Hubertusgarten (inexpensive)**
Bautzner Landstr. 89,
Tel. 460 47 00
Serves tasty game in hunt atmosphere

▶ ⑨ **Intermezzo (expensive)**
Am Taschenberg 3, tel. 491 27 12
The gourmet restaurant in Taschenberg Palais caters for every wish.

▶ ⑩ **Italienisches Dörfchen (moderate)**
Theaterplatz 2, tel. 49 81 60
Wonderful interior decoration by Hans Erlwein. Cooking ranges from German to Italian.

▶ ⑪ **Kö 5 (inexpensive)**
Königstr. 5
Tel. 802 40 88
Baroque inner courtyard and nice cellar bar,
reasonable prices for inner city

▶ ⑫ **Bauernstuben in Kügelgenhaus (inexpensive)**
Hauptstr. 13, tel. 563 31 26
Long-standing reputable restaurant in the Museum der Dresdner Frühromantik

▶ ⑬ **Le Boulevard (moderate)**
St. Petersburger Str. 34 (in Mercure Hotel Newa on Prager Str.), tel. 481 41 62
Uses light, fresh, seasonal produce

▶ ⑭ **Lesage (moderate)**
Lennéstr. 1
Tel. 420 42 50
Gourmet restaurant with cocktail bar and outdoor terrace; run by Kempinski Hotel / Taschenberg Palais.

Where to Eat and Stay in Dresden Plan

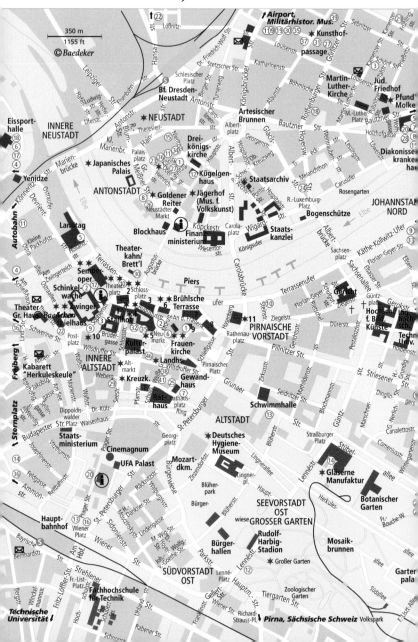

1 Schloss (palace)
2 Cathedral
3 Ständehaus (former parliament)
4 Fürstenzug

5 Johanneum
  (Transport Museum)
6 Sekundogenitur
7 Akademie

8 Albertinum
9 Coselpalais
10 Taschenbergpalais
11 Neue Synagoge

Where to eat

① Pulverturm
② Alte Meister
③ Bei Muttern
④ Brennnessel
⑤ Chiaveri
⑥ Fischhaus Alberthafen
⑦ Fischhaus
⑧ Hubertusgarten
⑨ Intermezzo
⑩ Italienisches Dörfchen
⑪ Kö 5
⑫ Bauernstuben im Kügelgenhaus
⑬ Le Boulevard
⑭ Lesage
⑮ Luisenhof
⑯ Oma

⑰ Opernrestaurant
⑱ Pattis
⑲ Schmidt's
⑳ Trompeter
㉑ Zum Alten Fährhaus
㉒ Restaurant im Schauspielhaus
㉓ Wenzel-Prager Bierstuben
㉔ Am Glacis
㉕ Brasserie
㉖ Canaletto
㉗ Caroussel
㉘ Schloss Eckberg
㉙ Balduccis Café Prag
㉚ Kahnaletto
㉛ La Villetta
㉜ Ristorante Rossini

㉝ Villa Marie
㉞ Cuchi Restaurant
㉟ Ogura
㊱ Cap Merlot
㊲ Espitas
㊳ Barcelona
㊴ El Perro Borracho

Where to stay

① Bülow Residenz Dresden
② Dresden Hilton
③ Kempinski Hotel
  Taschenbergpalais Dresden
④ Maritim Hotel
⑤ Schloss Eckberg
⑥ Hotel de Saxe
⑦ The Radisson SAS
  Gewandhaus Hotel Dresden

⑧ The Westin Bellevue
⑨ Am Blauen Wunder
⑩ Am Terrassenufer
⑪ art'otel Dresden
⑫ Artushof
⑬ Dorint Novotel
⑭ Hotel Dresden
  Elbflorenz
⑮ Martha Hospiz

⑯ Pullman Dresden Newa
⑰ Ringhotel
  Residenz Alt Dresden
⑱ Rothenburger Hof
⑲ Alpha-Hotel
⑳ Ibis Hotels Bastei, Königstein und Lilienstein
㉑ An der Rennbahn
㉒ Novalis garni

▶ ⑮ **Luisenhof (moderate)**
Bergbahnstr. 8, tel. 214 99 60
In-house patisserie, spacious
summer terrace and unique view
of the city; book a table by the
window!

▶ ⑯ **Oma
(inexpensive)**
Cossebauder Str. 15
Tel. 422 20 66
Twenties to Forties ambience,
nourishing food from grand-
mother's day.

▶ ⑰ **Opernrestaurant
(inexpensive)**
Theaterplatz 2, tel. 491 15 21
Small but good restaurant at the
opera house, predominantly Saxon
menu.

▶ ⑱ **Pattis (expensive)**
Merbitzer Str. 53, tel. 42 5 50
Gourmet restaurant – Mario Pattis
is one of the best chefs in Dresden.

▶ ⑲ **Schmidt's
(inexpensive)**
Moritzburger Weg 67
Tel. 804 48 83
International cuisine in designer
ambience by Deutsche Werkstätten Hellerau. With terrace.

▶ ⑳ **Trompeter
(inexpensive)**
Bautzner Landstr. 83
Tel. 268 31 23
Old-established, historic and rus-
tic atmosphere.

▶ ㉑ **Zum Alten Fährhaus
(inexpensive)**
Fährstr. 22 (Laubegast)
Tel. 257 18 42
Pleasant and good value, seating in
beer garden in summer

BOHEMIAN

▶ ㉒ **Restaurant im
Schauspielhaus (inexpensive)**
Ostra-Allee 2
Tel. 495 61 31
Bohemian and Saxon food in
ballroom atmosphere with view of
Zwinger

▶ ㉓ **Wenzel-Prager Bierstuben
(inexpensive)**
Königstr. 1, tel. 804 20 10
(see Baedeker Tip p.145)

FRENCH

▶ ㉔ **Am Glacis (expensive)**
Glacisstr. 8
Tel. 803 60 33
Gourmet restaurant with
French-Caribbean cuisine

▶ ㉕ **Brasserie (moderate)**
Ringstr. 1, tel. 49 4 90
In Radisson SAS Gewandhaus
Hotel – elegant

▶ ㉖ **Canaletto (expensive)**
Grosse Meissner Str. 15
(in Maritim Hotel Bellevue)
Tel. 804 36 45
With the famous Canaletto view of
Frauenkirche and Semper Opera;
Sun noon–3pm champagne buffet

▶ ㉗ **Caroussel
(expensive)**
Rähnitzgasse 19
Tel. 80 0 30
The kitchen crew in Hotel Bülow
Residenz serve exquisite food in a
Baroque setting

▶ ㉘ **Schloss Eckberg
(expensive)**
Bautzner Str. 134, tel. 80 9 90
Fine French and Mediterranean
cuisine with a wonderful view
of the Elbe valley.

ITALIAN

► ㉙ **Balducci's Café Prag (inexpensive)**
Seestr. 8, tel. 495 50 95
The master of the house, singer Giuseppe Balducci, often sings his favourite songs in the evening for his guests.

► ㉚ **Kahnaletto (moderate)**
Terrassenufer
Tel. 495 30 37
Restaurant ship with floating kitchen

► ㉛ **La Villetta (inexpensive)**
Augsburger Str. 43, tel. 31 59 90
Menu changes daily, also deli and wine dealers

► ㉜ **Ristorante Rossini (expensive)**
An der Frauenkirche 5 (in Hotel Dresden Hilton), tel. 864 28 55
Grand Italian style with typical contemporary design

► ㉝ **Villa Marie (moderate)**
(Blasewitz by Blaues Wunder bridge) Fährgässchen 1
Tel. 311 11 86
Tuscan cuisine, close to Blaues Wunder bridge: lovely villa handsomely furnished

JAPANESE

► ㉞ **Cuchi Restaurant (Inexpensive)**
Wallgässchen 5, tel. 86 27 50
Sushi and more; Sun brunch and Wed evening buffet

► ㉟ **Ogura (moderate)**
An der Frauenkirche 5
(in Hotel Dresden Hilton)
Tel. 864 29 75
One of Dresden's best Japanese restaurants; also sushi takeaway

A place to fall in love: the Villa Marie garden on the Elbe

MEDITERRANEAN

► ㊱ **Cap Merlot (inexpensive / moderate)**
Wallgässchen 2a, tel. 656 86 68
Acclaimed restaurant in old piano factory with light Mediterranean food; limited menu but good value for money

MEXICAN

► ㊲ **Espitas (inexpensive)**
Alaunstr. 57, tel. 456 85 25
Steaks, burritos, enchiladas on three floors – in the middle, an enormous bar. Popular with young people

SPANISH

► ㊳ **Barcelona (moderate)**
Weisse Gasse 6, tel. 485 25 83
It's hard to choose between almost 100 different tapas

► ㊴ **El Perro Borracho (Inexpensive)**
Alaunstr. 70, tel. 803 67 23
Tapas and wine in the Kunsthof-passage, worth experiencing the ambience

▶ RECOMMENDED RESTAURANTS IN THE SURROUNDING AREAS

BAD SCHANDAU

▶ **Lindenhof (inexpensive)**
Rudolf-Sendig-Str. 11
Tel. (03 50 22) 48 90
Regional cuisine, terrace

HOHNSTEIN / LOHSDORF

▶ **Zum Schwarzbachtal (inexpensive)**
Niederdorfstr. 3
Tel. (03 59 75) 80 3 45
Surrounded by meadows and woods: rural Saxony

KÖNIGSTEIN

▶ **Landgasthof Müller (inexpensive)**
Halbestadt 17

Vincenz Richter: a Meissen institution for fine wine

Tel. (03 50 22) 42 7 94
Beneath the Lilienstein on the Elbe with view of the fortress

MEISSEN

▶ **Bauernhäus'l (inexpensive)**
Oberspaarer Str. 20
Tel. (03 5 21) 73 33 17
Wines and garden

▶ **Domkeller (inexpensive)**
Domplatz 9
Tel. (03 5 21) 45 76 76
Panoramic view of the city

▶ **Vincenz Richter (moderate)**
An der Frauenkirche 12
Tel. (03 5 21) 45 32 85
Not be missed, guaranteed to provide good Saxon food and wines, since 1513

MORITZBURG

▶ **Adam's Gasthof (inexpensive)**
Markt 9
Tel. (03 52 07) 99 7 75
Good and pleasant, with beer garden

▶ **Churfürstliche Waldschänke (inexpensive)**
Tel. (03 52 07) 86 00
In game reserve, with beer garden; serves game and fish

PILLNITZ

▶ **Kaminrestaurant in Schloss-hotel Pillnitz (moderate)**
August-Böckstiegel-Str. 10
Tel. 26 1 40
Right by the Schloss – very good food

PIRNA

► **escobar (inexpensive)**
Obere Burgstr. 1
Tel. (03 5 01) 58 27 73
Restaurant-café-bar with Mediterranean food in Teufelserkerhaus

► **Romantikhotel Deutsches Haus (moderate)**
Niedere Burgstr. 1
Tel. (03 5 01) 46 88 00
Wonderful Renaissance house with wine tavern and garden service

► **Kostbar (inexpensive)**
Obere Burgstr. 11
Tel. (03 5 01) 58 55 36
Relaxed cocktail bar with small summer terrace, Mediterranean food, caters for vegetarians

RADEBEUL

► **Dampfschiff (inexpensive)**
Uferstr. 10
Tel. 833 97 49
Subtle fish dishes, summer terrace

► **Goldene Weintraube (inexpensive)**
Meissner Str. 152
Tel. 836 34 13
Good address, with Saxon and Italian cuisine

► **Spitzhaus (moderate)**
Spitzhausstr. 36
Tel. 830 93 05
Restaurant, beer garden and view of Elbe and vineyards

● BEER GARDENS IN DRESDEN

BEER TAVERNS

► **Am Thor**
Hauptstr. 35 (Neustadt)
Tel. 804 13 72
Vladimir Putin drank his Radeberger here.

► **Steigerstube**
(in Feldschlösschen brewery)
Budapester Str. 32, tel. 471 88 75
In listed engine house, with brewery museum

BEER GARDENS

► **Ball- and Brauhaus Watzke**
Kötzschenbrodaer Str. 1 (Pieschen)
Tel. 85 29 20
Watzke Pils and dark beer, monthly specials – seating by the Elbe, beneath the trees.

► **Brauhaus am Waldschlösschen**
Am Brauhaus 8b (Neustadt)
Tel. 811 99 22
Magnificent view of the Elbe from Dresden's oldest brewery, of 1836; live music daily, except Sun. Master brewer will explain the different stages of brewing (bookings, tel. 81 19 90).

► **Carolaschlösschen**
Tiergartenstr. 45 (Altstadt)
Tel. 250 60 00
Idyllical location on Carolasee lake

► **Elbsegler**
Grosse Meissner Str. 15
(in Hotel Bellevue), tel. 80 50
Under sail right by the water with Canaletto view; one of the three decks even has under-floor heating.

▶ **Elbterrasse Wachwitz**
Altwachwitz 14, tel. 26 96 10
Romantic spot with wholesome
food

▶ **Fährgarten Johannstadt**
Käthe-Kollwitz-Ufer 23b
(Neustadt)
Tel. 459 62 62
Hearty Saxon fare with view of the
Altstadt

▶ **Gare de la Lune**
Pillnitzer Landstr. 148 (Wachwitz)
Tel. 267 85 54
With beach chairs, deck chairs and
view of the Elbe

▶ **Körnergarten**
Friedrich-Wieck-Str. 26
(Loschwitz)
Tel. 268 36 20
Beer garden by Blaues Wunder
bridge

▶ **Radeberger Spezialausschank**
Terrassenufer 1
(beneath the Brühlsche Terrasse)
Tel. 484 86 60
Only place outside Radeberg for
natural, clouded Zwickelbier.

▶ **Saloppe**
Brockhausstr. 1 (Loschwitz)
Tel. (0172) 353 25 86
Summer pub with concerts and
parties

▶ **Schillergarten**
Schillerplatz 9
(near Blaues Wunder)
Tel. 318 30 20
Traditional inn with large beer
garden

▶ **Torwirtschaft Grosser Garten**
Lennéstr. 11
Tel. 459 52 02
Seating for 800 in this beer garden
by southern gatehouse of the
Grosser Garten main avenue

▶ **Wirtshaus Lindenschänke**
Altmickten 1, tel. 859 95 77
Sit beneath lime trees by the Elbe
in this romantic beer garden with
Bavarian food.

▶ **Yenidze**
Weisseritzstr. 3 (Altstadt)
Tel. 490 59 90
Loftiest beer garden in Dresden
with view over the town

Summer evening on the Elbe: mild air and chilled beer in Watzke beer garden

● CAFÉS IN DRESDEN AND SURROUNDING AREAS

IN ALTSTADT

▶ Aha
Kreuzstr. 7
Tel. 496 06 73
Café and whole-food restaurant

▶ Alte Meister
Theaterplatz 1a
Tel. 481 04 26
Museum café by day, restaurant with view of Theaterplatz in the evening

▶ Café in Italienisches Dörfchen
Theaterplatz
Tel. 49 81 60
Historic café with wonderful interiors and Elbe terrace, but traffic thunders over the cobbles directly below.

▶ Café Kreutzkamm
Seestr. 6
Tel. 495 41 72
Traditional Dresden bakery, founded 1825; speciality: pyramid cake

▶ Café No. 3
Weisse Gasse 3
Tel. 485 08 88
A sample breakfast No. 3: salmon, Italian salami, fruit salad and quark with honey

▶ Café Schinkelwache
Theaterplatz 2, tel. 490 39 09
The seats on Theaterplatz are very good for watching the world go by.

▶ Café Vis-à-Vis
An der Frauenkirche 5
(on the Brühlsche Terrasse)
Tel. 864 28 35
Enjoy the Elbe view in summer from the Brühlsche Terrasse.

▶ Coselpalais
An der Frauenkirche 12
Tel. 496 24 44
Late Baroque palais, authentically rebuilt – direct view of the Frauenkirche

▶ Lingner
Lingner-Platz 1
(in German Hygiene Museum)
Tel. 484 66 00
Splendid modern design; numerous breakfast options

▶ Rauschenbach Deli
Weisse Gasse 2
Tel. 802 65 03
Dresden's hip young people drink their latte macchiato here.

▶ Solino
Am Taschenberg 3
(in Kempinski Hotel Taschenberg Palais)
Tel. 491 26 57
Caffè and Bar Italiano

IN NEUSTADT

▶ Café L'art de vie
An der Dreikönigskirche 1a
Tel. 802 73 00
Snug little spot in inner courtyard close to Societätstheater; choose between sweet, hearty and refreshing

▶ Café Neustadt
Bautzner Str. 69, tel. 899 66 49
Wicked breakfast options!

▶ Kästner's Café
Alaunstr. 1
(off Albertplatz)
Tel. 810 40 50
Good prices – by the Erich Kästner memorial

Top café: Café Schinkelwache on Theaterplatz has atmosphere.

▶ **Pfund's Molkerei**
Bautzner Str. 79, tel. 80 80 80
Café over the »most beautiful
dairy in the world« with all sorts
of milk-mix drinks; also a small
dairy museum

▶ **Café zum Rosengarten**
Carusufer 12
Tel. 802 07 74
Set amidst rare species of roses by
the Elbe, with view of Altstadt
silhouette

▶ **Schwarzmarktcafé**
Hauptstr. 36
Tel. 801 08 33
Breakfast daily until 4pm, with
fabulous home-made jams

**IN THE SURROUNDING
AREAS**

▶ **Café Toscana**
(Blasewitz) Schillerplatz 11
Tel. 310 07 44
Good choice of cakes and tarts;
best view of Blaues Wunder bridge
from the winter garden.

▶ **Crêpes-Galerie im Bräustübel**
(Loschwitz) Am Körnerplatz 3
Tel. 314 12 99

▶ **Café am Rossplatz**
(Meissen) Rossmarkt 6
Tel. (03 5 21) 45 26 88

▶ **Café Zieger**
(Meissen) Rote Stufen 5
Tel. (03 5 21) 45 31 47
Try »Meissner Fummel«!

▶ **Schlosscafé**
Schloss Moritzburg
Tel. (03 52 07) 81 4 82
Wonderful café in what was once
the electors' hunting lodge

▶ **Parkcafé Pillnitz**
(Pillnitz) Orangeriestr. 26
Tel. 261 82 33
Directly opposite the Schloss

Health

Germany's healthcare system is excellent. Doctors and dentists are listed in the »Gelbe Seiten« (Yellow Pages) under »Ärzte« and »Zahnärzte« respectively. The US and UK consulates can point you in the direction of medical practitioners who speak English. **Medical help**

Pharmacies (Apotheken) are generally open Mon–Fri 9.30am–6.30pm, Sat 9.30am–2pm, sometimes longer. They are closed on Sundays. Every pharmacy displays in the window or door a list of pharmacies which run an emergency service outside these hours and on holidays. **Pharmacies**

PHARMACIES

► **Out-of-hours service**
Tel. (0900) 136 22 43, and see notices in pharmacies

► **Löwenapotheke**
Wilsdruffer Str. 5
Tel. 49 71 70

► **Sertürner-Apotheke**
Sternplatz 15
Ttel. 490 64 96

► **Apotheke Prager Strasse**
Prager Str. 3c
Tel. 490 30 14

MEDICAL HELP

► **Emergency services**
Tel. 112

► **Ambulance**
Tel. 19 2 22

► **Doctors on call**
Tel. 19 2 92

Information

▶ USEFUL ADDRESSES

TOURIST INFORMATION IN DRESDEN

► **Tourist Information Dresden**
Prager Str. 2a, D-01069 Dresden
Tel. 49 19 20, fax 49 19 22 44
Opening hours: Mon–Fri
10am–6pm, Sat 10am–4pm

► **Tourist Information Dresden**
Schinkelwache am Theaterplatz
Opening hours: Mon–Fri
10am–6pm, Sat, Sun 10am–4pm

FURTHER INFORMATION

► **Dresden Werbung und Tourismus GmbH**
Ostra-Allee 11, D-01067 Dresden
www.dresden-tourist.de
Tourist information:
Tel. 49 19 21 00

City tours, excursions,
interpreters: tel. 49 19 21 00
Package deals: tel. 49 19 21 20
Accommodation: tel. 49 19 22 22
Ticket service: tel. 49 19 22 33
Tickets for Grünes Gewölbe:
Tel. 49 19 22 85
Dresden Card: tel. 49 19 22 81

TOURIST INFORMATION IN SURROUNDING AREAS

► **Tourist Information Meissen**
Markt 3, D-01662 Meissen
Tel. (03 5 21) 41 9 40, fax 41 94 19
www.touristinfo-meissen.de

► **Tourist Information Moritzburg**
Schlossallee 3b
D-01468 Moritzburg
Tel. (03 52 07) 85 40, fax 85 4 20
www.kulturlandschaft.
moritzburg.de

► **Tourist Service Pirna**
Am Markt 7, D-01796 Pirna
Tel. (03 5 01) 46 5 70, www.pirna.de

► **Tourist Information Radebeul**
Pestalozzistr. 6a
D-01445 Radebeul
Tel. (0351) 831 19 05, fax 831 19 02
www.radebeul.de

► **Tourismusverband Sächsische Schweiz**
Am Bahnhof 6
D-01814 Bad Schandau
Tel. (03 50 22) 49 50, fax 49 5 33
www.saechsische-schweiz.de

► **Tourist Information Stolpen**
Schlossstr. 14a, D-01833 Stolpen
Tel. (03 59 73) 27 3 13, fax 24 4 38
www.stolpen.de

WEBSITES IN ENGLISH

► **www.dresden.de**
Official city website – useful links

► **www.dresden-tourist.de**
Accommodation, restaurant guide,
events and Semper Opera tickets

► **www.skd-dresden.de**
Website for the state museums and
collection, with information on
museums, exhibitions and events

► **www.dresden-theater.de**
Official Saxon theatre page:
Felsenbühne programmes,
Zwinger concert information
and tickets

► **www.vvo-online.de**
City and transport information
system with timetables and traffic
updates

► **www.elberadweg.de**
Cycle guide for Elberadweg (Elbe
cycle route) from Bad Schandau to
Dessau with information about
the route, accommodation and
sights worth seeing

GERMAN-LANGUAGE WEBSITES

► **www.sz-online.de**
Website of the regional newspaper.
Saxony and Dresden news, ticket
service and city plan – Thu:
PluSZ-Veranstaltungsmagazin
(events)

► **www.cybersax.de**
Online version of city magazine
SAX: parties, events, city and
cultural politics, tickets

► **www.dresden-nightlife.de**
Guide to gastronomy, culture,
parties, tickets

► **www.kneipensurfer.de**
Gastro, pub and club guide

Language

GERMAN

General

Yes / No	Ja / Nein
Perhaps. / Maybe.	Vielleicht.
Please.	Bitte.
Thank you. / Thank you very much.	Danke. / Vielen Dank!
You're welcome.	Gern geschehen.
Excuse me!	Entschuldigung!
Pardon?	Wie bitte?
I don't understand.	Ich verstehe Sie / Dich nicht.
I only speak a bit of ...	Ich spreche nur wenig ...
Can you help me, please?	Können Sie mir bitte helfen?
I'd like ...	Ich möchte ...
I (don't) like this.	Das gefällt mir (nicht).
Do you have ...?	Haben Sie ...?
How much is this?	Wieviel kostet es?
What time is it?	Wieviel Uhr ist es?
What is this called?	Wie heißt dies hier?

Getting acquainted

Good morning!	Guten Morgen!
Good afternoon!	Guten Tag!
Good evening!	Guten Abend!
Hello! / Hi!	Hallo! Grüß Dich!
My name is ...	Mein Name ist ...
What's your name?	Wie ist Ihr / Dein Name?
How are you?	Wie geht es Ihnen / Dir?
Fine thanks. And you?	Danke. Und Ihnen / Dir?
Goodbye! / Bye-bye!	Auf Wiedersehen!
Good night!	Gute Nacht!
See you! / Bye!	Tschüss!

Travelling

left / right	links / rechts
straight ahead	geradeaus
near / far	nah / weit
Excuse me, where's ..., please?	Bitte, wo ist ...?
... the train station	... der Bahnhof

... the bus stop	... die Bushaltestelle
... the harbour	... der Hafen
... the airport	... der Flughafen
How far is it?	Wie weit ist das?
I'd like to rent a car.	Ich möchte ein Auto mieten.
How long?	Wie lange?

Traffic

My car's broken down.	Ich habe eine Panne.
Is there a service station nearby?	Gibt es hier in der Nähe eine Werkstatt?
Where's the nearest gas station?	Wo ist die nächste Tankstelle?
I want	Ich möchte ...
... liters / gallons of ...	Liter / Gallonen (3.8 l) ...
... regular./premium.	.... Normalbenzin./Super.
... diesel.	... Diesel.
... unleaded	... bleifrei.
Full, please.	Volltanken, bitte.
Help!	Hilfe!
Attention!/Look out!	Achtung!/Vorsicht!
Please call ...	Rufen Sie bitte ...
... an ambulance.	... einen Krankenwagen.
... the police.	... die Polizei.
It was my fault.	Es war meine Schuld.
It was your fault.	Es war Ihre Schuld.
Please give me your name and address.	Geben Sie mir bitte Namen und Anschrift.
Beware of ...	Vorsicht vor ...
Bypass (with road number)	Ortsumgehung (mit Straßennummer)
Bypass (Byp)	Umgehungsstraße
Causeway	Brücke, Pontonbrücke
Construction	Bauarbeiten
Crossing (Xing)	Kreuzung, Überweg
Dead end	Sackgasse
Detour	Umleitung
Divided highway	Straße mit Mittelstreifen
Do not enter	Einfahrt verboten
Exit	Ausfahrt
Hill	Steigung / Gefälle/unübersichtlich (Überholverbot)
Handicapped parking	Behindertenparkplatz
Junction (Jct)	Kreuzung, Abzweigung, Einmündung
Keep off ...	Abstand halten ...
Loading zone	Ladezone
Merge (merging traffic)	Einmündender Verkehr
Narrow bridge	Schmale Brücke

No parking	Parken verboten
No passing	Überholen verboten
No turn on red	Rechtsabbiegen bei Rot verboten
U Turn	Wenden erlaubt
No U turn	Wenden verboten
One Way	Einbahnstraße
Passenger loading zone	Ein- und Aussteigen erlaubt
Ped Xing	Fußgängerüberweg
Restricted parking zone	Zeitlich begrenztes Parken erlaubt
Right of way	Vorfahrt
Road construction	Straßenbauarbeiten
Slippery when wet	Schleudergefahr bei Nässe
Slow	Langsam fahren
Soft choulders	Straßenbankette nicht befestigt
Speed limit	Geschwindigkeitsbegrenzung
Toll	Benutzungsgebühr, Maut
Tow away zone	Absolutes Parkverbot, Abschleppzone
Xing (crossing)	Kreuzung, Überweg
Yield	Vorfahrt beachten

Shopping

Where can I find a ...?	Wo finde ich ... eine / ein ..?
... pharmacy	... Apotheke
... bakery	... Bäckerei
... department store	... Kaufhaus
... food store	... Lebensmittelgeschäft
... supermarket	... Supermarkt

Accommodation

Could you recommend ... ?	Können Sie mir ... empfehlen?
... a hotel / motel	... ein Hotel / Motel
... a bed & breakfast	... eine Frühstückspension
Do you have ...?	Haben Sie noch ...?
... a room for one	... ein Einzelzimmer
... a room for two	... ein Doppelzimmer
... with a shower / bath	... mit Dusche / Bad
... for one night	... für eine Nacht
... for a week	... für eine Woche
I've reserved a room.	Ich habe ein Zimmer reserviert.
How much is the room...?	Was kostet das Zimmer...?
... with breakfast	... mit Frühstück

Doctor

Can you recommend a good doctor?	Können Sie mir einen guten Arzt empfehlen?
I need a dentist.	Ich brauche einen Zahnarzt.
I feel some pain here.	Ich habe hier Schmerzen.
I've got a temperature.	Ich habe Fieber.
Prescription	Rezept
Injection / shot	Spritze

Bank / Post

Where's the nearest bank?	Wo ist hier bitte eine Bank?
ATM (Automated Teller Machine)	Geldautomat
I'd like to change dollars/pounds into euros.	Ich möchte Dollars/Pfund in Euro wechseln.
How much is ...	Was kostet ...
... a letter ...	... ein Brief ...
... a postcard ...	... eine Postkarte ...
to Europe?	nach Europa?

Numbers

1	eins	2	zwei
3	drei	4	vier
5	fünf	6	sechs
7	sieben	8	acht
9	neun	10	zehn
11	elf	12	zwölf
13	dreizehn	14	vierzehn
15	fünfzehn	16	sechzehn
17	siebzehn	18	achtzehn
19	neunzehn	20	zwanzig
21	einundzwanzig	30	dreißig
40	vierzig	50	fünfzig
60	sechzig	70	siebzig
80	achtzig	90	neunzig
100	(ein-)hundert	1000	(ein-)tausend
1/2	ein Halb	1/3	ein Drittel
1/4	ein Viertel		

Restaurant

Is there a good restaurant here?	Gibt es hier ein gutes Restaurant?
Would you reserve us a table for this evening, please?	Reservieren Sie uns bitte für heute Abend einen Tisch!

The menu please!	Die Speisekarte bitte!
Cheers!	Auf Ihr Wohl!
Could I have the check, please?	Bezahlen, bitte.
Where is the restroom, please?	Wo ist bitte die Toilette?

Frühstück / Breakfast

Kaffee (mit Sahne / Milch)	coffee (with cream / milk)
koffeinfreier Kaffee	decaffeinated coffee
heiße Schokolade	hot chocolate
Tee (mit Milch / Zitrone)	tea (with milk / lemon)
Rühreier	scrambled eggs
pochierte Eier	poached eggs
Eier mit Speck	bacon and eggs
Spiegeleier	eggs sunny side up
harte / weiche Eier	hard-boiled / soft-boiled eggs
(Käse- / Champignon-)Omelett	(cheese / mushroom) omelette
Pfannkuchen	pancake
Brot / Brötchen / Toast	bread / rolls / toast
Butter	butter
Zucker	sugar
Honig	honey
Marmelade / Orangenmarmelade	jam / marmelade
Joghurt	yoghurt
Obst	fruit

Vorspeisen und Suppen / Starters and Soups

Fleischbrühe	broth / consommé
Hühnercremesuppe	cream of chicken soup
Tomatensuppe	cream of tomato soup
gemischter Salat	mixed salad
grüner Salat	green salad
frittierte Zwiebelringe	onion rings
Meeresfrüchtesalat	seafood salad
Garnelen- / Krabbencocktail	shrimp / prawn cocktail
Räucherlachs	smoked salmon
Gemüsesuppe	vegetable soup

Fisch und Meeresfrüchte / Fish and Seafood

Kabeljau	cod
Krebs	crab
Aal	eel
Schellfisch	haddock

Hering	herring
Hummer	lobster
Muscheln/Austern	mussels/oysters
Barsch	perch
Scholle	plaice
Lachs	salmon
Jakobsmuscheln	scallops
Seezunge	sole
Tintenfisch	squid
Forelle	trout
Tunfisch	tuna

Fleisch und Geflügel / Meat and Poultry

gegrillte Schweinerippchen	barbecued spare ribs
Rindfleisch	beef
Hähnchen	chicken
Geflügel	poultry
Kotelett	chop / cutlet
Filetsteak	fillet
(junge) Ente	duck(ling)
Schinkensteak	gammon
Fleischsoße	gravy
Hackfleisch vom Rind	ground beef
gekochter Schinken	ham
Nieren	kidneys
Lamm	lamb
Leber	liver
Schweinefleisch	pork
Würstchen	sausages
Lendenstück vom Rind, Steak	sirloin steak
Truthahn	turkey
Kalbfleisch	veal
Reh oder Hirsch	venison

Nachspeise und Käse / Dessert and Cheese

gedeckter Apfelkuchen	apple pie
Schokoladenplätzchen	brownies
Hüttenkäse	cottage cheese
Sahne	cream
Vanillesoße	custard
Obstsalat	fruit salad
Ziegenkäse	goat's cheese
Eiscreme	ice cream
Gebäck	pastries

Gemüse und Salat / Vegetables and Salad

gebackene Kartoffeln in der Schale	baked potatoes
Pommes frites	french fries
Bratkartoffeln	hash browns
Kartoffelpüree	mashed potatoes
gebackene Bohnen in Tomatensoße	baked beans
Kohl	cabbage
Karotten	carrots
Blumenkohl	cauliflower
Tomaten	tomatoes
Gurke	cucumber
Knoblauch	garlic
Lauch	leek
Kopfsalat	lettuce
Pilze	mushrooms
Zwiebeln	onions
Erbsen	peas
Paprika	peppers
Kürbis	pumpkin
Spinat	spinach
Mais	sweet corn
Maiskolben	corn-on-the-cob

Obst / Fruit

Äpfel	apples	Birnen	pears
Aprikosen	apricots	Orange	orange
Brombeeren	blackberries	Pfirsiche	peaches
Kirschen	cherries	Ananas	pineapple
Weintrauben	grapes	Pflaumen	plums
Grapefruit	grapefruit	Himbeeren	raspberries
Zitrone	lemon	Erdbeeren	strawberries
Preiselbeeren	cranberries		

Getränke / Beverages

Bier (vom Fass)	beer (on tap)
Apfelwein	cider
Rotwein / Weißwein	red wine / white wine
trocken / lieblich	dry / sweet
Sekt, Schaumwein	sparkling wine
alkoholfreie Getränke	soft drinks
Fruchtsaft	fruit juice
gesüßter Zitronensaft	lemonade
Milch	milk
Mineralwasser	mineral water / spring water

Literature

Fritz Löffler: *Das alte Dresden* (Old Dresden)
This classic by Dresden's well-known conservationist first appeared in 1955 and has gone through several editions. It tells the story of ancient buildings, and those that have vanished.

Erich Kästner: *Als ich ein kleiner Junge war* (When I was a little boy)
The great writer's childhood reminiscences can almost be classed as a love letter to his home town.

Victor Klemperer: *I Shall Bear Witness – The Diaries of Victor Klemperer*
Klemperer was a Jewish professor of languages, who survived the Nazi period as he was married to a gentile and at the end of the war went into hiding. Two moving a revealing volumes cover the years 1933–41 and 1942–45.

Heinz Quinger: *Dresden und Umgebung* (Dresden and surroundings)
History and art in the Saxon capital, amply and informatively illustrated

Katrin Nitzschke: *Dresden – Ein Reiselesebuch* (Dresden – a travel reader)
Dresden's eventful history in entertaining literary form.

Tony Sharp: *Pleasure and Ambition: The Life, Loves and Wars of Augustus the Strong*
How Saxony's most famous ruler tried to leave his mark on the European stage – and what distracted him from his pursuit of power

Frederick Taylor: *Dresden – Tuesday, 13 February 1945*
Background and events to the destruction of Dresden by the Royal Air Force, including eyewitness accounts.

Lost Property Offices

► **Fundbüro der Stadt Dresden**
Hamburger Str. 19
Tel. 488 42 80
Opening hours: Tue, Thu
8am–noon, 2pm–6pm

► **Fundbüro der Deutschen Bahn AG**
In Bahnhof Dresden-Neustadt
Tel. 461 56 01

Money

Since 2002 the euro has been the official currency of Germany.

Euro

Citizens of EU members countries may import to and export from Germany unlimited amounts in euros.

Currency regulations

The bureau de change in the tourist office opposite the cathedral has long opening hours. Cash dispensers operated by various banks are thick on the ground in the city centre and never far away in the suburbs, so that money can be obtained without problems round the clock by using credit and debit cards with a PIN.

Bureaux de change and cash dispensers

The major international credit cards are accepted by banks, most hotels, car rentals and many restaurants and shops. Credit cards have limits.

Credit cards

If bank cards or cheque and credit cards should get lost, you should call your own bank or credit card organization to make sure they are immediately stopped. It is a good idea to make a note of the telephone number on the back of the card.

Loss of bank cards and credit cards

● CONTACT DETAILS FOR CREDIT CARDS

In the event of lost bank or credit cards you can contact the following numbers in UK and USA (phone numbers when dialling from Germany):

► **Eurocard/MasterCard**
Tel. 001 / 636 7227 111

► **Visa**
Tel. 001 / 410 581 336

► **American Express UK**
Tel. 0044 / 1273 696 933

► **American Express USA**
Tel. 001 / 800 528 4800

► **Diners Club UK**
Tel. 0044 / 1252 513 500

► **Diners Club USA**
Tel. 001 / 303 799 9000
Have the bank sort code, account number and card number as well as the expiry date ready.
The following numbers of UK banks (dialling from Germany) can be used to report and stop lost or stolen bank and credit cards issued by those banks:

► **HSBC**
Tel. 0044 / 1442 422 929

► **Barclaycard**
Tel. 0044 / 1604 230 230

► **NatWest**
Tel. 0044 / 142 370 0545

► **Lloyds TSB**
Tel. 0044 / 1702 278 270

Museums and Exhibitions

Guided tours Guided tours of museums in the state collections are arranged by the publicity department (tel. 491 42 00), and regular ones are listed at www.skd-dresden.de.

Prices and discounts An annual pass for the state collections costs €20, a day pass €12, and €7 for discounts. They are valid for all museums in the state collections, but not for special exhibitions.

◉ DRESDEN'S MUSEUMS

i The top museums

- Gemäldegalerie Alte Meister
- Galerie Neue Meister
- Grünes Gewölbe
- Rüstkammer
- Deutsches Hygiene-Museum

DRESDEN'S STATE ART COLLECTIONS

▶ **Gemäldegalerie Alte Meister (Old Masters)**
▶Gemäldegalerie Alte Meister

▶ **Galerie Neue Meister (paintings since 19th century)**
▶Galerie Neue Meister

▶ **Grünes Gewölbe (Green Vault)**
▶Schloss

▶ **Kunstgewerbemuseum (arts and crafts)**
▶Pillnitz

▶ **Kupferstichkabinett (drawings, engravings)**
▶Schloss

▶ **Mathematisch-Physikalischer Salon**
▶Zwinger

▶ **Münzkabinett (coins)**
▶Albertinum, ▶Schloss

▶ **Museum für Sächsische Volkskunst (Saxon folk art)**
▶Jägerhof

▶ **Porzellansammlung (porcelain)**
▶Zwinger

▶ **Puppentheatersammlung (puppet theatre)**
▶Jägerhof

▶ **Rüstkammer (armoury)**
▶Zwinger

▶ **Skulpturensammlung (sculpture)**
▶Albertinum, ▶Zwinger

ART

▶ **Kunsthalle (art gallery)**
▶Kunstakademie

▶ **Städtische Galerie (city gallery)**
▶Stadtmuseum

HISTORY / CULTURAL HISTORY

▶ **Buchmuseum (book museum)**
▶Sächsische Landesbibliothek (Saxon state library)

In the German Hygiene Museum visitors embark on a journey to discover mankind.

▸ **Verkehrsmuseum
(transport museum)**
▸Johanneum

INDIVIDUALS

▸ **Erich Kästner Museum**
▸Neustadt, Innere Neustadt

▸ **Carl Maria von Weber Museum**
▸Hosterwitz

▸ **Josef Hegenbarth Archive**
▸Loschwitz

▸ **Käthe Kollwitz Museum**
▸Moritzburg

▸ **Karl May Museum**
▸Radebeul

▸ **King Johann exhibition**
▸Schloss Weesenstein

▸ **Kraszewski Memorial**
▸Neustadt,
Äussere Neustadt

▸ **Leonhardi Museum**
▸Loschwitz

▸ **Palitzsch Museum, Prohlis**
▸Famous People,
Johann Georg Palitzsch

▸ **Richard Wagner Museum,
Graupa**
▸Pillnitz, surrounding area

Newspapers and Periodicals

Newspapers
Dresden has three daily newspapers. The most important is the *Sächsische Zeitung*. The others are the *Dresdner Neueste Nachrichten* and the tabloid *Sächsische Morgenpost*.

City magazines
Sax is a monthly magazine for city politics and culture; the coverage includes party scene and detailed events calendar. *Dresden* is a free magazine covering culture and events.

Post and Telecommunications

Public
telephones
Public telephones normally only accept Deutsche Telekom phone-cards, available in 5, 10 and 20-euro denominations from post offices and newsagents.
International calling cards offer more competitive rates (www.com-fi.com). There are a large number of call shops which offer cheap rates for calls abroad.

Mobile
phones
The German mobile networks function throughout the country with providers such as T-Mobile, E-Plus, Base and O2. It is worth checking on roaming tariffs, which can be pricey, before you leave.

POST OFFICES

► **Postamt 1**
Königsbrücker Str. 29 (Neustadt)
Opening hours: Mon–Fri
9am–7pm, Sat 10am–1pm

► **Postamt 12**
Webergasse 1 (Altmarktgalerie)
Opening hours: Mon–Sat
9.30am–8pm

DIALLING CODES

► **Dialling codes to Dresden**
from Germany 0351
from the UK and Republic of
Ireland:
Tel. 00 49 351
from the USA, Canada and
Australia:
Tel. 00 11 49 351
It is not necessary to dial the 0351

area code for local calls within
Dresden.

► **Dialling codes from Germany**
to the UK: tel. 00 44
to the Republic of Ireland:
Tel. 00 353
to the USA and Canada: tel. 00 1
to Australia: tel. 00 61
The 0 that precedes the subsequent
local area code is omitted.

DIRECTORY ENQUIRIES

► **National**
Tel. 11 833

► **International**
Tel. 11 834

► **Enquiries in English**
Tel. 11 837

Prices · Discounts

The Dresden City Card costs €21.00 per person, is valid for 48 hours   Dresden Cards
and allows free travel by public transport in tariff zone Dresden (for
timetable and prices tel. (01 80) 22 66 22 66), free entry to state collection museums and the German Hygiene Museum, and also reduc-
tions on city tours, paddle-steamer trips, theatre tickets, and in some
restaurants and shops. Children up to 6 years of age travel free on
public transport, two children up to age 15 get free entry to state collection museums incl. special exhibitions. Explore the greater Dresden area with the **Dresden Regio Card**, valid for 72 hours, price €29.
It offers the same benefits as the Dresden City Card and also free
travel in the surrounding region. **Order Dresden Cards** on tel.
49 19 22 81, fax 49 19 21 16, www.dresden-tourist.de, or in the tourist
information offices (► Information).

On weekdays small groups of up to 5 can explore the whole of Sax-   Saxony ticket
ony on regional trains at a good price (one day costs €21) with the
Saxony ticket (information: www.bahn.de, tel. 11 8 61).

Minimumtwo nights: price includes Dresden City Card and a choice   Dresden Days
of events. Book the Dresden Days package deals with the Dresden
Werbung und Tourismus GmbH (► Information), tel. 49 19 21 20.

Elbe cyclist
ticket

Book overnight accommodation in advance and get discounted rail travel with the Elbe Radler Ticket (Elbe cyclist ticket): book with Dresden Werbung und Tourismus GmbH (▸ Information), tel. 49 19 21 20.

Out-of-term
accommodation

During the vacation period students can get inexpensive overnight accommodation in one of the hostels via student services, tel. 46 97 50.

Shopping

Shopping
districts

Prager Strasse used to be considered an elegant place to stroll and shop, but today it just has the usual selection of large chain stores. The Altmarktgalerie, by contrast, has a lot to offer. There is more chance of finding something out of the ordinary in the Neustadt district. You'll find top quality shops along Königstrasse, and something unusual might take your fancy in the streets of Äussere Neustadt beyond Albertplatz.

Souvenirs ▸

Popular souvenirs and gifts from Dresden are porcelain (especially from Meissen), wood carving from the Erzgebirge, Dresden Christstollen, and illustrated publications from the state collections.

▶ SHOPPING ADDRESSES

STOLLEN

▸ **Bäckerei Hinkel**
Loschwitzer Str. 52
(Schillergalerie Blasewitz)

▸ **Bäckerei Kreutzkamm**
Seestr. 6
The speciality here is called Baumkuchen

▸ **Bäckerei Matzker**
Johannes-Brahms-Str. 26
Tel. 202 40 03
Tours of the bakery are possible.

▸ **Schaubäckerei Scheinert**
Bautzner Landstr. 64
Tel. 268 38 74

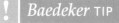

! | *Baedeker* TIP

Sachsenmarkt
Dresden's largest produce market with 200 stalls: open-air shopping every Friday 8am–5pm along Lingnerallee at the Deutsches Hygiene-Museum. Fresh fruit and vegetables, farmyard eggs, sausage and cheese, gourmet food, crafts, much of it sold by the producers.

CERAMICS AND PORCELAIN

▶ **Am Goldenen Reiter**
Hauptstr. 17 – 19
Old Meissen porcelain

▶ **Bunzlauer Keramik**
Bautzner Str. 81

▶ **Porzellanmanufaktur
Meissen**
in Hotel Dresden Hilton, An der
Frauenkirche 5
at Karstadt, Prager Str. 12
in ▶ Meissen: Talstr. 9 and
Burgstr. 6

SAXON FOLK ART AND CRAFTS

▶ **Kunsthandwerk
an der Kreuzkirche**
Kreuzstr. 6

▶ **Kunsthandwerkerpassage**
Hauptstr. 9 – 19
Folk art from the Erzgebirge,
Dresden specialities

▶ **Martina Seifert**
Bautzner Str. 79 (Neustadt)

▶ **Sächsische Werk-Kunst-Stube**
Wallstr. 1

WINE FROM SAXONY

▶ **Wein und Spirituosen Kontor**
Königstr. 4

▶ **Sächsische Winzergenossen-
schaft Meissen**
Bennoweg 9, D-01662 Meissen

▶ **Vintners and
wine taverns**
▶ Food and Drink

ART, BOOKS, DESIGN

▶ **art+form**
Bautzner Str. 11

---

i Rewarding areas for shoppers

- Altstadt: Altmarkt-Galerie (Webergasse)
- Innere Neustadt: between Hauptstrasse (arcades with craft shops and workshops) and Königstrasse (elegant and exclusive fashion and design, antiques)
- Äussere Neustadt: Kunsthofpassage, cool and fashionable shops around Alaunstr., Louisenstr., Böhmische Str. and Görlitzer Str. (retail therapy and coffee shops for the young scene).
- Loschwitz: Körnerplatz and Friedrich-Wieck-Strasse (little shops in half-timbered houses selling crafts, books and antiques).

Graphic art, photographs, art prints, a wide variety of gifts from pens to jewellery, books and CDs

▶ **Jo+Co**
Prager Str. 10 and
Böhmische Str. 14
Design for the home and kitchen,
knick-knacks

▶ **Kunsthofpassage**
Alaunstr. / Görlitzer Str.
Fashion, jewellery, books etc. in a
number of courtyards between
Alaunstr. and Görlitzer Str.

FASHION AND ACCESSORIES

▶ **Shirley Hoffmann
Goldschmiede**
Königstr. 11

▶ **Kalahari**
Bischofsweg 28
African crafts, wine and books

▶ **Atelier Jappée
Hutdesign Jacqueline Peevski**
Bautzner Str. 6 (am Albertplatz)
Hat designer

▶ **Le Bagage**
Königstr. 8
Ladies' handbags, luggage

▶ **Bärbel Drexel Shop**
Königstr. 1
(Passage beim Wenzel)
Natural products

▶ **Calzadór**
Rothenburger Str. 32
(Neustadt)
Wide range of shoes

▶ **Harlem**
Alaunstr. 53
Sporty and trendy

▶ **Ultramaringelb**
Görlitzer Str. 23
Young designer fashion, inventive
accessories

SECOND-HAND BOOKS

▶ **Antiquitäten und Kunst**
Obergraben 2
Books, furniture, toys

▶ **Dresdner Antiquariat**
Wilsdruffer Str. 14
Humanities and social sciences

▶ **Historica-Antiquariat**
Heinrichstr. 6
History, Saxony

Sport and Outdoors

SPORT AND FACILITIES

FOOTBALL

▶ **Rudolf-Harbig-Stadion**
Lennéstrasse
tram:
R.-Harbig-Stadion (line 13).
The top spectator sport is of
course football, which has a long
tradition in Dresden (▶ Famous
People, Helmut Schön). The main
team in the city, FC Dynamo, is
having a spell of bad luck (tickets:
www.dynamo-dresden.de).

PFERDERENNEN

▶ **Galopprennbahn
Dresden-Seidnitz**
Oskar-Röder-Straße 1,
Tel. 256 10 18,
S-Bahn: Bhf. Reick (S 1)
Horse racing, both on the flat and
steeplechases at weekends and on
some Wednesdays.

OUTDOOR SWIMMING POOLS

▶ **Freibad Cotta**
Hebbelstr. 33
Water slide and volleyball court

▶ **Freibad Mockritz**
Münzteichweg
Natural lake with an area for non-
swimmers and a playground

▶ **Stausee Cossebaude**
Meissner Str.
Beach on a lake

▶ **Strandbad Wostra**
Trieskestr. 22
(Kleinzschachwitz)
Opposite the Elbe island at Pillnitz
on the Zschieren bank of the Elbe;
nudist bathing

► **Moritzburg lakes**
(► Sights from A to Z, Moritzburg). There are bathing sites on the following lakes in this area: Mittelteich, Dippelsdorfer Teich (Strandbad Friedewald), Oberer Waldteich and Niederer Waldteich

► **Bilzbad Radebeul**
Meiereiweg 108
Friedrich Eduard Bilz was an advocate of natural healing and founder of Germany's first »light and air« bath. In 1911 he bought this swimming bath with the world's first wave machine, which is still regularly in operation!

SWIMMING INDOORS

► **Erlebnisbad Elbamare**
Wölfnitzer Ring 55,
Tel. 41 00 90

► **Georg-Arnhold-Bad**
Hauptallee 2
(at the Grosser Garten)
tel. 494 22 03

BOWLING

► **U. S. Play**
Lommatzscher Str. 98 (in the Elbe-Park), tel. 851 16 66

CLIMBING

The Elbsandsteingebirge (Elbe sandstone mountains) is a popular area for climbing. Information from Sächsischer Bergsteigerbund, tel. 494 14 15, Outdoortours, tel. (03 59 71) 56 9 07 and www.klettern-sachsen.de

JOGGING

Some good places for jogging are the banks of the Elbe (Neustadt side), the Grosser Garten and the Dresdner Heide.

At the top: climbers in Bielatal in Saxon Switzerland

CYCLING

► **Cycle hire**
Dresden-Neustadt rail station
Tel. 461 56 01, hours:
Mon–Fri 6am–noon,
12.30pm–8pm, Sat, Sun 8am–noon, 12.30pm–8pm.
From the city centre it is possible to cycle throught the Elbe meadows on the Elbe cycle path (Elberadweg) as far as the Czech border, or downstream to Meissen (www.elberadweg.de). The city is bordered to the northeast by the Dresdner Heide, where there are many cycle paths.

ICE SKATING

► **Ice rink
and Eissporthalle**
In the Ostra-Sportpark on Pieschener Allee, tel. 496 40 24
Ice rink: mid-Oct to early March.
Eissporthalle: early Sept to mid-April.

SPORTS AND LEISURE CENTRES

▶ **U 1 Sport- und Freizeitzentrum**
Ullersdorfer Platz 1
(at Kurhaus Bühlau)
Tel. 267 85 75,
Tram: Bühlau (lines 11, 51)
Bowling, billiards, fitness

▶ **XXL Freizeit**
Breitscheidstr. 40, tel. 25 45 80
S-Bahn: Bhf. Dobritz (S 1)
Bowling, climbing, volleyball and more

TENNIS

There are many tennis courts in the city, e.g. in Waldpark Blasewitz, in Weisser Hirsch in Kurparkstrasse, on Pieschener Allee, Wiener Strasse, Burgenlandstrasse and near the Technische Universität.

HIKING

Hikers go to the Dresdner Heide, to the Moritzburg lake district and the Sächsische Schweiz.
Information and maps for the Sächsische Schweiz:
Nationalparkzentrum
Bad Schandau
Dresdner Str. 2b
Tel. (03 50 22) 50 2 40

Theatre · Concerts

Musical tradition   Dresden's musical tradition is the most ancient part of its cultural life and today is characterised by three outstanding ensembles: the Staatskapelle Dresden, which has existed for almost 450 years; the Dresden Philharmonie; and the world-renowned Kreuzchor. Annual highlights are the Dresden music festival (tel. 47 85 60) and the Dixieland festival (▶Festivals, Holidays and Events).

▶ THEATRE, OPERA, DANCE, MUSIC

TICKET SERVICE

▶ **Schinkelwache am Theaterplatz**
Tel. 491 17 40, fax 495 12 76
Opening hours: Mon–Fri
10am–6pm, Sat 10am–1pm
Booking fee for advance tickets!

▶ **Box office in the Kulturpalast**
Schlossstr. 2 (on Altmarkt)
Tel. 486 66 66, fax 486 63 40
Opening Hours:
Mon–Fri 10am–7pm,
Sat 10am–2pm

▶ **Box office in the Florentinum**
Ferdinandstr. 12, tel. 86 66 00

▶ **Sax-Ticket**
Königsbrücker Str. 55
Tel. 803 87 44

MAJOR THEATRES

▶ **Sächsische Staatsoper Dresden**
Theaterplatz 2 (Semper Opera),
www.semperoper.de
Programme /
ticket availability: tel. 491 17 40
Bookings: tel. 491 17 05

Standby: tel. 491 17 77
Classical opera – the Sächsische
Staatskapelle is one of the longest-
established orchestras in the
world.

► **Schauspielhaus**
Postplatz
Programme: tel. 491 35 70
Tickets: tel. 491 35 55
Classical and contemporary

► **Kleines Haus**
Glacisstr. 28, tel. 491 35 55
Fri »Neubau« night: documentary
films in the afternoon, contemporary productions in the evening,
then party with DJ all night long

► **Landesbühnen Sachsen**
Meissner Landstr. 152
Tickets: tel. 895 42 14
Repertoire: plays, musicals,
concerts, ballet.

SMALL THEATRES
► **Festspielhaus Hellerau**
Karl-Liebknecht-Str. 56
Tel. 883 37 00
Ambitious contemporary (dance)
theatre in Hellerauer Festspielhaus

► **Hoftheater**
Hauptstr. 35 (Weissig)
Tel. 250 61 15
Rural theatre: devised and owned
by Saxony's best-known actor Rolf
Hoppe, who is also chief per-
former; the programme includes
plays, readings, jazz and children's
theatre.

► **Kleine Szene der
Sächsischen Staatsoper**
Bautzner Str. 107 (Neustadt)
Programme (recorded message):
tel. 491 17 31, tickets: tel. 491 17 05
Musicals

i Don't miss the music!
■ Semper Opera
■ Operetta: Staatsoperette
■ Dresdner Philharmonie
■ Hofkirche organ concerts
■ Zwinger serenades in summer
■ Kreuzchor

► **Komödie Dresden**
Freiberger Str. 39
(in World Trade Centre)
Tel. 86 64 10
Light entertainment, often farces
and comedies with celebrity cast

► **Projekttheater**
Louisenstr. 47
Tel. 81 07 60
Alternative theatre, dance, no
regular ensemble

► **Riesa efau**
Adlergasse 14/16
Tel. 866 02 11
Concerts, readings, theatre and
cinema

► **Societätstheater**
An der Dreikönigskirche 1a
Tickets: tel. 803 68 10
Modern intimate theatre

► **1001 Märchen**
Weisseritzstr. 3
(in Yenidze cupola)
Tel. 495 10 01
Fairy tales for young and old,
evening performances with belly
dancing

► **Theater Junge Generation**
Meissner Landstr. 4
Tel. 429 12 20
Theatre for children and young
people

▶ **Theaterhaus Rudi**
Fechnerstr. 2a, tel. 849 19 25
Amateur theatre, concerts, cinema, children's events and puppets

▶ **Theaterkahn Dresden Brettl**
Terrassenufer
(beneath Augustusbrücke)
Tel. 496 94 50
Afloat on the Elbe: musical and literary discoveries

▶ **Trocadero Sarrasani Theater**
Grosse Meissner Strasse
(between Blockhaus and Hotel Westin Bellevue)
Tel. (0700) 727 727 264
Dinner and variety show with top performers. Westin chef Holger Bartkowiak creates a 4-course meal.

PUPPET THEATRE AND PANTOMIME

▶ **mai hof puppentheater Weissig**
Hauptstr. 46

Tel. 269 00 72
For young and old!

▶ **Mimenbühne Dresden**
Maternistr. 17
Tel. 796 14 00
Pantomime and cabaret, incl. children's programme

▶ **Puppentheater im Rundkino**
Prager Str.
Tel. 496 53 70
Theatre for children and adults, programme from Grimm to Shakespeare

▶ **Puppentheater Sonnenhäusl, Grosser Garten**
Tel. 445 68 70
Programme information:
Tel. (0173) 924 36 84

CABARET AND REVUE

▶ **Breschke & Schuch Cabaret**
Wettiner Platz 10
Tel. 490 40 09

Large auditorium: the Semper Opera is always well attended.

Puts on its own productions and hosts visiting shows.

► **Carte Blanche**
Priessnitzstr. 10
Tel. 20 47 20
First Dresden transvestite revue – an entertaining performance

► **Comedy**
Katharinenstr. 11
Tel. 89 96 00 00
Plenty of laughter on Saturday evenings in the garage Comedy Club

► **Herkuleskeule**
Sternplatz 1, tel. 492 55 55
Political cabaret, rather more bite to it since German unification

► **Wechselbad**
Maternistr. 17
Information/bookings:
Tel. 796 11 55
Hot address for cabaret, comedy and visiting shows

OPEN AIR THEATRES

► **Felsenbühne Rathen**
Ticket office: tel. (03 50 24) 77 70
Magical natural theatre

► **TheaterRuine St Pauli**
Königsbrücker Platz
Tel. 272 14 44
May–Sept, open air performances of plays and concerts

► **Freilichtbühne Grosser Garten**
Tel. 445 68 46
Classical, rock and pop concerts and festivals

► **Parktheater**
Palaisteich, Grosser Garten
Grosser Garten office:
tel. 44 55 66 00
Baroque park theatre

► **More stages for open-air performances**
Zwinger, Schloss, Schloss Pillnitz, Barockgarten Grosssedlitz and Palais in Grosser Garten

OPERA / OPERETTA

► **Sächsische Staatsoper Dresden**
Theaterplatz 2 (Semper Opera)
Programme, ticket availability:
tel. 491 17 40
Ticket office:
tel. 491 17 05
Standby:
tel. 491 17 77
Classical opera, very sought after – get tickets in good time!

► **Kleine Szene der Sächsischen Staatsoper**
Bautzner Str. 107 (Neustadt)
Programme (recorded message):
tel. 491 17 31, tickets: tel. 491 17 05
Musicals

► **Staatsoperette Dresden**
Pirnaer Landstr. 131
Tickets: tel. 207 99 29
Operettas and dance revue

► **Landesbühnen Sachsen**
Meissnerstr. 152
Tickets: tel. 895 42 14
Repertoire: plays, musicals, concerts, ballet

ORCHESTRA / CHAMBER MUSIC / CHOIRS

► **Dresdner Philharmonie**
Location: Kulturpalast on Altmarkt
Tickets: tel. 486 63 06
Fax 486 63 53
On the night: tel. 496 63 30

Jazz, jazz, jazz

Tonne, founded in 1977 under the name IG Jazz, became the leading jazz club in the GDR. Today, in the Neue Tonne below the restaurant Le Maréchal de Saxe at König-strasse 15 (Neustadt), well-known national and international jazz musicians perform (tel. 820 60 17).

Founded in 1870, very highly regarded in musical world

► **Dresdner Sinfoniker**
Location, programme:
Tel. 490 36 05
www.dresdner-sinfoniker.de
Europe's top symphony orchestra for world premieres exclusively of contemporary music

► **Dresden Zentrum für zeitgenössische Musik**
Location: Karl-Liebknecht-Str. 56 (Hellerau), tel. 26 46 20
Renowned modern music centre

► **Hochschule für Musik »Carl Maria von Weber«**
Main venue:
Aula Blochmannstr. 2/4
Opera tickets available two weeks in advance from the Musikhoch-schule, Wettiner Platz 13, tel. 49 23 60, tickets for chamber music concerts on the door. Free entry most days to further concerts in the Aula Blochmannstrasse

► **Kreuzchor**
Location: Kreuzkirche on Alt-markt
Tel. 496 58 07, advance tickets in the Kreuzkirche
Kreuzchor vespers on some Sat-

urdays, Jan–Easter 5pm; Easter–Dec 6pm

► **Sächsische Staatskapelle Dresden**
Location:
Semper Opera, Theaterplatz 2
Programme,
Ticket availability: tel. 491 17 40
Tickets: tel. 491 17 05
Standby: tel. 491 17 77
One of the oldest-established orchestras in the world

FURTHER CONCERT VENUES IN DRESDEN

Kulturpalast, Schloss Albrechts-berg, Hofkirche (concerts on the Silbermann organ: Wed, Sat 11.30am–noon; April–Dec 3rd Thu in month 7.30pm sacred organ music), Martin Luther Kirche and Marcolini Palais in Dresden-Friedrichstadt

ROCK AND POP
► **Alter Schlachthof**
Gothaer Str. 11/Ecke Leipziger Str.
Tel. 858 85 29
One of Dresden's most popular concert venues; programme ranges from classical via pop and rock to musical

► **Scheune**
Alaunstr. 36 – 40
(Neustadt)
Tel. 804 55 32
Party, theatre and concert location for the young and wild, with popular Scheune café – truly legendary

► **Star Club**
Altbriesnitz 2 a
Tel. 421 03 02
Rock club in converted cinema, all the Indie greats play here.

Tours · Guides

City walks are organised by the tourist office (▶Information). They last approx. 90 min and start in front of the main office in Prager Strasse, on request also from other locations.

City walks

City tours are offered by various companies and start several times a day from Postplatz, Hauptbahnhof and Theaterplatz/Augustusbrücke. The tours listed below vary in length and theme.

City tours

A steamship cruise is a wonderful scenic experience. Cruises are possible all year round (reduced winter timetable), and can be combined with hiking or sightseeing.

Steamship cruise

There are several 90-minute trips each day with a sightseeing commentary. From the main landing-stage at Terrassenufer beneath the Brühlsche Terrasse (with ticket sales) boats go to the Sächsische Schweiz or downstream along the Weinstrasse to Meissen. Passengers can leave and join the ship at any point on scheduled routes. In the evenings there is jazz and Dixieland (May–Oct; Fri, Sat from 7.30pm), and summer night cruises (May–Sept, Sat from 8pm) with dance and buffet. The Sächsische Dampfschifffahrtsgesellschaft fleet operates the oldest paddle-steamer fleet in the world – nine paddle steamers listed for technical conservation – as well as two large and two smaller modern motor boats. Seven of the nine paddle steamers were launched in the 19th century: *Stadt Wehlen* (1879), *Diesbar* (1884), *Meissen* (1885), *Pillnitz* (1886), *Krippen* (1892), *Kurort Rathen* (1896) and *Pirna* (1898).

> **!** *Baedeker* TIP
>
> **Igeltour**
>
> Igeltour has made a good name for itself among the more unconventional guided walks, cycle and bus tours, not restricted to tourist highlights. Themed guided walks include Jewish Life in Dresden, Art Nouveau and Elbe Schloss Parks (information and booking: igeltour Dresden, Pulsnitzer Str. 10, D-01099 Dresden, tel. 804 45 57, fax 804 45 48, www.igeltour-dresden.de).

▶ SIGHTSEEING INFORMATION

▶ **Bus tour of Dresden**
Königstr. 6
D-01097 Dresden
Tel. 899 56 50, fax 899 56 60,
Departs from Theaterplatz, Augustusbrücke; round trips by day and in the evening, tours of the Zwinger

▶ **Hamburger Hummelbahn**
Feldschlösschenstr. 8
D-01069 Dresden
Tel. 494 04 04
Departs from Postplatz/Zwinger; city tours, Stollen tours, trips to the Radeberger brewery

! Baedeker TIP

An unconventional city tour
They are small and highly manoeuvrable, bright yellow and extremely comfortable: modern rickshaws, an opportunity to enjoy the passing scenes of the city without the noise of an engine. The customers are not part of a tourist horde, as there are seats for just two persons in the back (information and reservations: tel. 803 07 70).

▶ **Sachsen Show Dresden**
Altcoschütz 6a, D-01189 Dresden
Tel. 403 44 77, fax 403 44 78
Saxon history and stories

▶ **Dresdner Verkehrsbetriebe AG**
Trachenberger Str. 40,
D-01129 Dresden
Tel. 857 22 01 / -10 11
Bus tours from the main rail station or Postplatz; tram tours from Postplatz; also tours of the Zwinger and Semper Opera, wine-tasting at the Sächsisches Staatsweingut (state winery) in Schloss Wackerbarth

▶ **Sächsische Dampfschifffahrt (steamships)**
Hertha-Lindner-Str. 10,
D-01067 Dresden
Tel. 866 09 40, www.saechsische-dampfschifffahrt.de

Transport

Local Transport

Travel network plan, see p.132

Intersections

The most important means of public transport are trams and buses, and the S-Bahn (city and suburban railway). Important points of intersection for the three different forms of transport are, in Altstadt: Hauptbahnhof, Pirnaischer Platz, Postplatz and Strassburger Platz; and in Neustadt: Albertplatz and Bahnhof Neustadt.

S-Bahn

The S-Bahn goes out to Radebeul, Sächsische Schweiz, Tharandter Wald, Dresden Heide and the Meissen wine-growing district.
S 1: Meissen-Triebischtal – Radebeul – Dresden-Neustadt – Dresden-Hauptbahnhof – Heidenau – Pirna – Rathen – Königstein – Schöna
S 2: Dresden-Hauptbahnhof – Bahnhof Dresden-Neustadt – Dresden airport
S 3: Dresden-Hauptbahnhof – Freital – Tharandt

Tickets

Tickets for bus, tram, cable railway and Elbe ferries are obtainable from ticket machines, kiosks, newspaper kiosks, and in the buses or trams themselves. It is worth buying a ticket for several journeys, or for a period of time. Multi-journey tickets, a 24-hour ticket, family day pass, one-week pass and one-month pass are on offer. Short journey tickets are valid for four stops. S-Bahn tickets are sold at the stations.

⏵ TRANSPORT INFORMATION

INFORMATION ABOUT LOCAL TRANSPORT

www.vvo-online.de/en/index.aspx
(site in English)

▶ Dresden Transport
Tel. 857 10 11, www.dvbag.de

▶ Upper Elbe Transport
Tel. (0180) 22 66 22 66

▶ Rail enquiries
Tel. 11 8 61

TAXI

▶ Radio taxi
Tel. 21 12 11

▶ Taxi and limousine service
Tel. 88 88 88 88 (8 x 8)
On this number you can also
order a velotaxi!

ELBE FERRIES IN CITY AREA

▶ Kleinzschachwitz – Pillnitz
Mon–Fri 4.30am–0.30am;
Sat, Sun, holidays 5.30am–0.30am
Passenger and car ferry

▶ Tolkewitz – Niederpoyritz
Mon–Fri 5am–8pm; Sat, Sun,
holidays in summer 8am–8pm, in
winter 10.30am–6pm

▶ Johannstadt – Neustadt
April–Oct
Mon–Fri 6am–8pm,
Sat, Sun, holidays 8.30am–8pm

ELBE FERRIES IN SURROUNDING AREAS

The Elbe ferries in surrounding
areas link Cossebaude-Gohlis with
Radebeul-Serkowitz, Heidenau
with Birkwitz, Pirna with Copitz,
Krippen with Postelwitz.
There are Elbe ferries also in
Rathen, Wehlen, Königstein, Bad
Schandau and Schmilka

STEAMSHIPS

▶ City Tours/Sightseeing, Steamships

BREAKDOWN ASSISTANCE

▶ Allgemeiner Deutscher Automobilclub (ADAC)
Tel. (0180) 222 22 22

▶ ACE breakdown service
Tel. (01802) 34 35 38

▶ Automobilclub von Deutschland (AvD)
Tel. (0180) 990 99 09

CAR PARKS

▶ Centrally located underground parking
Frauenkirche; Kempinski Hotel/
Taschenberg Palais (Kleine
Brüdergasse); Karstadt (Waisen-
hausstrasse); Semper Opera (Am
Zwingerteich)

▶ Large central car parks
Altstadt: Altmarkt (Ferdinand-
shof), Kulturpalast
Neustadt: Bautzner Str/Glacisstr,
Palaisplatz, Theresienstrasse

PRIVATE CAR TRAVEL-SHARE

Dr-Friedrich-Wolf-Str. 2,
D-01097 Dresden
www.mitfahren-online.de
Tel. (01 8 05) 19 33 19

Tarifzone Radebeul 52

Travellers with Disabilities

Tours and brochure The Dresden Werbung und Tourismus GmbH (▸ Information) arranges bus tours and excursions for travellers with disabilities; it provides a brochure *Dresden without Barriers* (tel. 49 19 21 00, fax 49 19 21 16, e-mail: info@dresden-tourist.de). The brochure lists accommodation and restaurants that cater for the disabled, and gives information about access, guided tours of churches, the zoo, and museums, and addresses from mobility service to dialysis centre.

⏵ USEFUL ADDRESSES

DISABILITY SUPPORT

▸ **Silvia Müller**
Dr.-Külz-Ring 19, tel. 488 28 32

▸ **Social services/
disability support**
Riesaer Str. 7, tel. 488 49 71

TRAVEL

▸ **Travel for the disabled**
Tel. 850 02 23
(daily 6am–9pm)

▸ **Travel for the disabled /
Volkssolidarität**
Tel. 413 21 69

▸ **Taxi**
Book through
German Red Cross
Tel. 85 00 20
Mon–Sat 5am–6pm
(▸Transport, taxi).

Weights and Measures

IMPERIAL/
METRIC MEASURES

1 inch = 2.54 centimetres
1 centimetre = 0.39 inches
1 foot = 0.3 metres
1 metre = 3.3 feet
1 mile = 1.61 kilometres
1 kilometre = 0.62 miles
1 kilogram = 2.2 pounds
1 pound = 0.45 kilograms
1 gallon = 4.54 litres
1 litre = 0.22 gallons

The metric system is used in Germany. Visitors should keep in mind that a comma is used for decimals (2,5 not 2.5) and a point, when used, indicates thousands (2.500 instead of 2,500).

When to Go

It's worth visiting Dresden at any time of year, but May to September is the best time to enjoy the lovely surroundings, on foot or in the beer gardens. The winter is really cold and often windy, yet Dresden has its own charm at this season too; culturally there is something on offer the whole year round, and there are exceptional museums.

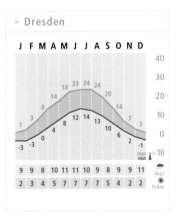

► Dresden

Tours

YOU DON'T KNOW WHERE
TO START? HERE ARE A FEW
TIPS FOR ITINERARIES. KEEP
SOME TIME FOR WALKS IN
THE BEAUTIFUL AREAS AROUND
DRESDEN TOO!

TOURS OF DRESDEN

The silhouette of Dresden is like an architectural painting set in the Elbe valley. The city has a lively cultural scene and night life, and not far away is the romantic scenery of the Sächsische Schweiz. You will experience many sides of the city on these four tours.

← *The park of Schloss Pillnitz*

Getting Around in Dresden

Dresden is a popular tourist destination all year round, and especially from spring to autumn, so it's advisable to book accommodation in good time. The city can cater for a top-level cultural break, and for active rest and relaxation in idyllic surroundings, and even for those who brave a city trip with kids. A car is not usually necessary because most of the sights are in the historic centre and can best be reached on foot. There are trams and buses to other city districts, and the S-Bahn suburban railway runs to destinations such as the Sächsische Schweiz (Saxon Switzerland). To explore the city by public transport it's worth buying a Dresden City Card, and to include the whole region there is a Dresden Regio Card. In four days you can see a lot of Dresden, and a whole week is ideal if hiking through the Sächsische Schweiz is to be included.

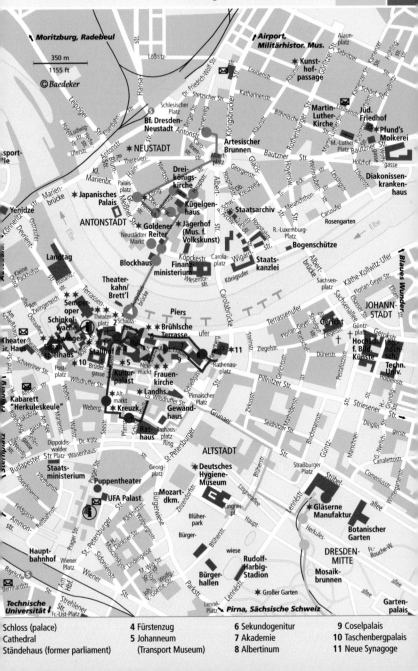

Schloss (palace)
Cathedral
Ständehaus (former parliament)

4 Fürstenzug
5 Johanneum
(Transport Museum)

6 Sekundogenitur
7 Akademie
8 Albertinum

9 Coselpalais
10 Taschenbergpalais
11 Neue Synagoge

Tour 1 If Time is Short

Start : Postplatz
End: Weisse Gasse

Duration: approx. three hours

The Altstadt (Old Town) has to be seen, because that's where Dresden reveals its Baroque splendour. Everything is close at hand, and one highlight follows another, inviting visitors to stroll, admire, linger – and come again.

Flying visit

If you are just going to spend three hours in Dresden, it's a good idea to wander through the Altstadt: starting from Postplatz, take a look at the ❶ ✶✶ **Zwinger palace,** apogee of Baroque architecture, the world-famous ❷ ✶✶ **Semper Opera** on Theaterplatz and the ❸ ✶✶ **Schloss** with its Hausmannturm; from the viewing platform it's possible to see the entire Altstadt. The ❹ ✶✶ **Hofkirche** on Schlossplatz needs to be seen inside as well as out. Then climb the steps to the ❺ ✶✶ **Brühlsche Terrasse** by the Elbe, drink a cup of coffee in Café Vis-à-Vis and stroll past the ❻ **Albertinum** to the ❼ ✶ **Neue Synagoge,** an example of award-winning modern architecture. Then go back in the direction of **Neumarkt** to the ❽ ✶✶ **Frauenkirche,** whose 95m/320ft dome, known as the stone bell, can

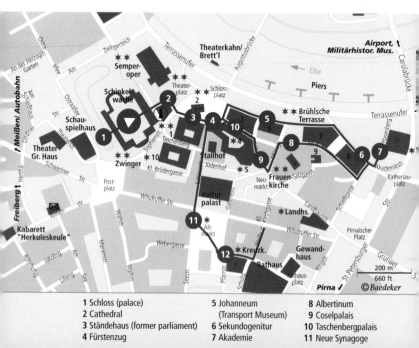

1 Schloss (palace)
2 Cathedral
3 Ständehaus (former parliament)
4 Fürstenzug

5 Johanneum
  (Transport Museum)
6 Sekundogenitur
7 Akademie

8 Albertinum
9 Coselpalais
10 Taschenbergpalais
11 Neue Synagoge

be seen from afar, and to the transport museum in the **❾** ✶ **Johanneum**; go along Augustusstrasse past the **❿** ✶ **Fürstenzug** (Procession of Princes), the ancestral portrait gallery of the Wettin dynasty on 24,000 porcelain tiles, and then left along Schlossstrasse to **⓫** ✶ **Altmarkt** and the **⓬** ✶ **Kreuzkirche**, where a famous choir, the Kreuzchor, can be heard on some Saturdays. The most enjoyable end to this flying visit is in Café No. 3 in Weisse Gasse.

If there is still an hour to spare, take a quick look at the ✶ ✶ **Gemäldegalerie Alte Meister (gallery of Old Masters)** in the Zwinger's Semper Gallery to see the *Sistine Madonna*, or – if you prefer – the porcelain collection, or the Grünes Gewölbe treasury collection in the ✶ ✶ **Schloss**.

Tour 2 For Art Lovers

Start : Postplatz   **Duration:** 1 day
End : Carolasee, a lake in the Grosser
Garten

The Altstadt breathes history and culture, and holds exciting discoveries in store: Old Masters in the Zwinger or a visit to the Semper Opera, a viewing of the Fürstenzug (Procession of Princes) or the Frauenkirche. If the cultural marathon has strained your eyes, a walk in the Grosser Garten will bring relief.

The tour takes a whole day, and begins on Postplatz. From here you can already see the Zwinger palace, Dresden's most famous Baroque building. As you walk towards it, on the right is the **❶ Taschenberg Palais**, which has been converted into a luxury hotel. Enter the inner courtyard of the **❷** ✶ ✶ **Zwinger** through the Glockenspiel Pavilion; the palace houses the porcelain collection, the geological collection, and the Mathematisch-Physikalischer Salon. From the Wallpavillon steps lead up to the Nymphenbad. Going in the direction of the Elbe, pass beneath the arched gate on the north side of the Zwinger, the Semper Gallery with the collection of Old Masters in the ✶ ✶ **Gemäldegalerie Alte Meister** and the armoury, out onto the magnificent **❸** ✶ ✶ **Theaterplatz**. The great attraction on Theaterplatz between Zwinger and Elbe is the ✶ ✶ **Semper Opera**; why not treat yourself to a performance in the evening? Between Theaterplatz and Schloss, on Schlossplatz, is the former **❹** ✶ ✶ **Hofkirche**, now the Cathedral Sanctissimae Trinitatis, which is worth seeing inside too. Straight ahead there is a view across the Elbe and Augustusbrücke (bridge) to the ✶ **Neustadt**. On the southern side of Schlossplatz is the ✶ ✶ **Schloss**, currently still under renovation, with the Georgentor, Hausmannturm, Kupferstichkabinett (collection of prints and drawings) and Grünes Gewölbe (Green Vault with jewels and

Walk through
800 years of
Dresden

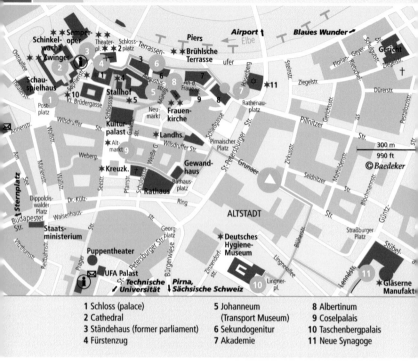

1 Schloss (palace)
2 Cathedral
3 Ständehaus (former parliament)
4 Fürstenzug
5 Johanneum (Transport Museum)
6 Sekundogenitur
7 Akademie
8 Albertinum
9 Coselpalais
10 Taschenbergpalais
11 Neue Synagoge

other treasures). The climb up the Hausmannturm in the Schloss is rewarded by a wonderful view of the city. Down to the Georgentor again, and outside, to the right, Augustusstrasse goes in the direction of Neumarkt, past the ✶ **Fürstenzug** (Procession of Princes). From here there is a view of the magnificent ✶✶ **Frauenkirche**, but before going there, the route passes the ❺ ✶ **Johanneum** with the transport museum to the right, as far as Schlossstrasse, and back to Schlossplatz, then up the steps by the Ständehaus (Estates House) to the ❻ ✶✶ **Brühlsche Terrasse** and old fortress walls with a view of the Elbe. Café Vis-à-Vis is a good place for a break; a little further on is the **Kunstakademie**, then comes the **Albertinum** with the ✶✶ **Gemäldegalerie Neue Meister** (painting since the 19th century) and Brühlscher Garten, and then the ❼ ✶ **Neue Synagoge**.

The Brühlsche Terrasse opens up by the Semper Monument, between Albertinum and Kunstakademie, to give access down to a section of the old **Dresden fortress**. Looking towards Neumarkt, you can see the dome of the ❽ ✶✶ **Frauenkirche**, where there is a guided tour. The walk continues from Neumarkt along Galeriestrasse, past

*The Schloss and Hofkirche in the evening sun, →
seen from the opposite bank of the Elbe*

the **Kulturpalast**, to ❾ ✶ **Altmarkt**. On the south-east corner of Altmarkt stands the ✶ **Kreuzkirche**, home to a famous choir, the Kreuzchor, for the last 700 years. Behind it rises a second tower, which belongs to the **Rathaus** (town hall). If you are interested, and not too exhausted, this would be a good moment to visit the ❿ ✶ **Deutsches Hygiene-Museum**: the quickest way to get there is by tram from Pirnaischer Platz to Zirkusstrasse. From the Hygiene Museum it's possible to see the ✶ **Gläserne Manufaktur** (Factory of Glass), where the luxury VW Phaeton limousine is assembled; it is situated on the edge of the **Grosser Garten**. Bring the tour to a fitting close with a ride on the ⓫**park railway** through the Grosser Garten to the Carolaschlösschen, and enjoy a well-earned sojourn in the café or a boat trip on the lake.

Tour 3 A Stroll around the New Town

Start: Schlossplatz **Duration:** approx. 3 hours
End: Albertplatz

This walk focuses on the Innere Neustadt (Inner New Town), which has been characterized as »smart, polished and classy«. Königstrasse is full of fine small shops, and is also home to the legendary jazz club Neue Tonne.

From the ❶**Altstadt**, take Augustusbrücke (bridge) across the Elbe; the ❷**Blockhaus** is immediately to the left, on the Neustadt side. ❸**Neustädter Markt** is dominated by the ❹ ✶ **Goldener Reiter** (Golden Rider), a statue of Augustus the Strong in the style of a Roman emperor, with scale armour on a leaping steed. From Neustädter Markt follow Hauptstrasse, a pedestrian zone planted with plane trees. It's worth making a detour to the left, into ❺ **Obergraben** where there are passages with art and craftwork. The ❻ **Kügelgenhaus** (Hauptstrasse 13; ▶ Neustadt, Innere Neustadt), now Museum der Dresdner Frühromantik and devoted to the early Romantic period, was the home of Gerhard von Kügelgen, painter and professor at the Akademie, where important figures of the Romantic era in Germany used to meet. In the rear courtyard of house no. 19 the Societätstheater has been performing since its restoration in 1999; originally founded in 1750, it is the oldest civic theatre in Germany. It's nice to relax in the theatre's small Baroque garden, or in the café L'Art de Vie. The walk continues to the ❼**Dreikönigskirche** (Church of the Three Kings); from the church tower there is a view over the Neustadt roofs all the way to the Altstadt. Opposite the church is the market hall of 1899 with the Schwarzmarktcafé (»black market café«)

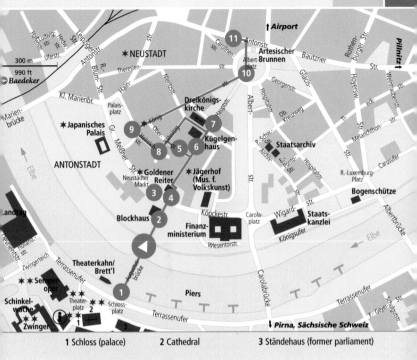

1 Schloss (palace)   2 Cathedral   3 Ständehaus (former parliament)

on the ground floor. On the first floor the Automobilmuseum (▶ Neustadt, Innere Neustadt) displays cars from the era of Soviet occupation and GDR, 1945 to 1990. At Rähnitzgasse 8 is Kunsthaus Dresden, the ❽**city gallery for contemporary art** (▶ Neustadt, Innere Neustadt). The route continues past renovated buildings and shops to ❾✶ **Königstrasse**, an elegantly restored shopping district, and now Dresden's finest Baroque street.

Looking back towards the Elbe, there is a striking view of the ✶ **Japanisches Palais**. At the end of Königstrasse lies ❿**Albertplatz**, a busy traffic hub. In the middle is the atmospheric Doppelbrunnen (double fountain) of 1894: *Stille Wasser* (Still Waters) and *Stürmische Wogen* (Stormy Waves) by Robert Diez. Villa Augustin (Antonstrasse 1) houses the interactive ⓫**Erich Kästner Museum** (▶Famous People), which provides an original approach to the author and his work.

! *Baedeker* TIP

Wenzel's hearty fare

At the Wenzel-Prager Bierstuben (Königstr. 1) high-quality Bohemian and Czech food is served in beautiful vaulted cellars and in summer in a beer garden. How about Karlsteiner roast meats with Bohemian dumplings, washed down with cool, dark Staropramen beer and followed by a pancake dessert? We wish you »Dobro chut«!

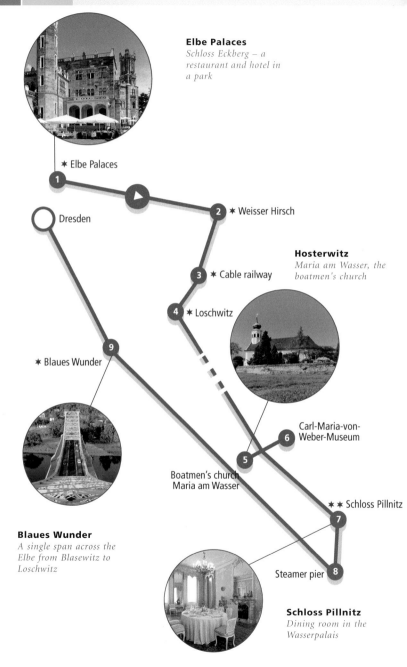

Elbe Palaces
Schloss Eckberg – a restaurant and hotel in a park

✳ Elbe Palaces

① ▷ ② ✳ Weisser Hirsch

○ Dresden

③ ✳ Cable railway

Hosterwitz
Maria am Wasser, the boatmen's church

④ ✳ Loschwitz

⑨ ✳ Blaues Wunder

Carl-Maria-von-Weber-Museum

⑥

⑤

Boatmen's church
Maria am Wasser

✳✳ Schloss Pillnitz

⑦

Blaues Wunder
A single span across the Elbe from Blasewitz to Loschwitz

Steamer pier ⑧

Schloss Pillnitz
Dining room in the Wasserpalais

Tour 4 For Walkers

Start: Theaterplatz
End: Terrassenufer

Duration: approx. 1 day

The air is fresh, the panorama magical, the villas and Elbe palaces are enchanting, Pillnitz Schloss and park pretty as a picture – this walk is guaranteed to raise your spirits.

The tour needs good weather: first take tram no. 11 from Theaterplatz to Schloss Albrechtsberg for the three ❶**Elbschlösser**, palatial residences enthroned high up on the slopes above the Elbe. Two tram stops further on (Plattleite) the walk sets out through the elegant villa district of ❷ ✶ **Weisser Hirsch**. Then take the ❸ ✶ **cable railway** to ❹ ✶ **Loschwitz**; don't miss the little Schillerhaus as you stroll around. From Körnerplatz the bus (no. 83) goes in the direction of Pillnitz; a break en route at **Hosterwitz** is recommended. Get off the bus at the stop marked Van-Gogh-Strasse in order to look at the ❺**boatmen's church »Maria am Wasser«**. At Dresdner Strasse 44 the ❻**Carl Maria von Weber Museum** has been set up in the composer's summer residence. The next bus (no. 83) finally takes the doughty walker to ❼ ✶ ✶ **Schloss Pillnitz** (bus stop Pillnitzer Platz), to join the idlers in the park. Directly beneath the palace grounds is the ❽ **paddle steamer** landing stage, and the return trip along the river is delightful, under the ❾ ✶ **Blaues Wunder bridge** and back past the Elbe palaces to Dresden.

> **✔ DON'T MISS**
>
> - A break at the Luisenhof, »Dresden's balcony«, at the Weisser Hirsch with a superb view of the city and the Elbe valley
> - A cold beer at Körnergarten under the Blaues Wunder bridge
> - The museum of arts and crafts (Kunstgewerbemuseum) at Schloss Pillnitz
> - A trip on a paddle steamer from Pillnitz back to Dresden

Excursions

Few large cities have such charming surroundings as Dresden, which is really fortunate in this respect. If at all possible explore the Sächsische Schweiz on foot, take a trip to Schloss Moritzburg and pay a visit to the Erzgebirge.

On the outskirts of the city are both the heath **Dresdner Heide**, and ✶ **Hellerau** garden city. Highly recommended destinations a little further afield are the porcelain town of Meissen, the town of **Radebeul**, the Baroque garden jewel **Großsedlitz** and Stolpen Castle.

Close by

✳ Müglitz valley	Take S-Bahn S 1 to Heidenau and from there the regional train to Altenberg. The train goes through the lovely Müglitz valley, past ✳ **Schloss Weesenstein** and then via the **clockmakers' town of Glashütte** (30km/18mi south) to the mining town of Altenberg (48km/30mi south) in the Erzgebirge.

Ferdinand Adolph Lange founded the first German precision clock-making factory in Glashütte in 1845, others followed and made Glashütte into the centre of clock and watch-making in the Erzgebirge. Lange & Söhne produce top-quality clocks by hand: manufacture and showroom (Altenberger Strasse 15) can be viewed by appointment, tel. (03 50 53) 44 0.

The original Glashütte factory and clock museum (Altenberger Strasse 1) runs a guided tour through the entire manufacturing process (Mon–Fri 10am, 1pm by appointment, tel. (03 50 53) 46 4 64).

Altenberg	The ✳ **Pinge** in Altenberg is an area of subsidence around 12ha/30 acres in size that can be viewed on an educational mining trail (alone or guided, May–Oct, Wed 1.30pm from rail station). There are also guided tours of the exhibition mine Neubeschert-Glück-Stollen (opening hours: Sat–Thu 10am–4pm).
Frauenstein in the Erzgebirge	An exhibition in Schloss Frauenstein (40km/25mi south) tells the story of Johann Gottfried Silbermann, born in Kleinbobritzsch in 1683, who built organs of unusual clarity and resonance.
Tharandt	For the 6000ha/15,000-acre Tharandt forest conservation area (22km/14mi southwest), take S-Bahn S 3 to Tharandt. The town became known for its forestry school founded in 1811 by Johann Heinrich Cotta, now the forestry section of the Technische Universität Dresden. Around 2000 different species flourish in the **arboretum**, including exotic specimens such as 190-year-old North American tulip trees, southern European sweet chestnuts, or snowdrop trees that flower in May, maples, magnolias and rhododendrons (open: Apr–Oct, Mon, Wed, Thu, Sat, Sun 8am–5pm, Tue 8am–3.30pm). More in-depth studies are possible in the Schweizerhaus (open: Mon–Thu, Sat–Sun 1.30pm–3.30pm), which has a museum of forest botany and a forest experience workshop for children and young people (open: April–Oct Sat–Thu 8am–5pm, Thu until 3.30pm). The ancient tradition of the hunt in Tharandt Forest is brought to life in an exhibition in the former Schösserei (»shoot«) of the hunting lodge **Jagdschloss Grillenburg**. This is all that remains of the lodge that Elector Augustus built in the mid-16th century to help dispel his black moods (open: Thu–Sun 10am–5pm).
Stolpen	The fate of Augustus the Strong's most famous mistress, Countess Cosel (▶Famous People), is inextricably linked with the small town

All in a row: Natural basalt formations from Stolpen Hill →
were used to build the castle.

Dresden *Tourist Highlights*

★ ★ Top sights
★ Outstanding sights

★ Altmarkt
★ Fürstenzug
★ Johanneum
★ Kreuzkirche
★ Kupferstichkabinett (Schloss)
★ Landhaus (Stadtmuseum)
★ Mathematisch-Physikalischer Salon (Zwinger)

★ ★ Brühlsche Terrasse
★ ★ Frauenkirche
★ ★ Gemäldegalerie Alte Meister
★ ★ Galerie Neue Meister
★ ★ Grünes Gewölbe (Schloss)
★ ★ Hofkirche
★ ★ Porcelain collection (Zwinger)
★ ★ Armoury (Zwinger)
★ ★ Schloss
★ ★ Semper Opera
★ ★ Theaterplatz
★ ★ Zwinger

★ Taschenbergpalais
★ Neue Synagoge
★ Gläserne Manufaktur
★ Königstrasse (Neustadt)
★ Pfund's Molkerei (Neustadt)
★ Kunsthofpassage (Neustadt)

★
Market square ▶

of Stolpen and its castle. The town, situated on a basalt knoll 20km/ 13mi east of Dresden, can be reached by taking bus (no. 261) in the direction of Sebnitz. Since a disastrous fire raged in the town in 1723, most of the Altstadt buildings date from the 18th century. The market square, which is indeed almost square in shape, is very impressive. Next to the Rathaus (town hall) of 1660 (its date 1549 refers to the grant of heraldic arms), the Löwenapotheke (pharmacy) of 1722 with its gilded arms is one of the most remarkable buildings. The Altes Amtshaus (government building) bears the Saxon electors' arms, as does the Neues Amtshaus, now the Sparkasse bank, which also has its date, 1673. After the Order of the Garter was awarded by the English monarch to the Electors Johann Georg II and Johann Georg IV (1660 and 1693 respectively) for their service in the Turkish wars, the order's motto was also added: »Honi soit qui mal y pense«.

★
Burg Stolpen ▶

The castle, Burg Stolpen, towers above the market. Collections and exhibitions relating to castle and town history, and special displays, can be viewed in the 13 historic castle rooms and cellar and dungeon area. The extended castle precinct has four courtyards and four commanding towers. A magnet for the general public is the Johannisturm of 1509, generally known as the Coselturm. Here Countess Cosel lived – against her will – in three rooms, which now house a commemorative exhibition. After the countess had enjoyed the favours of Augustus the Strong for nine years, and he had even given her written promises of marriage and had three children with her, he was made king of Poland and took a Polish mistress. Countess Cosel's star declined. She fled to Berlin, but was exchanged for Prussian prisoners and banished to Stolpen at the age of 36; she died and was buried there 49 years later.

The ✳ **Burgbrunnen (castle well)** was completed in 1630. It is 82m/270ft deep, the deepest basalt well in the world; the surface of the water at a depth of 75m/250ft can only be seen in a mirror. From the chapel tower platform there is a wonderful view of open countryside. On the west side of the castle the ✳ **basalt formations** take the form of beautiful octagonal pillars; inside the castle courtyard they are arrayed like organ pipes.

🕐
Opening times:
April–Oct daily
9am–6pm;
Nov–March daily
10am–4pm
Guided tours (including night tours):
tel. (03 59 73)
23 4 10

Sights from A to Z

RICHARD WAGNER CONDUCTED AT THE OPERA HOUSE IN DRESDEN AND LAUDED THE ORCHESTRA AS A »MAGIC HARP«. TODAY THE QUALITY OF PERFORMANCES STILL MAKES IT A TOP ATTRACTION!

Albertinum

G 7 / 8

Location: Brühlsche Terrasse
Plan of inner city: B 3

Tram: Synagoge (nos. 3, 7); Pirnaischer
Platz (nos. 1, 2, 3, 4, 7, 12)

The massive Albertinum was erected on the foundations of the arsenal of 1559–63 below the Brühlscher Garten to house the sculpture collection. It derived its name from the ruling monarch of the time, King Albert (1873–1902), and since 1931 has also held the art of the Galerie Neue Meister.

Opening hours:
Closed for renovation, scheduled to re-open in 2010

The cellar vaulting, ground floor with Tuscan pillars, the two west portals and parts of the façade are original. Carl Adolf Canzler was responsible for the new building (1884–87); the bronze façade reliefs are by Robert Diez (1909). The museum space was divided between the ► Galerie Neue Meister (picture gallery for painting since the 19th century), the Skulpturensammlung (sculpture collection) and the Münzkabinett (coin collection). After the completion of restoration work and a new flood-proof store and workshop building, the Galerie Neue Meister and Skulpturensammlung will be reopened here.

Sculpture collection

Opening hours:
On view in the Zwinger until reopening

The Skulpturensammlung was founded by Augustus the Strong; he purchased antique sculpture between 1717 and 1728 and set up the earliest collection of antiquities outside Italy. It provided an almost seamless overview of the technical and artistic development of sculpture in ancient times. From 1748 Johann Joachim Winckelmann, founder of modern archaeology and art history, worked here on his seminal papers. Outstanding treasures include the Athena Lemnia after Phidias, and three Herculanean women and dancing maenad by Skopas. Renaissance and Baroque sculpture is represented by masterpieces by Filarete, Giambologna and Adrian de Vries, and marble sculptures by **Balthasar Permoser**. A selection of 19th and 20th-century works was taken to the ► Galerie Neue Meister. Some of the medieval sculpture can be viewed in the Albrechtsburg in Meissen there (►Meissen).

Münzkabinett

Opening hours:
Special exhibitions in the Hausmannturm at the Schloss

The Dresden Münzkabinett (coin cabinet) grew out of a section of the electors' Kunstkammer, which makes it one of the oldest as well as largest collections of its kind.

It offers a seamless presentation of European coin systems in all currency periods since Greek and Roman antiquity, and comprises well over 200,000 coins, medals, banknotes, stamps, seals and mint equipment, with a complete collection of more than 20,000 Saxon coins and medals. The Münzkabinett is to be given a new permanent home in the Schloss.

✳ Altmarkt

Location: central Altstadt
Plan of inner city: B 3

Tram: Altmarkt (nos. 1, 2, 4); Weber-gasse (nos. 6, 8, 9, 11, 12, 47)

Altmarkt, the old market place first mentioned in 1370, is the historic city centre.

Originally only 1.3ha/3.7 acres in size, it served not only as market but also as the scene of lavish festivals, jousting and animal fights until the building of the Zwinger in the early 18th century; elegant shops, coffee houses and pastry shops such as Kreutzkamm, founded in 1825 and popular for its pyramid cakes, excellent eating-places and inns tempted people into the heart of Dresden. Many who came to fame lived there for a while, including Ludwig Tieck, Anton Graff, Heinrich von Kleist and Carl Maria von Weber. On the north side of Altmarkt stood the 13th-century town hall, which was demolished at Augustus the Strong's behest in 1707. Not until 1741–45 were sev- **History**

View from Rathaus tower over the Kreuzkirche and Altmarkt to the Schloss; a little further to the right, off the picture, is the dome of the Frauenkirche.

eral dwelling-houses in the northwest corner converted into a new town hall, to plans by Johann Christoph Knöffel; this became the old town hall when the new one, the present ►Rathaus on Dr Külz Ring, was ready for use in 1910. The south side of Altmarkt was occupied by a store, Kaufhaus Renner. The Kreuzkirche was originally not part of Altmarkt; it stood behind the southeast corner, pushed back by Kaufhaus Renner and the houses on the east side. In 1849 Altmarkt was the focal point of Dresden's May uprising. Thereafter the inner city was declared an exclusion zone up to the time of the Weimar Republic: no political gathering was allowed. The air attack of February 1945 destroyed everything on Altmarkt; a few days later the market place was the scene of one of the saddest chapters in Dresden's history: the bodies of victims of the air raid were transported to the market place and burnt on pyres constructed with tramlines.

After total wartime destruction the east and west sides were **rebuilt** from 1953 to 1956 as they are today to designs by Herbert Schneider and Johannes Rascher in traditional brickstyle. The space »created« by the bombs was allowed to remain, so the market place seemed very empty in spite of the new buildings. The façades of the newly erected residential blocks with shops, cafés and restaurants on the lower floors have design elements that draw on Dresden Baroque. A key feature of the current appearance of the market place is the long arcade on the west side, behind which is a smart new shopping centre, Altmarkt-Galerie. The most extensive restoration of the square's pre-war structure was initiated after German unification. On the south side, towards Dr Külz Ring and ► Prager Strasse, which had not been built up after 1945, new shops and commercial premises were constructed in the

New glamour behind an old façade: Altmarkt-Galerie

The Blaues Wunder is the backdrop for the dragon boat race held annually during the Elbhangfest.

all length is 226m/250yd. Regarded as a miracle of technology in 1891, the bridge was given the name Blaues Wunder (Blue Miracle), which in German has two meanings: it is figuratively a »sheer miracle«, and literally blue in colour from the protective coating on its massive yet filigree steel construction. The Blaues Wunder became a city emblem; at the same time the beauty of its construction enhances the Elbe scenery. When comprehensive restoration work took place in 1985 it was decided to remove trams from the bridge because of the strain through increasing use by cars. The SS made

preparations to blow up the bridge in May 1945, but this was prevented by the intervention of two Dresden citizens: a plaque at the Blasewitz end of the bridge (1993) commemorates master plumber Erich Stöckel and telegraph worker Paul Zickler for their heroic deed.

✷✷ Brühlsche Terrasse

F / G 7

Location: Altstädter Elbufer (Terrassenufer)	**Tram:** Theaterplatz (nos. 4, 8, 9); Pirnaischer Platz (nos. 1, 2, 3, 4, 7, 12);
Plan of inner city: B 3	Synagoge (nos. 3, 7)

The Brühlsche Terrasse owes its name to Count Heinrich von Brühl, who laid out a garden that became known as the »Balcony of Europe«, a place for fashionable society to stroll.

Promenade
The Brühlsche Terrasse extends along the old foundations of Dresden's fortress complex, above the bank of the Elbe. Count Heinrich von Brühl, a confidant of Friedrich August II (Augustus III), received the land as a gift from his royal friend. He turned it into a private pleasure garden and built several structures, of which only two have survived: the Delfinbrunnen (Dolphin Fountain), and the ornamental fountain that was once in front of the Brühlsches Palais and now stands on the north side of the Ständehaus (Estates House). The Russian governor of Dresden, Prince Repnin-Volkonsky, ordered that

Brühlsche Terrasse Plan

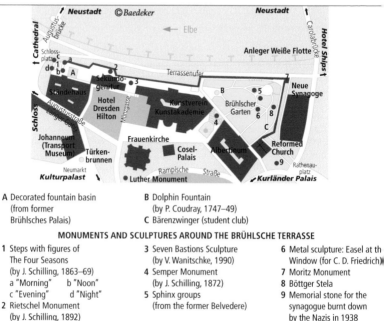

A Decorated fountain basin
    (from former
    Brühlsches Palais)

B Dolphin Fountain
    (by P. Coudray, 1747–49)

C Bärenzwinger (student club)

MONUMENTS AND SCULPTURES AROUND THE BRÜHLSCHE TERRASSE

1 Steps with figures of
    The Four Seasons
    (by J. Schilling, 1863–69)
    a "Morning"   b "Noon"
    c "Evening"   d "Night"

2 Rietschel Monument
    (by J. Schilling, 1892)

3 Seven Bastions Sculpture
    (by V. Wanitschke, 1990)

4 Semper Monument
    (by J. Schilling, 1872)

5 Sphinx groups
    (from the former Belvedere)

6 Metal sculpture: Easel at th
    Window (for C. D. Friedrich)

7 Moritz Monument

8 Böttger Stela

9 Memorial stone for the
    synagogue burnt down
    by the Nazis in 1938

the terrain be made available to the public in 1814. In the ensuing years, especially after the coffee houses opened, the view of the Elbe and Neustadt from the terrace made it an attractive promenade.

The **Ständehaus** (House of the Estates) is situated on the site of the earlier Brühlsches Palais, just at the top of the steps leading up to the Brühlsche Terrasse. The architect of the Berlin Reichstag, Paul Wallot, from 1894 professor at the ►

? DID YOU KNOW ...?

■ ... why the Brühlsche Terrasse is called the »Balcony of Europe«?
None other than Saxony's most famous enemy, King Frederick the Great of Prussia, is said to have coined the phrase, in recognition of its role as a meeting-point for travellers from all over the world – framed, moreover, by splendid buildings whose architecture shows the influence of various European countries.

Kunstakademie, planned the construction of the Ständehaus from 1896; it was built from 1901 to 1903 in a mixture of neo-Baroque and neo-Renaissance styles. The main façade with its sculptural ornamentation and central section framed by double columns faces Schlossplatz. On the Elbe side is a tower reminiscent of the Baroque towers of the Hofkirche and Kreuzkirche, crowned by Johannes Schilling's figure of Saxonia. The parliament of the Kingdom of Saxony met in the Ständehaus, as did the parliament of the Free State of Saxony during the Weimar Republic. Destroyed by fire in 1945 and then partially restored, it is now the seat of Saxony's Oberlandesgericht (higher law court).

★
Steps

A broad flight of steps designed by Gottlob Friedrich Thormeyer leads up to the terrace from Schlossplatz. The approach was once guarded by two sandstone lions; in 1863–68 they were replaced by a sculptural group by Johannes Schilling, the *Vier Tageszeiten* (Four Times of Day). Originally made of sandstone, the sculptures were gilded in 1883 and replaced by bronze casts in 1908.

Sekundogenitur

The first building is called the Sekundogenitur; it was erected in 1897 and replaced Count Brühl's library. Gustav Fröhlich designed the building in neo-Baroque form to match the style of the Brühlsches Palais. It provided exhibition space, and housed the royal graphics collection. This collection was assigned traditionally to the second-born prince, which explains the name Sekundogenitur (second birth). Between 1931 and 1945 it was used to display 19th-century art. It now belongs to the Hilton Hotel and houses a café.

Rietschel Monument

In front of the Sekundogenitur is a monument (1892) commemorating the sculptor **Ernst Rietschel**, who was appointed professor at the ►Kunstakademie in 1832. With him the importance of Dresden sculpture once more extended beyond the immediate region. Some of his sculptures and reliefs have survived in the city, such as the figures of Schiller and Goethe outside the ►Semper Opera, the figures

of children on the north side of the Sempergalerie, the Weber Monument and the head of the Luther Monument. His earliest work is the memorial to Friedrich August I in front of the ►Japanisches Palais. Ernst Rietschel's memorial, made by his pupil Johannes Schilling in 1872, stands on the site of the former garden pavilion of the Brühlsches Palais – Rietschel's atelier.

Seven Bastion Sculpture

A sculpture created by Vincenz Wanitschke in 1990 consists of the earth bursting open and ground markings; it refers to Augustus the Strong's decree of 1721, whereby the seven bastions of the royal and electoral residence of Dresden were to be named after the sun and the six planets known at the time.

Semper Monument

The memorial to Gottfried Semper (►Famous People) on the steps leading down to Georg-Treu-Platz is also by **Johannes Schilling**. A walk along the Brühlsche Terrasse from ►Theaterplatz makes it possible to trace this sculptor's language and form as they developed in expressive power over a period of 30 years. He established his fame with the group of the *Four Times of Day* (1863–68) on the steps leading up to the Brühlsche Terrasse; the Rietschel Monument (1872) is one of his most convincing works; there followed the bronze panther quadriga enthroned above the exedra of the ►Semper Opera with Ariadne and Dionysos, and the equestrian monument to King Johann on Theaterplatz (1889), the Semper Monument (1892) on the Brühlsche Terrasse and finally the decoration on the pediment of the Kunstverein (1894).

Casemates

At the foot of the stairs leading down from the Semper Monument is the entrance to the ►Fortress casemates.

Brühlscher Garten

Delfinbrunnen

In the east section of the Brühlsche Terrasse, Count Brühl had a garden made on the former Venus Bastion. The Delfinbrunnen (Dolphin Fountain, 1747–49) by Pierre Coudray dates from this time.

Sphinx groups

The two sphinx groups by Gottfried Knöffler at the tip of the bastion mark the former entrance to the Belvedere, which Johann Christoph Knöffel constructed as a successor to the first pleasure palace built in the 16th century. The fourth building on the site, of 1842, was a restaurant and concert venue until its destruction in 1945.

Memorial to C.D. Friedrich

The words inscribed on the metal sculpture *Staffelei am Fenster* (Easel by the Window, 1990) by Wolf-Eike Kuntsche in memory of **Caspar David Friedrich**, read: »The painter should not only paint what he sees, but also what he sees within himself. If he sees nothing with-

← *The Brühlsche Terrasse is a place to take a break and enjoy the view.*

in himself then he should also refrain from painting what he sees without. C. D. F.«

★
Moritz Monument

At the northeast corner of the terrace wall is a copy of the Moritz Monument, the oldest memorial in Dresden. Elector August had it made in 1553 for his brother Moritz who was killed at the battle of Sievershausen: Moritz with an hourglass hands the elector's sword to his successor. He had taken a stand against the pillaging raids of Margrave Albrecht Alcibiades of Brandenburg-Kulmbach with his infantry at Sievershausen. Although Elector Moritz paid for this battle with his life, yet the battle was won for electoral Saxony and its allies.

Böttger stela

At the behest of Augustus the Strong **Johann Friedrich Böttger** (▶Famous People) was confined in the vaults beneath the first pleasure palace. Böttger played a major part in the development of the first hard-paste white porcelain in Europe. A sandstone stela with a medallion portrait of Böttger (1982) in Meissen porcelain marks the spot in the east section of the Brühlscher Garten.

Reformed Church

The modest two-storey building opposite the main entrance of the ▶ Albertinum, used today by the Reformed Church and as an old people's home, was the garden office and nursery in Count Brühl's time.

Former synagogue

Next to it the sculpture of a seven-branched candelabra is a reminder of the synagogue built by Gottfried Semper that was destroyed in 1938; the ▶Neue Synagoge that replaced it stands on the Hasenberg.

Kurländer Palais

The Kurländer Palais, built in 1729 for minister Wackerbarth and visible on the far side of the crossroads, has been reconstructed as a hotel.

Cemeteries

The cemeteries of Dresden, the resting-place of many important persons, reflect the history of the city.

Eliasfriedhof

**Ziegelstrasse (F 8)
Tram (nos. 6, 13): Sachsenallee**

The Eliasfriedhof is the oldest and, from the point of view of cultural history, the most important of the city cemeteries. It was established in 1680 when a plague outbreak claimed thousands of lives in Dresden. Initially a poor people's cemetery, in the 18th century it became highly regarded as a place of burial. In 1724 it was extended according to plans by George Bähr. After its closure in 1876 it was soon forgotten and began to decay, and weathering caused many memorials, even artistically significant ones, to become indecipherable. It lies quietly under huge trees like a magic garden. It can be viewed **only as part of a guided tour**: (details tel. 251 62 11, Förderverein Elias-friedhof, www.eliasfriedhof-dresden.de).

Eliasfriedhof burials include:
Carl August Böttiger (1760–1835), archaeologist
Johann Christian Clausen Dahl (1788–1857), painter
Johann Christian Kirchner (1691–1732), sculptor
Wilhelm Gotthelf Lohrmann (1796–1840), first director of the Tech-nische Bildungsanstalt
Justine Renner, née Segedin (1763–1856), senator's widow and Schil-ler's »Gustel von Blasewitz«
Gottlob Friedrich Thormeyer (1775–1842), architect.

Trinitatisfriedhof

About a quarter-of-an-hour's walk east of the Eliasfriedhof lies the Trinitatisfriedhof, another oasis of peace. In the cemetery office by Entrance 1 there is a plan of the cemetery, on which a selection of graves are marked.

Fiedlerstrasse (F 9)
Tram: (no. 6): Trinitatisplatz

This »spacious cemetery« on Fiedlerstrasse became necessary when Napoleon won his last victory against the Prussian and Austrian troops at the battle of Dresden in 1813, and because of a nervous fe-ver that ravaged the population in 1815; later it was given the name »Trinity Cemetery«. By 1872 there were four sections, making up a unified whole designed by Gottlob Friedrich Thormeyer. The en-trance gate was immortalized by **Caspar David Friedrich** (►Famous People) in his painting *Friedhofseingang* (Cemetery Entrance), which can be seen now in the ►Galerie Neue Meister. To the right of the main entrance is a 10.25m/34ft obelisk for 75 revolutionaries who died in the May uprising in Dresden in 1849. Further important me-morials were made to designs by Caspar David Friedrich and sculp-ted by Ernst Rietschel. Important representatives of early Romantic art found their last resting-place here:

Caspar David Friedrich (1774–1840), painter
Carl Gustav Carus (1780–1869), physician, painter and philosopher
Kurt Arnold Findeisen (1883–1963), writer
Julius Otto (1804–77), court organist and Kreuzkirche cantor
Ferdinand von Rayski (1806–52), writer
Karl Gottlieb Reissiger (1798–1859), musician
Wilhelmine Schröder-Devrient (1804–60), actress and singer
Friedrich Kind (1768–1843), *Freischütz* librettist
Constantin Lipsius (1832–94), architect
Otto Ludwig (1813–65), writer
Julius Scholtz (1825–93), painter
Dr Friedrich Struve (1781–1840), inventor of artificially produced mineral water

Friedrich Wieck (1785–1873), musician and father of Clara Schumann

Ernst Rietschel (1804–61), sculptor

Johannstadt Jewish Cemetery

Fiedlerstrasse
(F 10)

Directly adjoining Trinitatisfriedhof is the Jüdischer Friedhof Johannstadt (Johannstadt Jewish Cemetery), created in 1868 after the closure of the Old Jewish Cemetery. Grave inscriptions attest the fearful suffering of Dresden's Jewish citizens during the Nazi years. Gottfried Semper's synagogue was burnt down in the 1938 pogrom night, and on this spot the first GDR synagogue was built to replace it in 1950. It served the Jewish community until the opening of the ▶Neue Synagoge in 2001.

Old Jewish Cemetery

Pulsnitzer
Strasse 10 (E 8)
Tram (nos. 3, 6, 7,
8, 11) to Albert-
platz, then to
Pulsnitzer Str
(no. 11)

Saxony's oldest remaining Jewish cemetery (Alter Jüdischer Friedhof) and the first burial place of the Jewish community in Dresden, who had to take their dead to Teplitz for burial prior to that, was established in 1751 close to the Martin Luther Church, and used until 1868.

In order to walk through the rows of graves in this green cemetery in a quiet corner of Dresden's Neustadt, contact the Jewish centre Hatikva for times of tours, or borrow the key (Hatikva opening hours: tel. 802 04 89: Mon–Thu 9am–noon, 1pm–4pm).

Alter Katholischer Friedhof

Friedrichstrasse
(F 8)
Tram (nos. 1, 2, 4,
6, 8, 9, 11, 12, 47)
to Postplatz,
then bus no. 94
to Krankenhaus
Friedrichstadt
⊘ Opening hours:
Daily 8am–4pm

The Old Catholic Cemetery, the most important Catholic cemetery in Saxony and the second-oldest in the city, was established in 1721. It served as burial place for prominent citizens of the Catholic faith, and for numerous Italians, including artists and musicians at the former Catholic ▶Hofkirche. In the 19th century Polish émigrés were buried here, and in 1945 Catholic priests who had been murdered in Dachau concentration camp, or who died in the air attack on Dresden.

In the chapel is the grave of sculptor **Balthasar Permoser** (1651–1732) with the Crucifixion group that he himself made. On the northern edge of the graveyard is the impressive memorial to the composer and court musician **Carl Maria von Weber** (1786–1826) by Gottfried Semper. Somewhat to the right of it is the grave of Countess von Kielmannsegg (1777–1863), favourite of Napoleon I. On the western edge are the graves of man of letters and philosopher Friedrich von Schlegel (1772–1829), and Johann Anton Dreissig (1774–1815), court organist and founder of the Singakademie. By the opposite cemetery wall lie: Gerhard von Kügelgen (1772–1820), painter and professor at the Akademie

Kazimierz Brodzinski (1791–1835), Polish national poet
Johann Georg von Sachsen (1869–1938), brother of the last Saxon king
Johann George Chevalier de Saxe (1704–74), son of Augustus the Strong and Countess Lubomirska, field marshal and reformer of the Saxon army.

Innerer Matthäusfriedhof

Behind the Matthäuskirche (St Matthew's Church) and diagonally opposite the Old Catholic Cemetery, the Innerer Matthäusfriedhof was established in 1725 as a Protestant cemetery. **Matthäus Daniel Pöppelmann** is buried in the crypt of the church. Those laid to rest in the cemetery include:
Johann Andreas Schubert (1808–70), designer of the first German locomotive, the first Elbe steamship and the Göltzschtal bridge
Wilhelm Walther (1826–1913), creator of the ►Fürstenzug

Friedrichstrasse (F 6)

Johannisfriedhof

The Johannisfriedhof throws an interesting light on the 19th-century. The entrance with chapel was created by Paul Wallot, architect of the Berlin Reichstag and the Ständehaus on the Brühlsche Terrasse. As Dresden grew into a major city at the end of the 19th century, further burial places became necessary. In 1881 the congregations of the Frauenkirche, Kreuzkirche and Johanniskirche in Tolkewitz/Tännicht opened the new Johannisfriedhof, a woodland burial ground that was subsequently enlarged considerably. Here the victims of the fight against the Kapp putsch of March 1920 were buried, as were 396 of the resistance fighters executed in Dresden from 1943 to 1945, and concentration camp prisoners. A massive monument honours Polish and Czech citizens murdered by the Nazis in Dresden. A grove of honour was created for the air raid victims of February 1945. The graves of many notable citizens of Dresden in this cemetery include those of:

Wehlener Strasse (F / G 12) Tram (nos. 4, 6, 10, 12) to Ludwig-Hartmann-Strasse

Otto Beutler (1853–1926), lord mayor
Bernhard Blüher (1864–1938), lord mayor
Ferdinand Dorsch (1875–1938), painter and professor at the Akademie
Hubert Georg Ermisch (1883–1951), architect and Zwinger restorer
Cornelius Gurlitt (1850–1910), composer
Eva Plaschke von der Osten (1889–1936), opera singer
August Toeplar (1836–1912), physicist and professor at the Technische Hochschule

Directly next to the Johannisfriedhof is the crematorium, opened in 1911; it is an important monumental building in German art nouveau style, designed by Fritz Schumacher. The sculptural decoration was provided by Georg Wrba. In the urn grove are the ashes of:

Crematorium urns

Heinrich Barkhausen (1881–1956), physicist and professor at the Technische Hochschule

Gotthardt Kuehl (1851–1915), painter and professor at the Akademie

Clara Salbach (1861–1944), actress

Karl Woermann (1844–1933), art historian

Städtischer Heidefriedhof

Moritzburger Landstrasse Tram no. 3 to Wilder Mann, then bus no. 80

The Heidefriedhof, which was laid out in the northwest of the city in 1934, is the site of an impressive place of memorial: a common grave for 20,000 victims of the bombing raids of February 1945, including the remains of those cremated on Altmarkt. Sandstone columns serve as reminders of the destruction in World War II of Coventry, Dresden, Leningrad, Rotterdam, Warsaw, Oradour and Lidice. The graves of the following are also on the Heidefriedhof:

Walter Weidauer (1899–1986), lord mayor 1946–1958

Otto Buchwitz (1879–1964), member of the Reichstag and president of the Saxon Landtag as member of the SED

Hans Grundig (1901–58), painter and rector of the School of Fine Arts

Lea Grundig (1906–77), painter and graphic artist

✶ Deutsches Hygiene-Museum

G 8

Location: Lingnerplatz 1	**Tram:** Hygiene Museum
Plan of inner city: C 4	(nos. 10, 13)

There is nothing in the world to match the German Hygiene Museum. It was founded after the first International Hygiene Exhibition in Dresden in 1911 at the suggestion of the major pharmaceutical manufacturer Karl August Lingner.

Opening hours: Tue–Sun 10am–6pm Guided tours for children: Sun 3pm for adults: Sat, Sun 2pm

Lingner focussed largely on educating the public and on preventative health measures, and spread his message by means of travelling exhibitions as well as by producing educational materials and publications about human beings and their bodies (► Baedeker Special p.172). On the occasion of the second International Hygiene Exhibition in 1930 the museum moved into its own premises.

Museum building

The museum building exemplifies the style of New Realism; it was designed by Wilhelm Kreis and built in the years 1928–30 in the axis of the ►Grosser Garten, and at the time was one of the largest and most modern museums anywhere. Its monumental exterior with classical features and an unpretentious, light, open interior make it an outstanding example of Dresden architecture of the 1930s. Resto-

The German Hygiene Museum looks at man and beast from an unusual perspective.

ration work completed at the end of 2005 returned the building almost to its original condition of 1930, evenly lit by means of frosted glass ceilings in the upper exhibition floor. If you need a break, try Café Lingner (hours: Mon–Fri 10.30am–midnight; Sat, Sun 9.30am–midnight).

The museum's mission is to go beyond health education, and to show how man is inextricably involved in biological, mental, social and cultural networks. On the upper floor the newly devised permanent exhibition entitled The Glass Human opened in 2004. The first room shows the history of the museum, and pictures of mankind as seen by modern science; then come the themes Food and Drink, Living and Dying, and Sexuality. Specially developed interactive modules encourage independent learning, experimentation and participation. In the Living and Dying section, old age simulators make visitors feel the burden of the years. There are also objects such as wax impressions of pathological conditions, anatomical models, laboratory samples, medical equipment and instruments, as well as exhibits on health care and education in the 20th century.

Exhibitions and activities

PROMOTING HEALTH

For Dresden the name of the manufacturer Karl August Lingner brings to mind Odol mouth-rinse – and much more. He was not solely preoccupied with his day-to-day business, but was inspired by the notion that his life's work would be of benefit to his fellow citizens and posterity.

Karl August Lingner was born in 1861. After an apprenticeship in commerce he lived for a time in Paris, and in 1888 he founded the firm of **Lingner & Kraft** in Dresden with Georg Wilhelm Kraft. They marketed products made by Kraft. The chemist Richard Seifert interested Lingner in bacteriological problems, and handed over to him an anti-bacterial substance which Lingner named »Odol« (tooth oil). Having separated amicably from Kraft, Lingner began to produce Odol in a garden shed with three assistants, and soon the mouth-rinse became the world-famous brand that it still is today, thanks to a distinctive publicity campaign and the equally distinctive bottle, with its neck curving sideways. What had started as a laboratory grew into a flourishing industrial enterprise.

Commitment to Prevent Disease

Supported by this healthy business, Lingner was able to devote himself to his own personal ambition: to improve the population's health through preventative measures and instruction. In 1897 he became a member of an association to support a children's hospital and infants' home, of which he became chairman in 1910. Here he

*Karl August Lingner
(painting by Robert Sterl)*

met renowned scientists from the fields of hygiene and health studies. In 1900 he had already founded a centre for dental hygiene, where Dresden's first dental health clinic was set up in 1907, catering for schools. In 1901 he founded the Disinfection Centre, to which a school was added not long after; on his initiative a public education hall with reading-room was established, Dresden's first public library.

His Goal: A Museum of Hygiene

Not content with all that, he organized an exhibition on »common diseases and how to combat them« at the Deutsche Städteaustellung (Exhibition of German Cities) of 1903. Its techniques and display anticipated much of what subsequently became, for a long time, the hallmarks of the first hygiene exhibition and museum. In 1905 preparations began for the first International Hygiene Exhibition, which finally took place in 1911 and attracted more than five million visitors. This success encouraged him to turn the exhibition into a permanent museum. On 3 March 1913 an association for a national hygiene museum was formed, but it took almost 20 years for the **museum** to open in its own building. Lingner did not live to see it. He died on 5 June 1916.

Most of his fortune passed to the Lingner Foundation, which used the money to fund various public health projects. Since 1922 his body has lain in a mausoleum at the foot of Villa Stockhausen, known today as **Schloss Lingner**. The Lingner works remained in Dresden until 1938, then moved to Berlin, and later to Düsseldorf; today their successor company Lingner & Fischer is located in Bühl in the province of Baden, in the southwest of Germany.

The display was completed in 2005 with three further sections: Movement; Remembering, Thinking, Learning (featuring progress in brain research); and Beauty, Skin and Hair. There are guided tours for wheelchair users, for blind, partially sighted and deaf visitors, and also for those with learning difficulties. The special exhibitions are remarkable, and for the most part originally conceived.

> ## ! Baedeker TIP
>
> ### Play and learn
>
> On Sundays and public holidays children can assess their bodies from 10am to 2pm at activity stations, practise microscopy or test their taste-buds. In the school holidays, too, children can experiment here, do research, play and make things (bookings, tel. 03 51 / 4 84 66 70). In the new children's museum there is an interactive display of the five senses.

One of the main attractions is the **Glass Woman**, with which the museum had a sensational success in 1930. Nine copies of this life-size model of the human organism, covered with a transparent skin, were made before World War II; they were displayed in all large European cities and drew innumerable visitors. It took the technicians nine months to produce one of these models, with artificial organs, and they used 13km/8mi of coloured copper wire to display the nervous and vascular systems.

Dreikönigskirche

F 7

Location: Hauptstrasse

Tram: Neustädter Markt (nos. 4, 8, 9); Albertplatz (nos. 3, 6, 7, 8, 11)

The Dreikönigskirche (Church of the Three Kings) in ►Neustadt has had a turbulent history. In the Dance of Death taken from the Georgentor of the Schloss, it possesses one of Dresden's most important works of art.

Haus der Kirche
In 1429 the Hussites almost entirely destroyed the first Dreikönigskirche, a Gothic building of 1404. Rebuilding was not completed until 1525, and the great fire of 1685 in Altendresden destroyed this second church. The third Dreikönigskirche was erected between 1686 and 1691, but in 1731 it got in the way of new plans for Altendresden's redevelopment and was demolished at the behest of Augustus the Strong; it had to give way to the new Hauptstrasse, which together with the Elbe bridge created the link between Altstadt and Neustadt. The fourth Dreikönigskirche, erected by George Bähr and Matthäus Daniel Pöppelmann in the years 1732–39, with an 87.5m/288ft tower that was not completed until 1857, burnt down in 1945. Not until 1994 was the rebuilding of the church, stage by stage, complete; in the process it was converted into an ecumenical conference

and meeting centre, the Haus der Kirche (House of the Church). The dedication coincided with the first session of the newly elected Saxon parliament in October 1990. The house continued to be used for such sessions until the new parliamentary building (►Sächsischer Landtag) was completed in 1994. The Baroque altar by Benjamin Thomae was gravely damaged in the war; restored in a way that deliberately did not conceal the damage, it was returned to the church as a war memorial. Beneath the organ gallery is one of Dresden's most important surviving Renaissance monuments, the Dresden Dance of Death from the old Georgentor at the Schloss by Christoph Walther I. The 12.5m/40ft frieze, originally coloured and created in the years 1534–36, shows the Estates led by death, symbol of the transience of life on earth. Death with a serpent leads the first estate, the clergy. They are followed by the second estate, representing secular rulers, then by an army captain, a scholar and an artist. The fourth group is made up of women: an abbess, a burgher's wife and a farmer's wife. The last group, which was damaged in the Schloss fire of 1701 and renewed in 1840, shows a blind old man led by a usurer and a young boy, followed by Death with his scythe.

✱
◄ Dance of death

From the viewing platform at 45m/148ft there is an unparalleled view of Neustadt and the Altstadt silhouette (hours: daily 10am–5.30pm; Sun from 11.30am).

Tower view

The altar of the Dreikönigskirche (Church of the Three Kings) is an outstanding example of Saxon Baroque art, and one of the largest stone altars found anywhere.

Dresdner Heide

A – D 9 – 15

Location: northeast of city centre **Tram:** Schloss Albrechtsberg (no. 11)
S-Bahn: S 2 to Bahnhof Klotzsche

»Green Lung« The peaceful Dresdner Heide (Dresden Heath) extends right up to the edge of vibrant Neustadt. It is a wonderful, easily accessible woodland area of more than 50 sq km/19 sq mi with many watercourses, of which the longest is the Priessnitz. Augustus the Strong had the centuries-old irregular paths replaced with a spider-web system. For ease of management the so-called Cotta system was introduced in 1832–33, dividing the heath into numbered rectangular sections. A map is advisable for long walks; there are also cycle tracks.

Landmarks In the south of the heath is the 211m/692ft Wolfshügel hill; at its foot the King Albert Column was erected in 1903. The »Saugarten« is the centre of the heath; it was enclosed in 1560 as a place to keep wild boar for the court hunt. Not far to the northeast is the Heidemühle inn by the Grosse Hengstbrücke bridge, which is first mentioned in 1558.

★ Elbe Palaces (Elbschlösser)

E 10 / 11

Location: Bautzner Strasse 130–134 **Tram:** Schloss Albrechtsberg
(no. 11)

The three fine residences known as the Elbschlösser are superbly situated above a bend in the river Elbe at Loschwitz. All three were built in the historicist style typical of the second half of the 19th century.

Schloss Albrechtsberg Schloss Albrechtsberg is situated on the former Findlater vineyard which the Scottish peer Lord Jacob Findlater acquired c1800; on it he built a country house. In 1850 it passed into the ownership of Prince Albrecht von Preussen, who had the old building demolished. He commissioned Adolph Lohse, a pupil of Schinkel and Prussian chief architect, to design a mansion in neo-classical style. It was build in 1851–54 above the garden terraces. The sandstone building with square side towers, a great bay at the centre and an ornamental balustrade looks like a Renaissance villa on the outside.

The ownership of Schloss Albrechtsberg passed to the city of Dresden in 1925. After the war it was used by the Soviet military administration, in 1949 it became a hotel, in 1951 the »Pionierpalast«; today it houses Dresden's school for young artists, and a hotel and catering training school. The loveliest rooms are the Kronensaal

The Roman Bath in Schloss Albrechtsberg with atmospheric illumination

(Crown Room) and the Turkish Bath designed by Karl Diebitsch. He also designed the Roman Bath on the slope below the castle.

On some Sundays and public holidays there are guided tours be- ◄ Events tween 11am and 2pm. The Turkish Bath is often used as picturesque backdrop for fairytale readings; the Kronensaal is used for chamber music concerts (for dates and times of guided tours, readings and chamber music concerts, tel. 811 58 21 or 811 58 20).

At much the same time as he built Schloss Albrechtsberg, Adolph **Lingner Schloss** Lohse designed the neighbouring neo-classical Villa Stockhausen for **(Villa** Baron von Stockhausen. The show front of the two-storey sand- **Stockhausen)** stone-clad building overlooks the Elbe, and is flanked by a colonnade. The entrance faces the road; it has corner towers and is approached by a grand flight of steps. Villa Stockhausen was purchased in 1906 by Karl August Lingner (►Baedeker Special p.172) and soon became known as Schloss Lingner; after his death in 1916 it passed to the city. Lingner was buried in a small mausoleum (architect: Hans Poelzig) below the villa on the bank of the Elbe. In his will he laid down that a restaurant »with affordable prices« should occupy his home. After a lengthy period of remodelling a restaurant serving organic food opened here – just as he would have wished.

A little further upstream Schloss Eckberg, the last of the three Elbe **Schloss Eckberg** palaces, was built independently of the others in 1859–61, and designed in neo-Gothic-cum-Tudor style. The building is situated on a spur of the hill – hence its name – and was designed by Christian Friedrich Arnold, a pupil of Semper, for the magnate John Daniel Souchay. Today it is an exclusive hotel, popular with state visitors among others. On the terrace – with fabulous view of Blasewitz and the Blaues Wunder bridge – stands the *Sun Worshipper*, a bronze figure by art nouveau sculptor Sascha Schneider.

Festung Dresden (Kasematten)

G 7

Location: Georg-Treu-Platz
Plan of inner city: B 3

Tram: Synagoge (nos. 3, 7); Pirnaischer Platz (nos. 1, 2, 3, 4, 7, 12)

⏱ Opening hours: April–Oct daily 10am–5pm; Nov–March daily 10am–4pm

The structures below the ►Brühlsche Terrasse enable visitors to travel back in time to a Renaissance fortress. The casemates, artillery yard, guard posts and brick gate of 1556 – closed up 400 years ago – have all survived in their original form. Work began on a system of fortifications on the Elbe in the years 1519–29 under Duke Georg, and was continued from 1547 under Duke Moritz.

The construction of the tall arsenal, rising above the level of the walls, necessitated new and larger bastions, which were built by Paul Buchner from 1590.

Tour ►

The audio tour simulates life in the fortress with the sounds of trampling horses' hooves and a creaking spiral staircase. The tour of the casemates goes past the brick gate, beyond which a bridge over the fortress ditch led to the three bastions on the Elbe, and through a gate with notches marking high water levels from three centuries.

✶ ✶ Frauenkirche

G 7

Location: Neumarkt
Plan of inner city: B 3

Tram: Altmarkt (nos. 1, 2, 4)

No other building has such symbolic importance for the city of Dresden as the Frauenkirche: its burnt-out remains were once a reminder of the horror of war, and in its rebuilt form the church stands for the reconstruction of a new Dresden.

⏱ Open Church: Mon–Fri 10am–noon, 1pm–6pm; dome, daily 10am–1pm, 2pm–4pm

Until 1727 the church »Zu unser lieben Frauen« (Of Our Dear Lady), dating back to the 11th century, stood on the space that became ►Neumarkt. In the early 18th century this Gothic building no longer met the needs of the growing congregation, and had fallen into disrepair, so that in 1722 the city council commissioned its master carpenter **George Bähr** (►Famous People) to build a new Frauenkirche. Bähr produced several designs and at the behest of the elector's director of building, Christoph von Wackerbarth, he adopted some ideas from the competing design by Johann Christoph Knöffel. On 26 August 1726 the foundation stone was laid, and in 1727 building work, to which Johann Gottfried Fehre and Johann Georg Schmid also contributed, commenced. Doubtless George Bähr drew ◄ »Stone bell« inspiration from domes in Rome and Florence in his desire from the very beginning to create a tower-like building on an approximately square ground plan. With a height of 95.25m/312ft and a dome 23.5m/77ft in diameter, it is one of the most magnificent and monumental achievements of Protestant church architecture of the time, and **the most important stone dome north of the Alps**, blending high Baroque with early classical forms in perfect synthesis. The execution in stone of a dome ostensibly designed in wood and copper had been Bähr's plan from the beginning, but he did not reveal it until the necessary pillars and foundations had been completed. The aesthetic effect of the dome, which is concave at the base, in relation to the building as a whole demonstrated George Bähr's outstanding architectural skill. Increasingly the building aroused the interest of Augustus the Strong, who gave financial support to the project. Neither Augustus the Strong nor George Bähr lived to see its completion. The master builder died in 1738, five years before his pupil Johann Georg Schmid could bring to an end work which had lasted for 17 years. In the Seven Years' War the church withstood a three-day cannonade by Friedrich II's Prussian troops in 1760. Initially it also survived the catastrophic World War II bombing, but on 15 February 1945 the sandstone building collapsed from the heat.

Johann Christian Feige the Elder and Benjamin Thomae furnished the altar space constructed in the years 1733–39 with a sumptuous Baroque altar. This has now been reconstructed from 2,000 fragments, supplemented by new pieces. The interior of the church, with its four galleries, was designed to accommodate 3600 people, in

Altar space in white and gold

FRAUENKIRCHE (CHURCH OF OUR LADY)

✴ ✴ The restored Frauenkirche is as a symbol of reconciliation, and its dome crowns the city silhouette once more. 8390 sandstone blocks were salvaged from the ruins; the 3634 that were re-used are recognizable by their blackened colouring.

🕐 Opening hours:
Church Mon–Fri 10am–noon, 1pm–6pm
Ascent of dome daily 10am–1pm, 2pm–4pm

① Lower church
The lower church in the form of a Greek cross replaced the cemetery of the previous church. It was dedicated and made accessible in 1996.

② Altar
The altar space was one of two surviving parts in the ruins, towering above them for decades. The altar was reconstructed in 1999 from 2000 fragments and shows Christ on the Mount of Olives. The figure of Christ is original, the angel a replica. The scene is flanked by Moses and St Paul (on the left) and St Philip and Aaron (on the right). The nail cross on the altar table symbolizes reconciliation.

③ Organ
On the outside the mighty organ resembles the old Silbermann organ, but inside it was constructed with the most up-to-date technology by the Strasbourg organ builder Daniel Kern. Four manuals and 67 registers conjure the sound of 4790 pipes.

The ruins of the Church of our Lady with the monument to the reformer Martin Luther. The heap of rubble was a year-long reminder of the city's destruction.

④ Nave
The square base of the Baroque building measures 45 x 45 m / 148 x 148 ft. The round interior is encircled by eight supporting columns for the dome and four-storey galleries with seating for 1800. The lofty preaching space is a Protestant »tiered theatre« encircling the central pulpit.

⑤ Stairs
In addition to the altar space, part of tower E with its stairway survived, the only one remaining of four diagonally placed stairways. Each stairway tower is crowned by a lantern.

⑥ Dome
The inner dome soars 26m/85ft above the nave, and above that is George Bähr's exterior dome, famously known as the »stone bell«. Between the inner and outer walls, a ramp winds up; once donkeys carried stones up this way to build the dome. Today it is the route to the viewing platform, at a height of 68m/223ft. Goethe once admired this view.

⑦ Turmkreuz
Since 13 February 2000 the tower cross has once more shone out on top of the lantern, at a height of 92m/300ft. It was given to the city in token of reconciliation by Great Britain, and was made by the London artist Alan Smith, son of one of the Royal Air Force pilots who flew on the Dresden raid. The original was salvaged from the ruins in 1993 and now stands in the south of the nave.

Friedrichstadt (city district)

F 4 – 6

Location: west of Altstadt   **Bus:** Krankenhaus Friedrichstadt (no. 94)

Friedrichstadt, Dresden's first suburb, arose as a result of an official edict of 1670 that encouraged the setting up of craft workshops and manufacturing.

The settlement was named Friedrichstadt in 1730, after Augustus the Strong's »official« name of Elector Friedrich August I. Incorporated into Dresden in 1836, it developed during the 19th century into a manufacturing area, with horse-drawn train, river port and goods yard.

Friedrichstrasse was once the main street of Friedrichstadt. The painter Adrian Ludwig Richter was born in the garden house at no. 44; Paula Becker, later Modersohn-Becker, was born in 1876 in Friedrichstrasse. Professor Johann Andreas Schubert lived at no. 46 from 1842 until his death (►Famous People); he constructed the first Elbe steamship in 1837 and the first German steam engine, *Saxonia*, in 1839.

Friedrichstrasse

In the middle section of Friedrichstrasse is the Marcolini Palais. The first palais, begun in 1728, was designed by Johann Christoph Naumann for Princess von Teschen, Duchess of Württemberg and Teck, and was an unpretentious building. Count Brühl purchased it in 1736 and had Johann Christoph Knöffel extend it into a mansion; he also added the lateral wings. In 1774 the palais passed into the hands of Count Camillo Marcolini, cabinet minister of Augustus III; for him Johann Daniel Schade extended the east wing. Finally, in 1849 the palais was converted into a hospital. The entrance tract was retained with four lions, four herms and the Chinese and Pompeian rooms, which **Napoleon I** occupied in the summer of 1813. Here the discussion between Napoleon and Metternich took place which decided that Austria would join the Russian-Prussian alliance. The interior decoration of these rooms is still preserved. From 1847 to 1849 **Richard Wagner** lived in the east wing; here he composed parts of *Lohengrin* and wrote texts for *Siegfried's Death*.
By the southern boundary wall in the hospital grounds is the Neptunbrunnen (Neptune Fountain), Dresden's most splendid Baroque fountain, which was completed in 1744. It attracted the gaze of all who came here, with its width of more than 40m/132ft, three-storey construction and sculptural ornamentation. The design was by Zacharias Longuelune, and Lorenzo Matielli executed the sculpture.

Marcolini Palais (Krankenhaus Friedrichstadt)

✱
◄ Neptunbrunnen

The Matthäuskirche adjoins the Marcolini Palais. Pöppelmann, who is buried in the crypt, built this unpretentious church in 1728–30; the interior was re-done in 1882 in the manner of the age, and it was altered again after World War II.

Matthäuskirche

★ Fürstenzug

G 7

Location: Augustusstrasse
Plan of inner city: B 3

Tram: Theaterplatz (nos. 4, 8, 9);
Altmarkt (nos. 1, 2, 4)

The 102m/335ft-long Fürstenzug (Procession of Princes) on the exterior wall of the Long Corridor of the Stallhof commemorates 93 important persons from Saxony.

Ancestral portrait gallery in porcelain

The idea of an artistic design on the Langer Gang (Long Corridor) was not new, for in 1589 it had already been painted with a procession of horsemen in coloured limewash à la sgraffito, which had faded. From 1872 to 1876, on the occasion of the 800-year jubilee of the House of Wettin, Wilhelm Walther, professor at the Kunstakademie, painted his picture of the procession of Wettin princes on the wall, also using sgraffito technique. Because of weathering the painting had to be transferred to Meissen porcelain tiles: in the Meissen factory 24,000 porcelain tiles were fired and in 1907 they were fixed seamlessly to the 957 sq m/10,300 sq ft surface. These tiles survived

Family history on the wall: the Procession of Princes

the catastrophic bombings of 1945 undamaged! 93 persons are portrayed. The first in the line are the 35 rulers of the House of Wettin from 1123 to 1904 – margraves, dukes, electors and kings; Heinrich I (1089–1103), Heinrich II (1103–23) and the last Saxon king, Friedrich August III, are missing; King Georg was added later. The rulers are followed by representatives of arts and sciences from the Kreuzschule, Leipzig University and the Technische Bildungsanstalt in Dresden. The painter Adrian Ludwig Richter, sculptors Ernst Julius Hähnel and Johannes Schilling, and finally Walther himself with assistants and the director of the royal public library, Ernst Wilhelm Förstemann, bring up the rear of the procession.

◄ Detailed reproduction with explanation see pp.26

★ ★ Galerie Neue Meister

G 7 / 8

Location: Albertinum
Plan of inner city: B 3

Tram: Synagoge (nos. 3, 7); Pirnaischer Platz (nos. 1, 2, 3, 4, 7, 12)

The collection of paintings from the 19th century to the present was set up as an independent museum in 1931. The rebuilding of its home, the ►Albertinum, is scheduled for completion in 2010.

During the Third Reich the collection suffered irreparable damage: defamed by the Nazis as »degenerate art«, Expressionist pictures, particularly ones by the Dresden »Brücke« artists, and Cubist pictures were removed, and some were sold abroad. Other works, including ones by Böcklin, Feuerbach, Hodler, Thoma, Uhde and Liebermann, were burnt in the bombing raids of 1945.

Opening hours: Interim exhibition in the Sempergalerie until the Albertinum re-opens

Major Works

In addition to paintings the gallery has **sculptures** (►Albertinum) by the following artists: Rauch (room 9), Rietschel (room 13), Meunier (room 16), Kolbe (room 24), Rodin (rooms 4, 20), **Lehmbruck** (room 25), Albiker (room 29), Marcks and Hoffmann (room 30) and Seitz (room 31).

Rooms 5–8 present post-war German art. During the GDR era this consisted almost entirely of paintings in Social Realist style, but these paintings have now for the most part been confined to the store and replaced by an experimental juxtaposition of German art from east and west, including works by Morgner, Baselitz and Penck. The gallery has 41 pictures on permanent loan by one of the most important present-day artists, **Gerhard Richter**, who was born in Dresden, covering all phases of his artistic life; this is the largest collection of works by Richter in the world. In his early years he practised a painting technique based on banal photos that he came across by chance

Post-war German art

and transposed into black-and-white pictures, often without sharp focus, as in his painting *Secretary*. With the discovery of photography as the medium for new departures in art, his work has become highly significant for the renewal and reassessment of German art after World War II.

Romantic art The Romantics are exhibited in rooms 10 and 11, with room 10 devoted to **Caspar David Friedrich** (▶Famous People): *Barrow Grave in Snow*, *Two Men Gazing at the Moon*, *The Mountain Cross*. His late work *The Great Enclosure at Dresden* marks the culmination of painterly perfection in his art. The subject, the view across the Elbe, is hardly spectacular, yet it is nevertheless considered one of the incomparable masterpieces of European landscape painting; in this tranquil landscape the whole expanse of the cosmos seems captured as in a concave mirror. Room 11 shows *Oaks by the Sea* and *Moonlit Night near Rügen* by Carl Gustav Carus, and Johan Christian Dahl's *View of Dresden by the Light of the Full Moon*.

✔ DON'T MISS

- Room 7: German post-war art: (Gerhard Richter: »Secretary«)
- Room 10: Romanticism (Caspar David Friedrich »The Great Enclosure at Dresden«)
- Room 24: German Impressionism (Max Slevogt »Pirates«)
- Room 27: Expressionists (Ernst Ludwig Kirchner »Naked Girls Standing by the Stove«)

Classical art In the next room, room 12, are works from the first half of the 19th century, including Schnorr von Carolsfeld's *The Family of John the Baptist with the Family of Christ*, Koch's *Landscape with St Benedict* and Overbeck's *Italia and Germania*.

Late Romantic period The pictures in rooms 13 and 14 were painted around the middle of the 19th century by late Romantics such as Richter (*Harpist Returning Home*, *Crossing the Elbe at Schreckenstein*, *Bridal Procession in Spring*) and Rayski (*Grenadiers in Snow*, *Portrait of Chamberlain Julius Graf Zech-Burkersroda*).

Bourgeois Realism Paintings by one of the most important German Realists, Adolph Menzel, are on view on room 15: *Sermon in the Old Monastery Church in Berlin*, *Afternoon in the Tuileries Garden in Paris* and *Piazza d'Erbe in Verona*.

Germans in Rome Rooms 16 and 18 are devoted to paintings by Germans in Rome; among them are *Summer Day* by Böcklin, *Portrait of Auguste Schäuffelen* by Marées and a *Self-Portrait* by Thoma.

Munich painting c1900 Room 117 shows Munich regional painting *c*1900, such as Leibl's *Head of a Peasant Girl* and *Portrait of Wilhelm Schenk Freiherr von Stauffenberg*, and Trübner's *Girl with Folded Hands*.

Galerie Neue Meister Plan

1 Ackermann
2 Stella
3 Strawalde
4 Rodin
5 Morgner
6 Baumeister, Schumacher, Bastik, Weißberg, Graubner, Caro
7 Wols, Oelze, G. Richter, Szymanski, Uhlig, Göschel
8 Baselitz, Penck, Graf, Makolies, Madorf, T. Richter
9 Canova, Schadow, Rauch, Herrmann
10 C. D. Friedrich

11 Carus, d'Angers Dahl
12 Koch, Overbeck, Schnorr, Olivier
13 Richter, Rietschel
14 Rayski, Waldmüller
15 Menzel, Spitzweg, Gille
16 Meunier, Thoma
17 Leibl, Trübner
18 Marées, Böcklin, Uhde
19 Manet, Monet
20 Rodin
21 Degas, Gauguin
22 Kuehl, Liebermann
23 Corinth
24 Slevogt, Kolbe

25 Klinger, Sterl, Lehmbruck
26 Zwintscher
27 Schmidt-Rottluff, Kirchner, Nolde
28 Feininger, Klee, Glöckner
29 Lohse, Felixmüller, Albiker, Lange
30 Dix, Hoffmann, Grundig, Marcks, Blumenthal Lachnit
31 Hegenbarth, Rosenhauer, Körnig, Wigand, Seitz, Grzimek
32 Mattheuer, Tübke, Wolff, Förster, Tucholke, Antes

French Impressionism

Rooms 19 and 21 belong to the French Impressionists, including Degas (*Lady with Spyglass, Two Dancers*), Manet (*Lady in Pink*) and Monet (*Bank of the Seine near Lavacourt, The Peach Glass*).

German Impressionism

In the following rooms, 22–26, are works by German Impressionists such as *The Garden Room* and *Orphans in Lübeck* by Kuehl; *Portrait of Alfred von Berger* by Liebermann; Sterl's *Boat Haulers on the Volga* and Slevogt's *Portrait of the Dancer Marietta di Rigardo*.
Slevogt's picture of *Pirates* belongs to the cycle of his journey to Egypt in 1914, a pinnacle of his creative achievement – the gallery has 16 of these paintings. The treatment of the subject is astonishing: only part of the boat is visible on the left of the picture, which contributes to the sense of movement and atmosphere. The transience of the moment is emphasized by the manner in which the boat is

cut, by the dynamic handling of the brush and richly contrasting change of colours. Matter increasingly dissolves beneath the intense bright light.

German Expressionism Room 27 is devoted to German Expressionists, the artists of »Die Brücke«. Among the best known are **Kirchner** (▶ Famous People), represented by *Railway Cross-Over Löbtauer Strasse in Dresden* and *Naked Girls Standing by the Stove*; Nolde (*Sailors on the Yellow Sea*) and Schmidt-Rottluff (*After Bathing* and *Landscape in Rottluff*). Kirchner's *Naked Girls Standing by the Stove* is regarded as a successful early work, on the threshold of the mature »Brücke« style of the years 1909–10, and still visibly influenced by French Fauvism. Diverging from traditional notions of art, the »Brücke« artists embodied their idea of beauty in bright colours and a less refined, even coarse manner of painting.

The nude painting in contrasting primary colours arose from the practice called »quarter-of-an-hour life studies«: striving for the natural, the »Brücke« painters rapidly sketched unconstrained movement.

The triptych »War«, one of Otto Dix's chief works, was painted in Dresden.

Rooms 28–32 display painting between the world wars, and further German post-war art. Room 30 has outstanding inter-war paintings. **Otto Dix's** (▶Famous People) pictures put a gloss on nothing, but criticise the times by exaggerating reality, as in the painting *Woman with Child*. In his triptych *War* Dix succeeds in conveying his experience of war as the first of the great catastrophes of the 20th century with a gripping and admonitory power. In the same room is Hans Grundig's visionary triptych *Thousand-Year Reich* of 1935–38, which prophetically anticipates the events of World War II. With cold colours Grundig alienates Dresden city views. From left to right a spooky carnival procession intrudes; it is simultaneously a masked festival and gas-mask procession, taking as its theme human activity behind the mask of animals of prey. Grundig symbolizes individual powerlessness in *Sleepers on the Predella*. Further notable works are Lachnit's *Girl with Fur* and *Death of Dresden*.

Between the wars

The two last rooms, 31 and 32, once more present German post-war art with such works as Rosenhauer's *Child on Yellow Chair* and Tübke's *Requiem*. Mattheuer's *High-spirited Sisyphus and his People«*, painted in 1976, acquired astonishing contemporary relevance when the Berlin Wall fell, and came in a sense to represent the people's departure for new horizons in the GDR.

German post-war art

✱ ✱ Gemäldegalerie Alte Meister

F 7

Location: Zwinger, Sempergalerie
Plan of inner city: B 2

Tram: Postplatz (nos. 1, 2, 4, 6, 8, 9, 11, 12, 47); Theaterplatz (nos. 4, 8, 9)

The Old Masters picture gallery is one of the richest collections of 15th to 18th-century European painting, and therefore one of the most important collections of paintings in the world.

It started as the Kunstkammer (art cabinet), founded c1560 by Elector Augustus. In the late 17th century Augustus the Strong extended it systematically with the purchase, above all, of works by Italian and Dutch masters. During the reign of Augustus III in the mid-18th century the collection of the Wallenstein Gallery in Dux was acquired, with masterpieces formerly belonging to Italian or French owners and 69 pictures from the imperial gallery in Prague. The largest and most important purchase was that of 100 of the most valuable paintings from the collection of the Duke of Modena in 1745–46. This included such unique masterpieces as Titian's *Tribute Money,* four altar panels by Correggio, works by Veronese, Holbein, Rubens and Velázquez. Finally in 1754, at the behest of the elector, Raphael's *Sistine Madonna* was purchased from the monastery

Opening hours:
Tue–Sun
10am–6pm
Guided tours:
Fri, Sun 4pm

Gemäldegalerie Alte Meister *Plan*

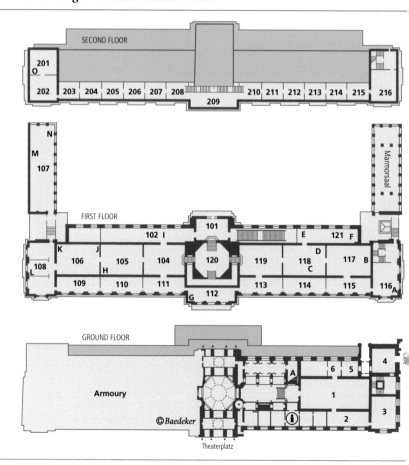

church of San Sisto in Piacenza. The beginning of the Seven Years' War halted the acquisition process, which did not begin again until the 19th century. The collection is remarkable for what is at times an unparalleled coherence and continuity of exhibits over long periods of time, especially of 15th to 17th-century Flemish and Dutch painting, 14th to 18th-century Italian painting, and 17th-century Spanish and French painting

War damage ► In 1942 a start was made on moving the works of art to safe locations. The bombing of 13–14 February 1945 destroyed all museum buildings, and 154 pictures were burnt, including works by Lucas

Cranach. During the war 206 paintings were lost, and a further 507 are listed as missing. The works that had been moved for safe keeping were found by Soviet troops, taken to the Soviet Union, and preserved in museums in Moscow, Kiev and Leningrad/St Petersburg. 1240 paintings were returned to Dresden in 1955, and have been back in the Sempergalerie since 1960.

Sempergalerie

The Gemäldegalerie Alte Meister is located in the Sempergalerie, designed by **Gottfried Semper** (►Famous People) to complete the Baroque ensemble of the ►Zwinger palace facing the Elbe. Opened in 1854, it gave Dresden at this early date an appropriately grand and

✔ DON'T MISS

- Canaletto: *Dresden from the Right Bank of the Elbe below the Augustusbrücke* (room 102)
- Giorgione: *Sleeping Venus* (room 118)
- Titian: *Tribute Money* (room 121)
- Raphael: *The Sistine Madonna* (room 117)
- Rembrandt: *Rembrandt and Saskia in the Parable of the Prodigal Son* (room 106)
- Rubens: *Bathsheba at the Well, Receiving David's Letter* (room 105)
- Lorrain: *Coastal Landscape with Acis and Galatea* (room 112)
- Vermeer: *Girl Reading a Letter at an Open Window* (room 108)

purpose-built exhibition space, something that only the Alte Pinakothek in Munich and the Altes Museum in Berlin provided in Germany at that time. The gallery had to be closed for renovation in 1988; after four years' of work, in 1992 the layout was once again much as Semper intended it to be. In the entrance are grisaille paintings and reliefs of great artists; the ornamentation of stairwell and vaulting has been restored.

The approach to the exhibition halls is dominated by large equestrian portraits of the two patrons Augustus III and Augustus the Strong. In the halls the paintings are hung as Semper intended, especially with regard to their positioning in two rows one above the other and the use of high-quality textiles to cover all the walls – Bordeaux red for the Italian, green for German and Dutch, grey for Spanish and French masters.

Important Works

Ground floor

Cityscapes by Canaletto ►

Rooms 2–6, which surround the Gobelinsaal (Tapestry Hall) on the ground floor, and rooms 102 and 203 on the upper floors, contain city views by Bernardo Bellotto, known as Canaletto (►Famous People), and works by 18th-century Dresden painters. Canaletto's painting *Dresden from the Right Bank of the Elbe below Augustusbrücke* is in room 102. The view Canaletto chose for this panorama has become a classic. In addition to compositional strength it demonstrates his consummate craftsmanship in the effects achieved in the reflection of the water and precise architectural details.

1st floor

16th and 17th-century Italian paintings ►

14th and 15th-century Italian painting ►

The rotunda on the first floor contains 16th and 17th-century Italian paintings of the Bologna school with major works by Annibale Carracci. From the rotunda the **Sistine Madonna**, the jewel of the collection, is visible at the end of the rooms devoted to Italian painting; in the opposite direction, at the end of the Dutch rooms, hangs Rembrandt's *Self-Portrait with Saskia*. The chronological sequence begins in room 116 in the west corner room with 14th and 15th-century Italian painting. The outstanding works here are Botticelli's *Four Scenes from the Life of St Zenobius*, Mantegna's *The Holy Family* and **Pinturicchio's *Portrait of a Boy*.**

It is said that Augustus himself pushed his seat to one side in Dresden →
Schloss for the »Sistine Madonna«: »Make way for the great Raphael!«

16th-century Italian painting

Sistine Madonna ▶

Next, in room 115, are 16th-century Italian paintings. In the main hall (room 117) the *Sistine Madonna* painted by Raphael *c*1513 is admired by all visitors. To the right of the Madonna kneels St Barbara, a 3rd-century martyr who for a time was imprisoned in a tower, as depicted above her shoulder, and who was subsequently beheaded for her faith.

On the other side is St Sixtus, also a martyr, and characterized as a 3rd-century pope by the tiara in front of him. One interpretation sees in Sixtus some similarity to Pope Julius II (Giuliano della Rovere), who commissioned the picture. Further indications are the acorn on the tiara, which occurs in all della Rovere family arms, and the veneration of St Barbara in this family. The picture may have been intended originally for Julius II's tomb. The two angels at the lower edge have become famous; they underline the distance between earth and heaven. Room 118 shows major works by Parmigianino and paintings from the Venice and Parma schools, including: Meloni's *A Pair of Lovers*, Parmigianino's *The Madonna with the Rose* and Titian's *Portrait of a Painter with Palm*. **Giorgione's *Sleeping Venus*** is amazing; it shows the consummately beautiful female body lying peacefully stretched out in antique nudity. This subject had not been painted in this way before Giorgione, but then artists were inspired by it for centuries.

15th and 16th-century Venetian painting

Room 121 holds works by important 15th-century artists, including **Messina's *St Sebastian***. Titian's early work *Tribute Money* focuses on a story from St Matthew's Gospel (Matthew 22: 21), with two heads and two hands: in answer to the Pharisee's question as to whether it was right to pay tribute to Caesar, Jesus asked for a coin and answered, pointing to the portrait of the emperor stamped on the coin: »Render unto Caesar the things which are Caesar's, and unto God the things which are God's.« In room 119 hang paintings by Tintoretto (*The Archangel Michael's Fight with Satan in the Form of a Dragon*) and Veronese (*The Madonna with the Cuccina Family*).

17th-century Italian painting

After room 119 come the smaller rooms 113 and 114 with Italian Baroque painting, for instance, Carracci's *The Genius of Fame*, Dolci's *St Cecilia at the Organ*, Guercino's *St Luke the Evangelist* and Strozzi's *Woman Playing the Gamba*.

17th-century French painting

Room 112 has French painting from the first half of the 17th century. Works by Nicolas Poussin (*Flora's Kingdom*) and Claude Lorrain form the nucleus of this group. Lorrain's *Coastal Landscape with Acis and Galatea* gives no suggestion that a catastrophe will soon invade this serenely illuminated landscape. The giant Polyphemus who is playing the flute on the hill to the right is jealous of the lovers Acis and Galatea in the foreground. At the moment captured in the picture the giant has yet to discover the lovers and hurl the rock that will dash Acis to pieces.

Next is room 111 with Flemish pictures of c1600; 17th-century Flemish paintings hang in the main halls (rooms 104 and 105). Flemish Baroque painting owes a great deal to the creative energy of **Peter Paul Rubens**; his work also had a great influence on Jordaens and van Dyck. Here are Van Dyck's *St Jerome*, Jordaens' *Diogenes with the Lantern, Looking for People at the Market* and Rubens' *Old Woman with Coals. Bathsheba at the Well, receiving David's Letter* is also by Rubens. This late work depicts an Old Testament story, according to which King David was inflamed with love for Bathsheba, his captain's wife, when he saw her beauty from the palace – at once he wrote her a love letter.

17th-century Flemish painting

Rooms 106 and 108–110 present painting of the Dutch school. In room 106 the spotlight is on Rembrandt.

His 1559 painting of *Rembrandt and Saskia in the Parable of the Prodigal Son* was originally in landscape format and was supposed to be about the prodigal son in the tavern with harlots. While he was working on it Rembrandt cut off the left side of the picture and turned it into a self-portrait with Saskia, his young bride.

Another notable painting is Rembrandt's *Samson Posing the Riddle at the Wedding Feast*. Rooms 108–110 show Claesz Heda: *Breakfast Table with Blackberry Pie* and *The Procuress* by **Vermeer van Delft**.

Vermeer's *Girl Reading a Letter at an Open Window* is full of the poetry of harmonious light and colour.

A letter, when it is written or read, always requires inner composure. Here the paper is the only counterpart of the person portrayed and the viewer can only guess at the dialogue; the contents remain hidden.

17th-century Dutch painting

◄ *Rembrandt and Saskia in the Parable of the Prodigal Son*

The Zwinger's Deutscher Saal (German Hall), room 107, presents early Dutch and German paintings. Early Dutch painting played an important part in overcoming formulaic medieval art by turning towards the precise depiction of reality, landscape and interiors, seen beautifully in Jan van Eyck's winged altar and *The Tax Collector* by Jan Massys.

The age of Dürer epoch was shattered by social and religious tensions, which were reflected in art too, for instance in Cranach the Elder's St Catherine's Altar; *The Seven Sorrows of Mary, Portrait of Bernhard von Reesen*, and the Dresden Altar by **Dürer**; and the *Portrait of Charles de Solier, Sieur de Morette* by **Holbein the Younger**.

Dutch and German painting of the 15th–16th centuries

Spanish paintings are exhibited in rooms 208–210, including important works of the 17th-century artistic flowering such as El Greco`s *The Healing of the Blind Man*, Murillo's *The Death of St Clare*, Ribera's *St Agnes in Prison*, and the *Portrait of a Man*, presumed to be master of the royal hunt Don Juan Mateos, by Velázquez. 14 of the Spanish paintings in the collection were bought from the estate of the exiled French king Louis Philippe and displayed in the newly opened Sempergalerie in 1855.

2nd floor

◄ 16th–17th century Spanish painting

18th-century Italian painting	The next rooms, 207–203, contain 18th-century Italian paintings, including *The Arts* by Batoni; Canaletto's *The Grand Canal in Venice with the Rialto Bridge*; and Tiepolo's *The Vision of St Anne*.
18th-century French painting	In room 202 French painting from the first half of the 18th century is on display. There are portraits of Dresden personalities, and also works by the masters of chivalric pageantry: *Noli me tangere* by Silvestre and Watteau's *Feast of Love*.
Pastels	Room 201 is the larger of two pastel cabinets (the other is room 215) with works by the following artists: Carriera (*Self-Portrait as Winter*), Liotard (*The Chocolate Girl*) and De La Tour (*Moritz Count of Saxony, Marshal of France*).
17th–18th century German, Austrian, Dutch, English and Swiss paintings	In the west wing of the upper floor, in rooms 211–216, the following works can be seen: Graff's *Self-Portrait Aged 58*, Angelika Kauffmann's *Portrait of a Lady as Vestal Virgin* and Mengs' *Self-Portrait in a Red Coat*.

✴ Gläserne Manufaktur

G 8

Location: Strassburger Platz

Tram: Strassburger Platz (nos. 1, 2, 4, 10, 12, 13)

Since 2000 the »Transparent Factory« has glittered on the former exhibition space in the Grosser Garten. It breaks with two time-honoured assumptions of industry, namely that factories don't have to be attractive but that they do have to be on the edge of town. The Kugelkino (Globe Cinema) in the factory is a citation of the Kugelhaus (Globe House) by Peter Birkenholz that stood on the exhibition space from 1928 to 1938, and was demolished by the Nazis because of its »un-German« architecture. Dresden architect Gunter Henn designed the car factory. Manufacture originally meant »making by hand«, and that is how the top model VW Phaeton is assembled here. It is a luxury limousine costing about €75,000 – and for that price the customer is allowed to see it being assembled, or even take a hand. Even those who don't want to pay that much for a car can have fun on the simulator (opening hours: accessible only on guided tours, daily 10am–5pm by appointment, tel. (0180) 589 62 68).

> **❗ Baedeker TIP**
>
> **Jazz brunch**
>
> On Sundays Lesage provides high-class surroundings for a tour: from 11am to 3pm there is a jazz brunch including a tour of the factory. The only disadvantage is that production line stops at weekends, so it is not possible to watch the assembly line in operation (tel. 420 42 50).

A glass »cathedral of the hi-tech age«, in which luxury vehicles are assembled by hand

★ Grosser Garten

G / H 8 – 10

Location: southeast of Altstadt centre   **Tram:** Strassburger Platz (nos. 1, 2, 4, 10, 12, 13); Zoo or Querallee (nos. 9, 13); Comeniusplatz (nos. 1, 2)

Of the 21 parks in Dresden, the Grosser Garten (Great Garden) is the most beautiful and, with an area of around 2 sq km/500 acres, also the largest.

It contains the zoo, the botanical garden, an open-air stage and the Parktheater at the pond of the Palais, where Augustus the Strong attended the opening performance in 1719. North of the Herkulesallee are the Sonnenhäusl puppet theatre and the park railway. Carolasee lake is popular for its rowing-boats, for a visit to the lakeside café and the Carolaschlösschen restaurant in summer, or for ice-skating in winter. Adjoining the Grosser Garten are the Bürgerwiese meadow, the ►German Hygiene Museum, the Georg-Arnhold-Bad (swimming pool) and the Rudolf-Harbig-Stadion, where FC Dynamo Dresden play. An eye-catching sight in the northeast corner is the ► Gläserne Manufaktur (Factory of Glass).

City oasis

Grosser Garten/Bürgerwiese Plan

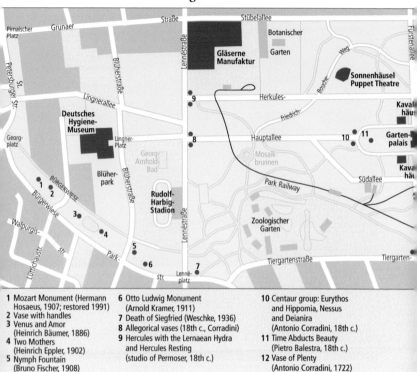

1 Mozart Monument (Hermann Hosaeus, 1907; restored 1991)
2 Vase with handles
3 Venus and Amor (Heinrich Bäumer, 1886)
4 Two Mothers (Heinrich Eppler, 1902)
5 Nymph Fountain (Bruno Fischer, 1908)

6 Otto Ludwig Monument (Arnold Kramer, 1911)
7 Death of Siegfried (Weschke, 1936)
8 Allegorical vases (18th c., Corradini)
9 Hercules with the Lernaean Hydra and Hercules Resting (studio of Permoser, 18th c.)

10 Centaur group: Eurythos and Hippomia, Nessus and Deianira (Antonio Corradini, 18th c.)
11 Time Abducts Beauty (Pietro Balestra, 18th c.)
12 Vase of Plenty (Antonio Corradini, 1722)

The Grosser Garten is not only important as a landscape garden, but with its Baroque Grosses Palais also possesses an architectural treasure with a fine exhibition. Its origins go back to 1676, when Elector Johann Georg II had a first garden made, in which construction of the Grosses Palais started two years later.

Augustus the Strong extended it to its present size according to plans by Johann Gottfried Karcher, who took the garden at Versailles as his model and conceived the large avenue layout. For ornamentation the elector had sculptures made or purchased, but very few have survived, mainly because the Prussians smashed or looted many of them in the Seven Years' War. In 1814 the Russian governor, Prince Repnin-Volkonsky, made the Grosser Garten accessible to the general public. From 1873 Friedrich Bouché re-shaped it in the style of an English landscape garden.

Garten Palais Next to the pond in the centre of the Grosser Garten stands the Grosses Palais. The palais was built in the years 1678–83 to designs

Stübelallee

N

300 m
990 ft

15

Neuer
Teich

ch-
Bouché-
Weg

Karcherallee

12

Hauptallee

14

steich

rktheater

Georg-Starcke-Weg

Südallee

**Open-Air
Stage**

eorg-Starcke-Weg

Carola-
see

**Carola-
Schlösschen**

Tiergartenstraße

© Baedeker

13 South entrance with sandstone lions
14 East main entrance,
   Meleager and Atalante, Venus and
   Adonis (Johann Christian Kirchner, 1719)
15 Hercules and the Dragon in the Garden
   of the Hesperides and Hercules with Busiris
   (studio of Permoser, 18th c.)

by Johann Georg Starcke on an H-shaped ground plan, modelled on French palaces but also revealing some influence of the traditions of the Italian villa and the German pleasure palace.

It is Saxony's earliest Baroque building, and an important example of early German Baroque architecture. The rich ornamentation is one of the great sculptural achievements of the late 17th century. The palais was never a residence, but used entirely as pleasure palace; eventually it housed the museum of classical antiquities, until it was destroyed in 1945. The **permanent exhibition** »Permoser in the Palais« on the ground floor presents a collection of Saxon Baroque sculpture, including prominent works such as Permoser's *Chronos* of 1705. Other figures have been removed from their original location and replaced by copies in order to prevent deterioration. These include the sculptural ornamentation from the Dresden Zwinger (opening hours: April–Oct Sat 2pm–6pm, Sun 11am–6pm; Nov–March Sat, Sun 11am–6pm). In addition, the door of the Grosses Palais is always open on Tuesdays at 2.30pm and 7.30pm for the »Offenes Palais« concert series.

🕐
◄ Concert series

At the end of the main avenue, on the corner with Lennéstrasse, are the classical gatehouses by Gottlob Friedrich Thormeyer.

The two large longitudinal avenues, the Hauptallee and Herkulesallee, were lined by sculptures in the 18th century.
Of those decorating the Hauptallee, two vases with allegories of the Four Elements and Four Continents have remained; in front of the Grosses Palais, two centaur groups; and by the pond the *Vase of Opulence* with a winged Psyche and scenes from the life of Alexander the Great, all by Antonio Corradini. Of the twelve original Hercules sculptures on the Herkulesallee, two have survived at the west en-

Avenues

★
◄ Sculptures

Boating on Carolasee

trance and two at the east entrance; they are from the workshop of sculptor **Balthasar Permoser**.

The **park railway** is fun; it crosses the Grosser Garten, and is 5.6km/3.5mi long. The conductor, station master and ticket inspector with hole-puncher are all children; only the engine-driver is a grown-up (hours: April–Oct 1.30pm–5pm; May–Sept 10am–6pm, Fri 1pm–6pm).

Around the Grosser Garten

Botanical garden
The 3.25ha/8-acre botanical garden was laid out in 1889–92 (Stübelallee 2b); in it the plant world of the earth's temperate, subtropical and tropical zones is arranged geographically (hours: April–Sept daily 8am–6pm; restricted in winter).

Zoo ▶
The zoo is in the southern part of the Grosser Garten. Founded in 1861, it was one of the earliest German zoos. The enclosure for big cats, the penguin pool and the giraffe house are new. Children especially enjoy the petting zoo and the tundra section with Arctic foxes and snowy owls (opening hours: summer 8.30am–6.30pm; winter 8.30am–4.30pm).

Bürgerwiese
For the Bürgerwiese (citizens' meadow) take a tram (nos. 9, 11, 13) to Lennéplatz. Mentioned as early as 1469, the Bürgerwiese was made into a public park between Rathaus (town hall) and Grosser Garten from 1835. The Potsdam landscape architect Peter Joseph Lenné laid out the Bürgerwiese in its present form after 1846. It is enhanced by sculptures (see plan p.198).

✱
Mozart Memorial ▶
The best is considered to be the Mozart Memorial of 1907 by Hermann Hosaeus: it shows not Mozart, but rather three female figures dancing round the name »Mozart«; they symbolize serenity, earnestness and charm.

✱
Christuskirche
South of the Grosser Garten in Dresden-Strehlen is the Christuskirche, which is visible from afar with its 66m/216ft twin-tower front (tram: nos. 9, 13 to Wasaplatz). This church, built of sandstone in 1903–05 by Rudolf Schilling and Julius Gräbner, was the first modern ecclesiastical building in Dresden. Its interior has a central plan without galleries; altar, pulpit and organ are in the choir recess. Most of the sculptural interior decoration, tending towards art nouveau, was the work of Karl Gross and August Hudler. It was largely destroyed in 1945 and restored in simplified form.

Serenity, Earnestness and Charm dance their round for Mozart at Bürgerwiese.

Großsedlitz

Location: 16km/10mi southeast of
Dresden

S-Bahn: S 1 to Heidenau-Großsedlitz,
then 20 min on foot

Großsedlitz has one of the finest Baroque gardens in Saxony.   History

Initially it was Count Wackerbarth who from 1719 had the land built
on and the park laid out to designs by Johann Christoph Knöffel.
After Augustus the Strong acquired the property in 1723, **Matthäus
Daniel Pöppelmann** and Zacharias Longuelune were also involved,
which means that Dresden's three best architects of the time were responsible for the park. Its extent and the gently curving slopes are
impressive. Over the years it suffered severely. First the Prussians
raged here in 1756. In 1813 the garden was again fought over, and in
the years up to 1846 it decayed. In 1861 the remaining sculptures,
the flight of steps and the orangery were restored. The Upper Orangery was designed by Knöffel and built in the time of Count
Wackerbarth. The Friedrichsschlösschen (little palace) was built in
1872–74 and replaced the earlier three-winged Friedrichsburg. The

Großsedlitz Baroque Garden *Plan*

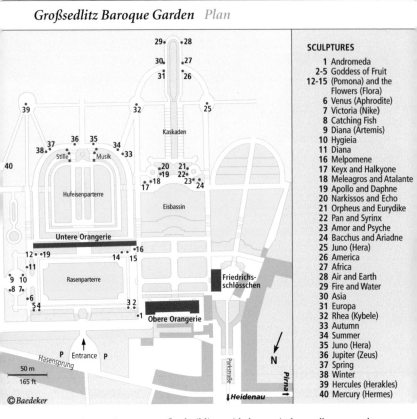

SCULPTURES

1 Andromeda
2-5 Goddess of Fruit
12-15 (Pomona) and the
Flowers (Flora)
6 Venus (Aphrodite)
7 Victoria (Nike)
8 Catching Fish
9 Diana (Artemis)
10 Hygieia
11 Diana
16 Melpomene
17 Keyx and Halkyone
18 Meleagros and Atalante
19 Apollo and Daphne
20 Narkissos and Echo
21 Orpheus and Eurydike
22 Pan and Syrinx
23 Amor and Psyche
24 Bacchus and Ariadne
25 Juno (Hera)
26 America
27 Africa
28 Air and Earth
29 Fire and Water
30 Asia
31 Europa
32 Rhea (Kybele)
33 Autumn
34 Summer
35 Juno (Hera)
36 Jupiter (Zeus)
37 Spring
38 Winter
39 Hercules (Herakles)
40 Mercury (Hermes)

🕐 Lower Orangery, a flat building with long window gallery, was designed by Longuelune. (hours: April–Sep 8am–8pm; Oct–Nov 8am–4.30pm).

★ ★
Baroque garden

The Baroque garden at Großsedlitz owes its fame to its **sculptural ornamentation**, although only 52 of the 360 original sculptures have survived. The sculptors included Johann Christian Kirchner with the *Four Seasons*, Benjamin Thomae with the groups of pairs of lovers from classical antiquity at the foot of the cascade and François Coudray with two sphinxes. Pöppelmann's *Still Music*, consisting of Baroque steps with curving balustrades and groups of putti, vividly animated in form, is particularly harmonious. There are always guided

Guided tours ►

tours on Sundays at 3pm. Summer concerts against the unusual backdrop of the Baroque garden are a wonderful experience! If you just want to enjoy the garden, find a seat in the Galeriecafé of the Upper Orangery, or in Friedrichsschlösschen restaurant – from both the view is superb.

✴ ✴ Hofkirche

Location: between Theaterplatz and
Schlossplatz
Plan of inner city: B 3

Tram: Theaterplatz (nos. 4, 8, 9); Postplatz (nos. 1, 2, 4, 6, 8, 9, 11, 12, 47)

**Two things about the Hofkirche (Court Church) are remarkable: it
is the largest church in Saxony with its ground area of 4,800 sq m/
51,666 sq ft, and it is an island of the Catholic faith in a sea of
Protestants.**

Although Augustus the Strong had converted to Catholicism in 1697,
it was left to his son Augustus III to have a grand new Catholic court
church built on ►Theaterplatz in the midst of a Protestant state. The
commission went to the Roman architect Gaetano Chiaveri, who was
succeeded in 1743 by Sebastian Wetzel and Johann Christoph
Knöffel, who in turn were followed by Julius Heinrich Schwarze.
Dedicated in 1751, the church was not actually finished until 1755.
The costs reached the substantial sum of 1 million talers. The Protestant citizens of the electoral capital declined to recognize the church
and denied it the right to ring its bells. Not until 1807, one year after
Napoleon had made Saxony a kingdom, did the church bells ring out
for the first time. In 1980 it was elevated to become the Cathedral
Sanctissimae Trinitatis (of the Most Holy Trinity) of the diocese of
Dresden and Meissen. Because it was aligned with the city fortifications, the longitudinal axis of the church does not run, as is usual,
from east to west, but rather from
northeast to southwest, adding an
extra ingredient to the city panorama. The architects created a sandstone basilica with an elaborate
86m/282ft tower, which is partially
free-standing; with the towers of
the ►Frauenkirche and ►Schloss it
is a prominent feature of the city
skyline. The long nave is higher
than the aisles, in the four corners
of which are chapels. The Hofkirche is distinctive not only for its
towers but also for 78 larger-than-life-size statues of saints by Lorenzo Matielli; 59 of them are on the balustrades; on the tower front are
the evangelists and apostles with the four cardinal virtues. In the
northwest corner a neo-Baroque bridge links the Hofkirche to the
Schloss. The most unusual feature of the Hofkirche interior is the
two-storey processional ambulatory inserted between the nave and
aisles, which was necessary because Catholic processions outside the
church were not allowed in Protestant Saxony. In the Hofkirche there

🕐
Opening hours:
Mon–Thu
9am–5pm,
Fri 1pm–5pm,
Sat 10am–5pm,
Sun noon–4pm

> **!** *Baedeker* **TIP**
>
> ### Sound of the Silbermann organ
>
> Concerts are held on the Silbermann organ in the
> Hofkirche. This historic instrument is the last
> remaining organ in Dresden made by Johann
> Gottfried Silbermann (organ recital: Wed, Sat
> 11.30am to noon; religious organ music: April to
> Dec. every third Thu in the month at 7.30pm).

◄ Interior

Former Catholic Hofkirche *Map*

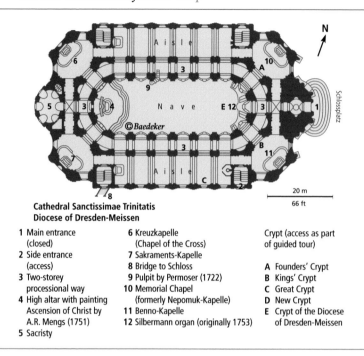

Cathedral Sanctissimae Trinitatis
Diocese of Dresden-Meissen

1 Main entrance
  (closed)
2 Side entrance
  (access)
3 Two-storey
  processional way
4 High altar with painting
  Ascension of Christ by
  A.R. Mengs (1751)
5 Sacristy

6 Kreuzkapelle
  (Chapel of the Cross)
7 Sakraments-Kapelle
8 Bridge to Schloss
9 Pulpit by Permoser (1722)
10 Memorial Chapel
  (formerly Nepomuk-Kapelle)
11 Benno-Kapelle
12 Silbermann organ (originally 1753)

Crypt (access as part
of guided tour)

A Founders' Crypt
B Kings' Crypt
C Great Crypt
D New Crypt
E Crypt of the Diocese
  of Dresden-Meissen

were at least 18 altars. In 1945 most of the interior burned out, the vaulting collapsed and the outer walls were damaged; only the tower remained intact. In the course of restoration the chapels were re-created, but the Bennokapelle was left without a frieze in the dome. The Kreuzkapelle (Chapel of the Cross) is adorned by altar paintings by Charles Hutin, while the Sakramentskapelle was painted by Stefano Torellis. The Nepomukkapelle was given a Pietà and a Meissen porcelain altar by Friedrich Press, and in 1973 it was re-dedicated as a memorial chapel for the victims of the Dresden bombing and rule of terror. The showpieces of the interior are the tall altar painting of *The Ascension* (1751) by Anton Raphael Mengs and the pulpit of 1722 by Permoser (►Famous People). Other items worthy of note are the organ by Gottfried Silbermann with a reconstructed organ case by Johann Joseph Hackl, and St Augustine and St Ambrose below, by Permoser; the 4.25m/14ft-high crucifix on the altar by the Augsburg silversmith Ignatz Bauer; and the old Hofkirche altar

★
◄ Pulpit

← *On the balustrades of the Catholic Hofkirche »saints and angels with flowing robes seem to storm heaven in ever-increasing ecstasy«.*

painting by Antonio Pellegrini in the processional ambulatory behind the main altar.

Crypt ► The crypt was the burial-place of the Catholic Wettin dynasty. 47 members of the princely Saxon line are buried in four crypt rooms; among them, in the founder's crypt, Elector Friedrich August II with his wife Maria von Habsburg. Here, too, in a simple box is the heart of Augustus the Strong, who was buried in Cracow Cathedral as king of Poland. In the Kings' Crypt lies King Johann in a magnificent bronze sarcophagus, and in the New Crypt Friedrich August III, the last Saxon king (guided tours: Mon–Thu 2pm; Fri 1pm; Sat 1pm, 2 pm; Sun 1pm).

Hosterwitz (city district)

Excursion

Location: eastern outskirts of the city

Tram: Schillerplatz (nos. 6, 12), then bus (no. 83) to Van-Gogh-Strasse

The best way to approach Hosterwitz is by water: this shows the little boatmen's church to best advantage.

Picturesque and tranquil: Maria am Wasser, a church on the Elbe

The small church in the Kirchgasse on the bank of the Elbe, charming in its simplicity, was built as a late Gothic hall church *c*1500; in 1774 it was given its Baroque turret above the west gable with a little onion dome. The interior of the church, with a flat ceiling, gallery and box pews above the sacristy, is also plain. It owes its designation as a boatmen's church to the river boatmen and towmen who had to load and unload their freight here at the Elbe ford, and took the opportunity to say their prayers at the same time. For a short viewing Mon–Thu during the day, see the administrator at Kirchgasse 6; in summer the church is open at weekends and there are occasional concerts.

Boatmen's church, Maria am Wasser

The court master of music Carl Maria von Weber (►Famous People) worked at Dresdner Strasse 44, a typical Saxon vintner's house and the property of vintner Gottfried Felsner, during the summer months of 1818–19 and 1823–24. Here he composed substantial parts of the operas *Freischütz* and *Euryanthe*, and the *Invitation to the Dance*. Visitors can see the rooms where Weber lived and worked, with music manuscripts and copious texts and visual documentation of his life and work (opening hours: Wed–Sun 1pm–6pm; guided tours by appointment, tel. 261 82 34). Lectures and concerts take place all year round in the house, and in summer also in the pretty garden.

Carl Maria von Weber Home

A 20-minute walk leads from the house through the wooded Keppgrund to the Keppmühle (mill), built in 1781, where a plaque records that Weber liked to spend time there.

Keppmühle

★ Jägerhof

F 7

Location: Köpckestrasse 1
Plan of inner city: A 3

Tram: Carolaplatz (nos. 3, 7, 8);
Neustädter Markt (nos. 4, 8, 9)

The Jägerhof (huntsmen's house) is one of the few pre-Baroque buildings to have survived, at least partially, in Dresden.

When Elector Augustus moved his hunt headquarters to Altendresden, present-day Dresden-Neustadt, in 1568, he found suitable premises in the farm buildings and offices of the former Augustinian Hermits' monastery of 1541. These were extended between 1582 and 1611, and completed in 1617 under Elector Johann Georg I. The chronicler Iccander acclaimed »the large and excellently furnished Jägerhaus« as one of the seven wonders of Dresden. When hunting lodges were built the Jägerhof dwindled into insignificance and served from 1830 to 1877 as a cavalry barracks. After that most of the buildings were demolished, and the rest decayed.

Museum of Saxon Folk Art

🕐 Opening hours:
Tue–Sun 10am–6pm

The best part of the Jägerhof, the west wing of 1617 with its richly decorated Renaissance gable and three stair towers, has survived. Since 1913 it has housed the folklore collections that were founded in 1897 and extended to become the first German folklore museum, the Museum für Sächsische Volkskunst. The majority of exhibits are Saxon folk art: painted furniture and household equipment such as bridal boxes, ceramics and pewter vessels, Saxon and Sorbian traditional costumes, lace and bobbin work, Erzgebirge carving, toys and colliers' items. There are frequent special exhibitions, and at Easter and in Advent demonstrations of traditional arts and crafts.

★ **Puppet theatre collection**

🕐

Since 2005 the upper floor has housed the puppet theatre exhibition of Dresden's state art collections. It has travelling marionettes of the 18th and 19th centuries, fantasy marionettes, handheld, rod and stick puppets of the 19th and 20th centuries, and Southeast Asian theatre figures (opening hours: Tue–Fri 10am–5pm; last Sunday in month 10am–5pm, incl. performances).

★ Japanisches Palais

F 7

Location: Palaisplatz   **Tram:** Palaisplatz (nos. 4, 9)

The Japanisches Palais is a fine example of the mode for the Far East of the first half of the 18th century. Today it houses several museums.

Chinese herm in the inner courtyard

Count Flemming had a »Dutch Palace« built on the Neustadt bank of the Elbe in 1715 by Johann Rudolf Faesch; it owed its name to the Dutch ambassador van Cranenberg, who was its first occupant. Augustus the Strong purchased it in 1717, in order to house his porcelain collection. Under Pöppelmann's direction work began in 1728 on extending the building into a four-winged complex and converting it into a porcelain palace. Augustus the Strong's plan to have the interior decoration made of porcelain failed, owing to lack of money. The portico relief of 1733 by Johann Benjamin Thomae recalls the dream of a porcelain palace: Saxon and East Asian porcelain producers pay homage to Saxonia. Chinese herms by Johann Christian Kirchner frame the inner courtyard and support the entablature of the staircases at the side of the ground floor hall. Further design features such as the curving roof form borrowed from Japanese architecture gave the palace its characteristic look, and ultimately its name. In 1785–86 Gottlob August Hölzer came up with a new design, because »chinoiserie« was no longer in fashion; classical antiquity was gaining in significance, so the sculpture collection took over. The house was given a new direction, articulated in an inscription on the entrance hall architrave: »MUSEUM USUI PUBLICO PATENS« (museum for public use). Gottfried Semper designed new rooms for the antiquities collection, with polychrome painting inspired by ancient models. Today the Japanisches Palais houses several museums.

The prehistory museum (Landesmuseum für Vorgeschichte) presents a changing programme of special exhibitions on Central European archaeology and the results of archaeological conservation work in Saxony(opening hours: daily 10am–6pm).

Regional prehistory museum
⊙

The ethnography museum (Staatliches Museum für Völkerkunde) grew out of the royal zoological and anthropological museum founded in 1875. The ethnographic collection goes back ultimately to the »Indianische Cammer«, a cabinet of artefacts and rarities founded in 1560 by Augustus I. The holdings include items from almost all cultural regions in the world, though the main focus is on Oceania and the Malay archipelago. In addition there is an anthropological collection, which started with the skulls and plaster casts of death masks collected by Carl Gustav Carus (► Famous People). Hours: Tue–Sun 10am–6pm.

State ethnography museum
⊙

The state zoological museum (Museum für Tierkunde) originated as the electors' cabinet for art and natural sciences. In 1720 an independent natural history collection was founded in the Zwinger; from 1875 the collection was part of the zoological and anthropological museum. Now it belongs to the state natural history collections. The most notable sections are the collection of beetles and the examples of extinct species, such as the Californian condor, a giant guillemot with skeleton and egg, and the skeleton of a sea cow that became extinct 300 years ago; only a small number of these items can be seen, in special exhibitions (hours: Tue–Sun 10am–6pm). The museum's ornithological collection is housed in the Kavaliershaus in ►Moritzburg.

Zoological museum

⊙

The French garden of the Japanisches Palais was once adorned with sculptures and was one of the most beautiful Baroque gardens on the Elbe; it was designed by Pöppelmann. From the central axis of the palace a flight of steps led down to the gondola landing-stage. Today the famous »Canaletto view« of Dresden's Altstadt is visible from the garden.

★
Palais garden

In front of the palace garden is the monument to Elector Friedrich August III, who reigned from 1763 to 1824, from 1806 as the first king of Saxony, King Friedrich August I. It was Ernst Rietschel's first monument, made in 1843.

Monument to King Friedrich August I

★ Johanneum (Transport Museum)

G 7

Location: Augustusstrasse 1　　　　**Tram:** Altmarkt (nos. 1, 2, 4)
Plan of inner city: B 3

The Johanneum was rebuilt soon after 1945, the only building on Neumarkt to be reconstructed. Since 1952 it has been home to the Verkehrsmuseum (Transport Museum).

🕐
Opening hours:
Tue–Sun
10am–5pm

The Johanneum was originally built in Renaissance style under Elector Christian I in 1586–91, probably to plans by Giovanni Maria Nosseni, in order to house stables. In the centuries that followed, the building largely forfeited its Renaissance character, especially because of its two-phase conversion (1722–29, 1744–46) to a picture gallery for the royal art collections by Georg Maximilian von Fürstenhoff and Johann Christoph Knöffel. This use as picture gallery from 1722 until the opening of the Sempergalerie in 1855 necessitated an extra floor and the row of large windows in what is now the main front. The double flight of steps dates back to 1729. The two side portals were retained from the original building. From 1872 to 1876 Karl Moritz Haenel converted the building in neo-Renaissance style into the »Johanneum«, after King Johann, and seat of the historical museum. After 1945 the Johanneum was the only building on ►Neumarkt to be reconstructed; since 1952 it has been open to visitors as a transport museum.

Türkenbrunnen　　The »Turks' Fountain« has been located in front of the Johanneum since 1866; it was originally put up on ►Neumarkt to commemorate peace after the Thirty Years' War.
In 1683, after Elector Johann Georg III returned triumphant from the war against the Turks, the goddess of peace, Irene, who crowned the fountain, was replaced by Conrad Max Süssner's figure of Victory.

Transport Museum

Railways ►　　The transport museum is one of the most visited museums in Dresden; its central focus is the history of technology in the GDR. An outstanding feature is the historic rail collection, which provides an overview from 1835 to the present day. The earliest of the original steam engines on display is *Muldenthal*, built in 1861, now the third-oldest engine in Germany. Further interesting items are the first experimental three-phase electric engine in the world, constructed in 1899, and regional transport vehicles such as a horse-drawn wagon of 1890 from the Great Berlin Horse Railway, and Saxony's oldest surviving tram cars.

The motor vehicle section has veteran cars and exemplars of East German and Saxon automobile history, including the first viable Daimler truck and a five-seater Böhmerland-Langtourenmobil of 1927.

◄ Motor vehicles

The air travel section ranges from hot air balloons to modern intercontinental passenger planes. The prize exhibits are the original of Hans Grade's famous monoplane and a replica of the 1894 Lilienthal glider.

◄ Air travel

In the navigation section there are numerous model ships, and information about chain-hauling navigation on the Elbe (opening hours: Tue–Sun 10am–5pm).

◄ Navigation

⊕

✶ Kreuzkirche

G 7

Location: east side of Altmarkt   **Tram:** Altmarkt (nos. 1, 2, 4)
Plan of inner city: C 3

The Kreuzkirche is the city's main Protestant church and for centuries has been home to a world-famous choir, the Kreuzchor.

The present church had three predecessors on this site and is the only historic building on ► Altmarkt. Constructed c1200 as Romanesque basilica, a Kreuzkapelle (Chapel of the Cross) was added in 1319 in order to preserve a fragment of the Cross of Christ donated almost 100 years earlier, in 1234. From this time on the church was always referred to as »Kreuzkirche«. It had an eventful history: the second Kreuzkirche, built in 1449, burnt down in 1491; during the Reformation the third Kreuzkirche became Dresden's main parish church. Canaletto often painted the church, but it was destroyed by Prussian bombardment in 1760. The building of the fourth Kreuzkirche was completed in 1792 by Johann Georg Schmid and Christian Friedrich Exner. The 94m/308ft tower was designed by Gottlob August Hölzer, and in simplified form it matches the tower of the ► Hofkirche. After it was destroyed by

A concert by the Kreuzchor is always an experience.

fire in 1897, Rudolf Schilling and Julius Gräbner rebuilt the church in neo-Baroque style. The Kreuzkirche was not spared in February 1945; the church and many of its furnishings were consumed by the flames. The bells, however, the second-largest peal in Germany after that in Cologne Cathedral, survived the fire unscathed. The church was re-dedicated in 1955, and liturgical services resumed with vespers and concerts performed by the Kreuzchor, but rebuilding work was not completed until 1982. The exterior of the present church is as Schmid and Exner designed it, with a unified structuring of pilasters and entablature on the late Baroque-Classical façade, and a semi-circular choir taking up the whole width of the church to the east.

Interior ► After the fire of 1897 the inside of the church was entirely reshaped by Schilling and Gräbner in neo-Baroque style with marked art nouveau influence. The interior of 1900 was reconstructed in roughcast by 1982 in very simplified form. The altar made in 1572 by Hans Walther II for the third Kreuzkirche has been in the church of St Johannis in Bad Schandau (► Sächsische Schweiz) since 1927. In the autumn of 1989 the Kreuzkirche was the assembly point and forum of the public movement for sweeping changes in society (hours: April–Sept, daily 10am–6pm; Oct–March, daily 10am–4pm; in Advent, 10am–8pm; guided tours Fri 10am–noon).

Tower ► From the tower there is a glorious panoramic view of the city, and far into the Elbe valley.

Kreuzchor The boys' grammar school, the Kreuzschule, was founded c1300 in the vicinity of the chapel of the Holy Cross. Here boys were trained as choirboys and altar boys: the beginning of the famous Kreuzchor. Today the choir has 80 members, and is accompanied for big concerts by the Dresden Philharmonic. The Kreuzchor sings vespers on some Saturdays, from January until Easter at 5pm, and from Easter to December at 6pm (tel. 496 58 07).

✸
Kreuzchor
vespers ►

Kunstakademie (High School for the Arts)

G 7

Location: Brühlsche Terrasse	**Tram:** Synagoge (nos. 3, 7); Pirnaischer Platz (nos. 1, 2, 3, 4, 7, 12)
Plan of inner city: B 3	

The Saxon Kunstakademie (High School for the Arts) was established in 1764 as the successor of one of the first fine arts training institutions in Germany, founded in 1680 and since 1705 known as the Sächsische Malerakademie (Saxon Painters' Academy).

In 1950 the Kunstakademie merged with the Kunstgewerbeakademie (Arts and Crafts Academy), which had existed since 1875, to form the Hochschule für Bildende Künste. In the 18th century the teach-

The Kunstakadamie, a temple to art on the Brühlsche Terrasse, was founded in 1894.

ers included Bernardo Bellotto (**Canaletto**). Famous artists who taught at the Kunstakademie during the next two centuries were the painters Adrian Ludwig Richter, Anton Graff, Robert Sterl, Oskar Kokoschka, Otto Dix, Hans Grundig, Joseph Hegenbarth, sculptor Ernst Rietschel and architects Gottfried Semper, Heinrich Tessenow and Wilhelm Kreis.

The academy building, now the seat of the Hochschule für Bildende Künste (High School for the Arts), was designed by Konstantin Lipsius and built from 1891 to 1894 on the ▶ Brühlsche Terrasse. The glass cupola, scorned when it was built and now referred to as »lemon squeezer«, has been crowned since 1894 by Robert Henze's symbolic figure of Fama, the goddess of renown, who looks out over Dresden.

Academy building

The **Kunsthalle**, an exhibition space for temporary exhibitions (including contemporary art), opened in the building in late 2005.

✳ Loschwitz (city district)

E / F 10–13

Location: upstream, east of city centre
Elbe boat: Landing-stage Dresden-Blasewitz

Tram: Schillerplatz (nos. 6, 12), then bus (no. 84) to Körnerplatz

Loschwitz is, all things considered, perhaps the prettiest district of Dresden. It stretches along the slopes above the Elbe.

From Blaues Wunder to Weisser Hirsch

There is no need to come here for Baroque architecture or works of art: in Loschwitz, take the cable car or funicular up the hill to admire the grand ▶ Weisser Hirsch villas and look down on the bridge known as the Blaues Wunder. Until the end of the 19th century the Elbe slopes were used as vineyards; Loschwitz was also a favoured residential area for the well-to-do, with its charming location and open countryside. An infestation with phylloxera during the last third of the 19th century put an end to the vineyards and Loschwitz developed entirely into a high-class residential area. Where Loschwitz borders on the Neustadt district, there is an ideal view across the Elbe to the Altstadt – for the time being: there are plans for a four-lane bridge for cars, even though the Elbe valley has been declared a World Heritage site by UNESCO.

Körner house

Körnerweg runs west from Körnerplatz. The friends of poet Christian Gottfried Körner, including Mozart, Goethe, Kleist, Novalis, the Humboldt brothers and the Schlegel brothers, met in the summer residence of Körner's parents' at no. 6 from 1785. The Körner frieze has been put back in place.

Schiller garden house ⊕

Schiller-Körner fountain ▶

The garden house of the Körner winery, a little vintners' hut, is in the parallel Schillerstrasse (no. 19; opening hours: May–Sept Sat, Sun 11am–5pm). Here Friedrich Schiller stayed as a guest of the Körners while completing *Don Carlos* in the years 1785 to 1787. Oskar Rassau made a memorial fountain in 1912–13. It is set into the winery wall

View from Weisser Hirsch of the cable car, Loschwitz, the Blaues Wunder bridge and Dresden's Elbe valley landscape

opposite Schiller's garden house and shows two farewell scenes: Friedrich Schiller leaves the Körner family after his second visit of 1801 (on the left); Theodor Körner bids farewell to his family in 1813 and goes to fight in the war against Napoleon, in which he lost his life (on the right).

Returning to Körnerplatz, go a little way up Grundstrasse to the former mill named Rote Amsel, a half-timbered building with a tower supported by atlas figures. Here the painter Eduard Leonhardi had his studio from 1880. In addition to his work there are temporary exhibitions of contemporary art here (hours: Tue–Fri 2pm–6pm; Sat, Sun 10am–6pm).

Leonhardi Museum

On the north side of Körnerplatz is the lower station of one of the oldest mountain railways in Europe, the funicular of 1895. In 4.5 minutes it covers a distance of 547m/600yd and ascends 99m/325ft to the district of ►Weisser Hirsch, where it is worth taking a stroll among the high-class villas. By the upper station is the Luisenhof restaurant, where there is a fantastic view of the Elbe valley and Dresden from the veranda (funicular hours: Mon–Fri 6am–8pm; Sat, Sun 8am–8pm).

✱ Funicular

An alternative is the cable car: a little to the east of Körnerplatz is the cable car station. It was built in 1898–1900, which makes it the oldest of its kind in the world. Driven by an electric motor and pulled by rope, it makes the 274m/300yd journey to the viewing platform on the Loschwitz heights, with an altitude difference of 84m/275ft, in 2.5 minutes (cable car hours: daily 10am–5.30pm).

✱ Cable car

Near the cable car lower station, on Pillnitzer Landstrasse, lies the Loschwitz church, built by George Bähr and Johann Christian Fehre in 1705–08. This octagonal Baroque hall church with a mansard roof and roof spire was burnt out in 1945; restoration work was completed in 1993. Its great treasure is a splendid Renaissance altar by Maria Giovanni Nosseni, which came from the demolished Sophienkirche on Postplatz (hours: usually, 8am–5pm).

Loschwitz church

Back at Körnerplatz, then down Friedrich-Wieck-Strasse towards the bank of the Elbe, there are still a few Loschwitz village houses, where arts and crafts are sold direct from the workshop. At the top there is also a striking pavilion-style classical memorial to Joseph Hermann, commonly referred to as the Senfbüchse (mustard pot). The Loschwitz sculptor Joseph Hermann designed it in 1869 and had it erected at his own expense in memory of his father, who saved the lives of two boatmen who had fallen into the stormy Elbe. Diagonally across the road is no. 10, where Friedrich Wieck lived until his death in 1873. He was a music teacher, father of pianist Clara Wieck and father-in-law of Robert Schumann. Further down the road is

Friedrich-Wieck-Strasse

◄ Joseph Hermann Memorial

◄ Friedrich Wieck Haus

Fährgut ► the Fährgut (ferry farm; no. 45), a half-timbered house of 1697 that was used to house a wine-press until 1839, and was then a farm occupied by the ferryman and his family until 1862. Next door, on Uferweg, is the 17th-century ferry house with hipped and mansard roof, one of the oldest half-timbered houses in Loschwitz. Don't miss the opportunity for rest and refreshment in the Körnergarten, right by the Elbe beneath the ►Blaues Wunder!

Joseph Hegenbarth archive | The Joseph Hegenbarth archive at Calberlastrasse 2, which branches off from Pillnitzer Landstrasse in the direction of Pillnitz, is dedicated to the work of painter and graphic artist Joseph Hegenbarth, who died in 1962. An outstanding book illustrator, he interpreted fairytales and sagas in pen and brush drawings and water-colours (hours: Thu 10am–noon, 2pm–4pm; Tue by appointment, tel. 268 33 35).

✶ ✶ Meissen

Excursion

| **Location:** 26km/16mi northwest of Dresden | **S-Bahn:** S 1 to Meissen |
| | **Elbe boat:** Landing-stage Meissen |

Meissen – a name that immediately brings to mind fine and, above all, expensive porcelain. Production of this »white gold« since 1710 has made the name of the town famous all over the world. Yet historically Meissen is also the »cradle of Saxony« with a history stretching back more than 1000 years.

History | In the course of subjugating the Slavs Heinrich I founded the castle of »Misni« c929. In 968 Meissen became an episcopal seat and developed into a strategic stronghold. The first settlement below the castle dates from the late 10th century; around 1000 it already had a market charter. The hereditary title of margrave of Meissen passed to the Wettin dynasty in 1125; in 1150 Meissen is recorded as a town. A short time later a planned settlement and the Gothic cathedral were built (1260–1410), as were the bishop's palace and the Albrechtsburg on the hill. After Saxony was divided and the court moved to Dresden, and the bishopric was dissolved at the Reformation, Meissen lost its political significance. In the Thirty Years' War Meissen was conquered by the Swedes and severely damaged by a

? DID YOU KNOW …?

■ … what »Meissner Fummel« means? It is a delicate pastry, hollow inside, which served more than one purpose: it is said the Augustus the Strong insisted that the carters who transported Meissen porcelain also took the pastries with them – but not so that they could eat it. If the Fummel was intact at the end of the journey, so was the porcelain!

Meissen *Plan*

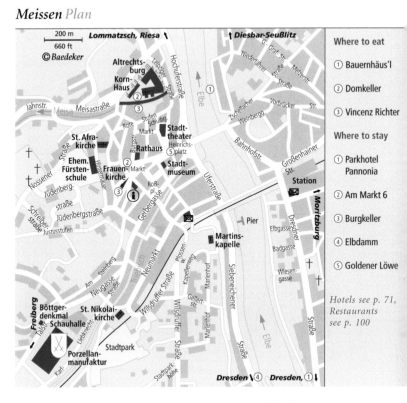

Hotels see p. 71,
Restaurants
see p. 100

◄ Guided tours

fearful conflagration. One-and-a-half hour walks round the historic old town are held in April and May daily at 1pm, from June to October at 1pm and 5.30pm (meeting point: tourist information office, Markt 3).

Castle Hill

Most visitors to Meissen are first drawn to Albrechtsburg castle, and the cathedral and canons' lodgings on the hill. Starting from the marketplace pass along Burgstrasse, where there are handsome Baroque and Renaissance houses on either side. At no. 27 is the oldest working pewter foundry in Germany, built in 1605; it has a small museum with workshop tours and foundry demonstrations. From the square, where Café Zieger is known for its »**Meissner Fummel**« (pastries), the Red Steps begin, which lead up past the Jahnaischer Friedhof (cemetery) to the castle bridge of 1228 and the cathedral square. In the middle castle gate there is a museum containing a Ludwig Richter exhibition (opening hours: daily 10am–5pm).

Ascent

Albrechtsburg *Plan*

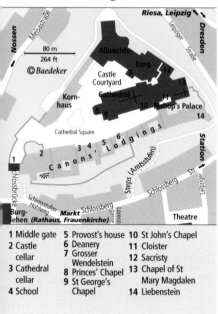

1 Middle gate
2 Castle cellar
3 Cathedral cellar
4 School
5 Provost's house
6 Deanery
7 Grosser Wendelstein
8 Princes' Chapel
9 St George's Chapel
10 St John's Chapel
11 Cloister
12 Sacristy
13 Chapel of St Mary Magdalen
14 Liebenstein

The castle hill became the actual nucleus of present-day Saxony when the German conquerors established the first fortifications in 929. The present Albrechtsburg Meissen, which was given its name in 1676 by Elector Johann Georg II in honour of Albrecht the Stout-Hearted, was chiefly built by the important late-medieval master builder **Arnold of Westphalia**, from 1471 to 1500, and extended c1520 by Jakob Heilmann of Schweinfurt. Although it is one of the most beautiful secular Gothic buildings in Germany, it also anticipates Renaissance elements. Its outstanding features are the large stone spiral staircase, in its time a unique technical achievement, and the very varied, richly decorated vaulting, as well as the reliefs on the first-floor balustrade panel made by Christoph Walther I in 1524, which are among a number of very well preserved early Renais-

✸ **Albrechtsburg**

sance works in Saxony. The painting of most of the rooms, however, was undertaken c1870 according to historicist notions; it illustrates the history of the castle and scenes from the life of Duke Albrecht.

🕑 On the second floor there is a display of medieval sculpture (hours: March–Oct, daily 10am–6pm; Nov–Feb, daily 10am–5pm; but closed in Jan).

✸✸ **Cathedral**

Meissen's Gothic cathedral, dedicated to St John the Evangelist and St Donatus, dominates the town silhouette. Building began c1260; it was extended in several phases up to 1410. In 1413 the west front with its twin towers collapsed after being struck by lightning, and was initially not rebuilt. In 1425 Friedrich the Quarrelsome, one of the most powerful Saxon princes, had a burial chapel added here, so that the west portal of 1400 became an inner portal. Between 1470 and 1477 Arnold of Westphalia added a third floor, and not until 1903–08 was the cathedral given its present 81m/266ft-tall spires, designed by Carl Schäfer.

Interior ▶

The sculptures dating from about 1260 are remarkable: portrayals of the founder, Emperor Otto I, with his consort Adelheid, St John the Evangelist and St Donatus in the choir, and St John the Baptist, Mary with Child and Stephen the Deacon in St John's Chapel, are from the workshop of Naumburg Cathedral. In the mid-16th century **Lu-**

cas Cranach the Elder's studio produced the painting on the lay altar, and in 1534 the master himself painted the triptych for St George's Chapel, in which Duke Georg and his wife Barbara are buried. Johann Joachim Kaendler made the crucifix and candelabra of Meissen porcelain in 1760 (hours: April–Oct, daily 9am–6pm; Nov–March, daily 10am–4pm; guided tours: every hour from 10am; organ music: May–Oct Mon–Sat 12 noon; concerts: Sat 6pm).

The west side of the cathedral square is taken up by the Kornhaus, which was built at the same time as the castle. On the side facing the town, on the extreme left, is the bishop's palace of 1597; its round tower is called Liebenstein and is a distinctive feature of the castle silhouette. Next to it are the canons' lodgings (Domherrenhöfe). House no. 5 is the former deanery (1526), no. 7 the provost's house (1497–1503). The porcelain modeller Johann Joachim Kaendler lived at house no. 8; no. 10 was the home of painter Georg Friedrich Kersting. No. 9 is the Domkeller, Meissen's oldest inn. It has chestnut trees on the terrace and a good view of the town.

Cathedral square

◄ Kornhaus and canons' lodgings

View from Blocksberg vineyards across the Elbe to the magnificent castle hill

Unterstadt (lower town)

★
Market

Rathaus ▶

The market square is dominated by the Rathaus (town hall) and Frauenkirche. Arnold of Westphalia was involved in the building of the late Gothic Rathaus of 1472 with its blind gables. Above the portal the »Meissen Jew's head« is displayed; the Jew's head adorned the helmets of the margraves of Meissen.

Among the handsome Renaissance and neo-Renaissance burgher houses the most notable are the Hirschhaus (Stag House, Markt 2), the partially Romanesque Bennohaus (Markt 9), named after its owner Bishop Benno, with niche seating in the portal and Gothic vault, and the Marktapotheke, opened in 1560, which was provided with a bow front in 1717.

Frauenkirche

The mid-15th century Frauenkirche has its chancel towards the market square, while the tower, which was newly erected in 1549 after a fire, is beyond the market. This late Gothic hall church is unusual in that the nave is wider than it is long. The most valuable church furnishing is the Gothic altar of 1480. In the tower hangs the world's first porcelain peal of bells, made in 1929 by Emil Paul Börner; the bells are rung daily at 6.30am, 8.30am, 11.30am, 2.30pm, 5.30pm and 8.30pm. Daily at 5.30pm Luther's »Ein' feste Burg ist unser Gott« is played. From the tower platform there is a view of the town and the river (hours: May–Oct daily 10am–noon, 1pm–5pm).

Historic Vincenz Richter wine tavern

Brauhaus and Tuchmachertor ▶

Next to the Frauenkirche there is an inviting 16th-century half-timbered house, the historic Vincenz Richter wine tavern.

Opposite the Frauenkirche tower lies the Bahrmann Brauhaus (brewery) of 1569 with its splendid Renaissance gable. The Tuchmachertor (Clothmakers' Gate) beside it is also a Renaissance monument, if only a replica.

Heinrichsplatz

Town museum ▶

🕐

Northeast of the main marketplace, the small marketplace leads to Heinrichsplatz, where there is a memorial to the founder of the town, Heinrich I. Behind it is the church, completed in its present form in 1457, of the Franciscan monastery founded in 1258. Today the church houses the Meissen Stadtmuseum (town museum) (hours: daily 10am–5pm).

Thürmer pianoforte museum

🕐

At Martinstr. no. 12 is the pianoforte factory founded in 1834 by Ferdinand Thürmer, open to visitors as pianoforte museum since 1999 (hours: Tue–Fri 3pm–6pm; Sat, Sun 10am–1pm, 3pm–6pm).

Afraberg (St Afra's Hill)

St Afra's church

Steps known as the Superintendenturstufen or Frauenstufen lead up St Afra's Hill from behind the Frauenkirche. St Afra's Church was built in about 1300 and has an altar carved by Valentin Otte in 1660;

the pulpit, also by him, is decorated with a depiction of Jonas and the whale (hours: June–Sept, Tue–Sun 10am–1pm, 2pm–5pm).

Adjacent to its back wall is the former Fürstenschule of St Afra, which moved into the Augustinian monastery at its dissolution in 1543. It was the state school of Saxony and prepared students for the university. Among its best-known students were Lessing, Gellert and Rabener.

Former Fürstenschule (royal school)

✱ ✱ Porcelain Manufacture

In 1863, when the premises of 1710 in the Albrechtsburg became too small, the world-famous factory moved to its present location at Talstrasse no. 9, approx. 10 minutes' walk from the marketplace. From April to October a city bus runs every half-hour between the Albrechtsburg, cathedral, town centre and porcelain factory. Opposite the factory a bust commemorates J.F. Böttger who, after substantial preparatory work by Ehrenfried Walther von Tschirnhaus, was a key figure in developing the first hard-paste porcelain in Europe (hours: May–Oct daily 9am–6pm; Nov–April daily 9am–5pm; guided tours available).

In the **showroom** on the first floor is a display of everything that has made **Meissen porcelain** famous throughout the world. Many of the 3,000 exhibits, some of which are changed every year, are still used as models for moulders and painters – the famous monkey orchestra, for example. In the course of its almost 300-year history the factory has produced more than 20,000 models. The tableware for twelve which changes every year is especially splendid. On the second floor is porcelain of all epochs, from a thimble to the 3.5m/11.5ft dinner

Meissen porcelain: famous, timeless, made by hand

Meissen porcelain for the tsa Lisotta, Catherine II's favourite d

Johann Joachim Kaendler made amusing and imaginative figures.

GET IT RIGHT FOR ME, BÖTTGER...

»... or I'll hang you!« With these words August the Strong rebuked his alchemist, Böttger, who had taken too long to produce any tangible result that could help to refill the state coffers. He realized that Böttger was never going to succeed in making gold – even if his experiments years before with the apothecary Zorn in Berlin had mysteriously yielded small golden-gleaming lumps – but porcelain, the white gold of the Chinese and Japanese, had to be possible!

Marco Polo had already brought back reports of exquisite receptacles, but not until the 17th century did the Dutch East India Company import vases, tiny cups and plates from the Far East, which came to be greatly coveted in the houses of noblemen and wealthy merchants. People tried to produce porcelain themselves, but initially such attempts led only to substitutes, such as **Delft faience** ware. The scientist Walther von Tschirnhaus was the first to produce a porcelain-like substance, in 1696. At about the

same time **Böttger** caught the attention of the Prussian king Friedrich I with his gold experiments, but fled to Wittenberg. Here fate caught up with him in the shape of Augustus the Strong, who transported him to the casemates of Dresden and made him work with **von Tschirnhaus**. In 1708 Böttger witnessed Tschirnhaus's success, after many attempts, in finding the earths which could indeed be shaped and fired as porcelain. Scarcely had Tschirnhaus discovered the secret when he died, but in 1709 the recipe was found in his will. Just one week later, on **28 March 1709**, Böttger was able to present his ruler with the first little jug made of white European porcelain.

Meissen Porcelain

On 6 June 1710 the »Royal Meissen Porcelain Factory of the Kingdom of Poland and Electorate of Saxony« was founded at Albrechtsburg castle in Meissen. Thirty staff were employed to experiment with porcelain recipes, firing, colour mixes and décor, until their product was deemed perfect. Böttger did not live to see the final triumph; he died in 1719. It was others who secured the subsequent reputation of Meissen porcelain: the painter **Johann Gregorius Höroldt**, who tried out innumerable colour combinations, and introduced painting in the »Indies style« and flower painting; and the sculptor **Johann Joachim Kaendler**, a modelling genius whose hands made fantasy figures in porcelain. One of his creations was the Swan Service for Count Brühl, the largest dinner service ever made, with more than 1000 pieces. If Böttger was the one who started it off, and Höroldt and Kaendler were the creative spirits, the production inspector Steinbrück had another brilliant idea

Barrel-type vessel of Meissen porcelain, painted by Johann Gregorius Höroldt (1725/30)

in 1722: he suggested using the swords of the Saxon electors as a trademark, for »in that way other nations would see that the wares bearing this sign were made in the principality of Saxony«, and today the cobalt blue **swords** beneath the glaze are still the Meissen trademark, one of the oldest in the world. They replaced earlier marks such as AR (Augustus Rex) and K.P.M. (Royal Porcelain Manufacture). The most sought-after motifs in the decoration of porcelain for everyday use still derive from the first decades of manufacture. First came painting in the »Indies« style with the famous red and green dragons, following the fashion of the time, and brightly coloured Chinese butterflies and landscapes of Höroldt's chinoiserie; then from 1735 there was native European flower painting (dried flowers, German flowers, and flower painting with insects, butter-

flies and gold decoration), extended to include **classical** Marcolini flower painting, Meissen rose and Biedermeier garden flowers; then hunting scenes and finally the Meissen classics of vine leaves and the ever-popular »onion pattern«. The decoration beneath the glaze was developed from the earliest stages of manufacture under the influence of East Asian models, where, however, the originals were not onions but pomegranates, peonies and bamboos. As far as figurative designs are concerned, Rococo genre scenes are still very much in demand. Not until art nouveau came on the scene was there anything of comparable originality. No other European porcelain can so justly claim first place for beauty and value as can the white gold of Meissen.

table decoration of 1749 for Augustus III. There have been regular concerts, since the year 2000, on the world's first organ with Meissen porcelain pipes. Today the Meissen factory employs 1230 persons and produces more than 150,000 items.

In the Meissen open workshop it is possible to trace the passage of a porcelain figure through the hands of turners, moulders, modellers (who join together the parts of the figures) and painters.
Meissen porcelain is on sale in the new visitor centre and shop, opened in 2005, and in the museum shop.

Open workshop

Not far from the factory, on Neumarkt, is the Nikolaikirche (Church of St Nicholas). It was founded in 1100 and extended in the 13th century, and has some remains of early Gothic wall-painting (hours: May–Sept Tue–Thu, Sun 2pm–4pm).

Nikolaikirche

⏲

Around Meissen

Steamers take passengers down the Elbe to Diesbar-Seusslitz, a romantic two-part village on either side of the river. It has the northernmost vineyards in Saxony, and some beautiful wine taverns.
The Baroque Schloss Seusslitz was built in 1726 and designed by George Bähr. The grounds include the Heinrichsburg and the former monastery church re-modelled in Baroque style, with four sandstone sculptures by Balthasar Permoser. The Schloss has no regular opening hours, but can be viewed by arrangement with the owners – ring the bell.

Diesbar-Seusslitz

◀ Baroque Schloss Seusslitz

Militärhistorisches Museum

Location: Olbrichtplatz 2   **Tram:** Stauffenbergallee (nos. 7, 8)

The leading military museum in Germany is scheduled to open in 2010 following conversion of the main arsenal building of 1873–76 on the site of the former barracks in Albertstadt district.

In the post-war years the Nordhalle was used for dances and other events, but in 1972 it became a military museum again, and was the GDR army museum until 1990. Today it is the Bundeswehr's most important museum, presenting military history from 1500 to the present day. One section juxtaposes the two German armies of the post-war years, the Bundeswehr of the Federal Republic and the Nationale Volksarmee of the GDR. Among the exhibits are the giant cannon named Faule Magd (Lazy Maid) of 1450, the first German submarine, *Brandtaucher*, of 1850/1851 and, outside, large-scale pieces of equipment of both post-war German armies.

⏲
Opening hours:
Tue–Sun
9am–5pm

Since summer 2004 work has been in progress on a further building designed by Daniel Libeskind. This will cut through the existing building and house the newly designed permanent exhibition, together with a new presentation entitled *Being a Soldier* past and present, with critique of pros and cons. While alterations are going on in the main museum, the collection is on view in temporary accommodation on the museum site.

Moritzburg

Excursion

Location: 14km/9mi northwest of Dresden

S-Bahn: S 1 to Radebeul-Ost, then by Lössnitzdackel train

A trip to the beautiful landscape of lakes and ponds at Moritzburg is a must for visitors to Dresden.

✳ ✳ Schloss Moritzburg, Hunting Lodge and Pleasure Palace

Architectural history

The electoral palace of Moritzburg glows in the Saxon Baroque colours: yellow ochre and white. It was designed to be a magnificent total work of art, incorporating landscape as well as buildings.

Duke Moritz, subsequently Elector Moritz, had a first hunting lodge built in the years 1542–46 to designs by Hans von Dehn-Rothfelser, and it was gradually extended to become a palace. Wolf Caspar von Klengel built the palace chapel in 1661–72, and Zacharias Longuelune, Matthäus Daniel Pöppelmann and Jean de Bodt created the palace in its present form, almost square and harmoniously symmetrical, under Augustus the Strong (1723–36). Sculptors of renown, such as Balthasar Permoser, Johann Christian Kirchner and Benjamin Thomae created the blithe Baroque balustrade statues for the approach and the terrace. The pond was made in 1730. Interior decoration was the responsibility of Raymond Leplat, with support from

! *Baedeker* TIP

Lössnitzdackel train

The steam train known as the »Lössnitz Dachshund«, built in 1884, is the oldest narrow-gauge train in Saxony. Not only steam fans enjoy the journey from from Radebeul Ost, past Schloss Hoflössnitz and through the Lössnitz valley to Moritzburg, where the Moritzburger Teiche are a nature reserve of lakes.

Blowing the horn for a merry hunt

court painter Louis de Silvestre and tapestry designer Pierre Mercier (hours: Nov–March, Tue–Sun 10am–4pm; Jan–Feb only at weekend; ⏲ April–Oct daily 10am–5.30pm).

The rooms are used as Baroque museum to display exquisite art and craft work from the 16th to the 18th century: porcelain, furniture, stoves, paintings and wall-coverings – Moritzburg is adorned with the largest collection of Baroque leather wall-coverings in the world. On the ground floor is Augustus the Strong's elaborate and exclusive Federzimmer (Feather Room), purchased in 1723 from feather decorator Nicolas Le Normand. The showpiece eiderdown is stuffed with hen, duck, jay, peacock and pheasant feathers. Tales from the Moritzburg kitchen are told in the ground-floor display on 17th and 18th-century kitchens.

Baroque museum

★
◀ Feather Room

◀ Kitchen tales

The first room on the first floor is the Steinsaal (Stone Hall), with antlers of elk, reindeer and red deer on the walls. Beyond it is the Monströsensaal (Hall of Monstrosities), with leather wall-coverings painted by court painter Lorenzo Rossi showing scenes with Diana, goddess of the hunt: Schloss Moritzburg regards itself as her residence. The room owes its name to the red deer trophies, which are without exception malformed and »monstrous«; above the main door hangs the Moritzburg 66-end set of antlers, the most desirable

★
◀ Leather wall-coverings in the Hall of Monstrosities

Moritzburg Plan

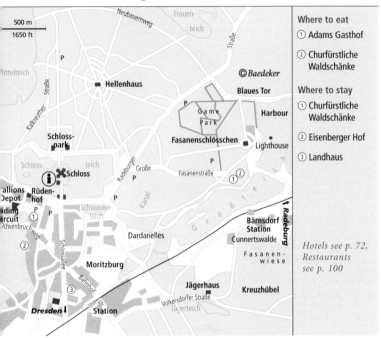

Where to eat
① Adams Gasthof
② Churfürstliche Waldschänke

Where to stay
① Churfürstliche Waldschänke
② Eisenberger Hof
③ Landhaus

Hotels see p. 72, Restaurants see p. 100

trophy in European hunting history. The two rooms on the left, the Augustzimmer, are draped with punched Moorish leather wall-coverings; on the right is the route through the Kurfürstenzimmer (Electors' Room) and Kupferzimmer (Copper Room) to the palace chapel. Johann Finck's painting of *The Ascension* adorns the chapel ceiling.

Palace chapel ► The marble *Man of Sorrows* is by Balthasar Permoser; an earlier version is in the Hofkirche in Dresden. The next rooms contain portraits of Augustus the Strong's mistresses by Louis de Silvestre and his workshop. Through the billiard room, also with hunt motif leather wall-hangings and one of the oldest billiard tables in Germany dating from c1700, are the Moritz Gallery with portraits of Saxon electors and the lacquered furniture room, which has not only East Asian lacquered furniture but also one of 18 so-called dragoon vases which Augustus purchased from

! **Baedeker TIP**

Explore the palace

Phone (03 52 07) 8 73 18 for guided tours of the palace – not only the rooms and park, but also to the »Secret Corners of the Palace«, the »Moritzburg Hunting Trophies« or to learn about the history and restoration of the leather wall-hangings, including a visit to the restorers' workshop.

the Prussian king for the price of 600 Saxon dragoons. Then comes the largest room, the dining hall, which was used for banquets, theatrical performances and concerts. The Baroque dining table is decorated in festive court style with a 66-piece porcelain dinner service. The dining hall, too, is adorned with antlers, including an uneven 24-end specimen, with 298.25 points, considered the mightiest red deer antler in the world. Also noteworthy is the so-called Willkom, the right branch of a 36-ender: new guests were welcomed by being allowed to drink wine out of the chalice-shaped crown of the discarded branch.

Further Sights

Through the Moritzburg woodland park a path leads eastwards to the Fasanenschlösschen (Little Pheasant Palace), regarded as one of the most important late Baroque buildings for the Saxon court. Friedrich August II had this exquisite little palace built and ornamented with chinoiserie in the years 1769–82 by Johann Daniel Schade and Johann Gottlieb Hauptmann, and used it as summer residence. Restoration work has returned it to its former glory with a display of Rococo interiors (tours April–Oct daily 10am–5pm, May–Sept until 6pm).

★ **Woodland park**

◄ Fasanen-schlösschen

From the Fasanenschlösschen there is a view of the little harbour on the lake. The lighthouse and landing-stage were also built by Friedrich August II so that he could embark here for boating parties. On the west bank were the so-called Dardanelles, artificial artillery bastions and ruins which gave a realistic framework to the »sea battles« put on for the entertainment of Saxon court society.

◄ Harbour

In the more northerly of the two cavaliers' houses the zoological museum (► Japanisches Palais) has its **Teich und Tier (pond and animal)** exhibition, drawing on the Moritzburg environs (opening hours: April–Oct; Wed, Thu, Sat, Sun 10am–5pm). The 40ha/100-acre **game enclosure** northwest of the Fasanenschlösschen dates back to the days of Augustus the Strong, who had his deer park here (hours: Jan–Feb, Sat, Sun 9am–4pm; March–Oct, daily 10am–6pm; Nov–Dec daily 9am–4pm; feeding time daily from 2.30pm).

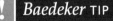

! **Baedeker** TIP

Coach trips

Have Schloss Moritzburg, the game enclosure and the lake scenery pass before your eyes and enjoy the view of them from a distance to the sound of horses' hooves. Bookings in Moritzburg: Bernd Haase, Fasanerie 6, tel. (03 52 07) 8 21 53; Rainer Herrmann, Berstr. 9, tel. (03 52 07) 8 17 09; or tourist information, tel. (03 52 07) 85 40.

The countryside around Moritzburg is a conservation area. There are six bathing sites on the 25 pools, some of them with camping facilities.

★ **Moritzburg Pools**

Moritzburg fishing ► A special event is the annual fishing of the palace pond, which takes place on the last weekend in October with demonstration angling, sales of fish and lively market bustle.

Käthe Kollwitz Memorial In the summer of 1944 the 77-year-old graphic artist, sculptor and painter Käthe Kollwitz moved from Berlin to the Moritzburg Rüdenhof (Meissner Str. 7) at the invitation of Prince Ernst Heinrich of Saxony. She had been persecuted by the Nazis and forbidden to practise her profession. Already ill, and no longer able to work, she died on 22 April 1945. Her apartment has been made into a place of memorial with a collection of graphics, photographs, diary entries and letters, and special exhibitions (hours: April–Oct, daily 11am–5pm; Nov–March, Tue–Sun noon–4pm).

Stallion depot
✷
Moritzburg stallion parades ► In 1828 the stallion depot was established at Moritzburg; today half-bloods are bred at the Saxon stud in Moritzburg for equestrian sports. Horse-lovers can experience the opening of the stallion parades (Hengstparaden) in September with a horseback fanfare procession and beat of the drum; historic equestrian events are re-created, and there are displays of daredevil Cossack riding.

✷ Neue Synagoge

G 8

Location: east of Brühlsche Terrasse
Plan of inner city: B 4

Tram: Synagoge (nos. 3, 7)

The synagogue designed by Gottfried Semper and inaugurated in 1840 was burnt down by the Nazis in the pogrom night of 9–10 November 1938 and then demolished. Exactly 50 years after the fire, on 9 November 1998, the foundation stone of a new building was laid on the same site.

History Of the original synagogue; only the Star of David was saved. Close to its site, opposite the ► Albertinum and below the ► Brühlsche Terrasse, is a commemorative stela in the form of a seven-branched candelabra.

Guided tours only:
Mon–Thu
bookings with
Hatikva e. V.
Tue 10am–noon,
1pm–3pm
Tel. 656 88 25

The Neue Synagoge building complex was designed by architects Wandel, Hoefer, Lorch and Hirsch of Saarbrücken and dedicated on 9 November 2001. Opposite the homogeneous, massive sandstone cube of the sacred building, on the other side of the inner courtyard with its plane trees and ground plan of the old synagogue marked out in shards of glass, is the glazed north façade of the community centre with café (opening hours: Tue–Fri 10am–6pm, Sat 11am–5pm, Sun 11am–4pm). The available site made it impossible to have the synagogue face east, as is customary. A startlingly simple archi-

The massive unadorned exterior of the synagogue houses a grandly designed inner space.

tectural solution to this problem was found: the building turns within itself like a screw, with every layer of masonry a little off the axis of the previous layer. At the entrance the Star of David saved in 1938 shines forth. Contrasting with the unadorned exterior, the grandly designed interior unites the congregation of 450 members beneath a gleaming gold metal tent. In 2001 the complex won the prize awarded by the German architectural critics, and in 2002 a World Architecture Award.

Neumarkt

Location: Altstadt centre
Plan of inner city: B 3

Tram: Altmarkt (nos. 1, 2, 4)

The buildings of Neumarkt, which appear at their most impressive on Canaletto's paintings, represented an outstanding achievement of European architecture. In 1945 all of them were severely damaged or completely destroyed.

Neumarkt, the »new market«, occupies the site of an old Slav settlement. This area was not enclosed within the city walls until the 16th century. Many of the residential buildings with their ornamented   **History**

New design ▶ Baroque and Rococo façades were architectural gems. Today Neumarkt is dominated by the rebuilt ▶Frauenkirche. The new plan envisages eight so-called quarters (Quartiere), which are intended to recall the old splendour. The Frauenkirche Quarter with a reconstruction of the Weigel Haus (Neumarkt 2) and Quarter II with the houses Zum Schwan and Zur Glocke are already complete.

Luther Memorial The memorial to Martin Luther, erected in front of the ▶ Frauenkirche in 1885, is by Ernst Rietschel and his pupil Adolf von Donndorf.

Statue of King Friedrich August II The 1867 statue of King Friedrich August II by Ernst Julius Hähnel shows the king holding the constitution which the revolution of 1830–31 compelled him to recognize. This memorial was returned to its original location in 2006.

Cosel Palais The splendid Cosel Palais was destroyed in the Second World War; it was rebuilt in 1998–2000 adjacent to the Frauenkirche as a café, true to its original design and incorporating some remains of the medieval city fortifications. Johann Christoph Knöffel built it in 1744–46. It takes its name from a former resident, Count Friedrich August von Cosel, son of Augustus the Strong and Countess Cosel. The Prussians destroyed it in 1760.

★ Neustadt (city district)

D – F 7 – 9

Location: north of the Elbe	**Tram:** Innere Neustadt: Neustädter Markt (nos. 4, 8, 9); Äussere Neustadt: Albertplatz (nos. 3, 6, 7, 8, 11)

It is easy to answer the question of where to go in Dresden for a shopping trip followed by a night out: the inner Neustadt for shopping, the outer Neustadt for pubs and restaurants.

History The settlement on the right bank of the Elbe, Altendresden, which was known by this name from 1370, received its town charter in 1403 and was united with Dresden in 1549. After burning down in 1685 it was rebuilt to plans by Wolf Caspar von Klengel as a unified Baroque city district within the old ring of fortifications and known as »Neue Stadt bey Dresden«, subsequently »Neustadt« (New Town). This part is today's Innere Neustadt, which suffered rather less severe bomb damage in February 1945 than did the Altstadt. While the ▶ Jägerhof, the Blockhouse on Neustadt market place, the ▶ Japanisches Palais and ▶Dreikönigskirche were rebuilt after the war, the numerous neglected burgher houses on Königstrasse and Rähnitzgasse were restored only in recent years.

Innere Neustadt

From the Altstadt the Augustusbrücke (bridge) leads to the
Neustadt, where the **Blockhaus**
stands on the left hand side of the
bridge. It is the only surviving
building by Zacharias Longuelune.
Begun in 1732, it was completed in
1755 as the Neustadt guardhouse
and after conversion in 1890 served
as the seat of the Ministry of War.
The market place **Neustädter
Markt** has been dominated since
1736 by the **Goldener Reiter**
(Golden Cavalier), designed by
Jean Joseph Vinache and cast in
iron and copper by gunsmith Ludwig Wiedemann. It represents Augustus the Strong in the guise of
Roman emperor with scale armour
on a leaping horse. The urban ensemble of buildings on Neustädter
Markt was almost entirely destroyed in February 1945. Nothing
remains of the one-time village
square of Altendresden; and only
the Nymphenbrunnen (Nymph
Fountains) at the Neustädter Rathaus by Benjamin Thomae date
back to 1742.

Pottery market beneath the Golden Cavalier

Hauptstrasse leads off the market place and follows the course of the **Hauptstrasse**
old Neustädter Hauptstrasse. It is worth making a detour on the left-
hand side, opposite the Jägerhof, into the Obergraben with its art
and craft passages. In the courtyards of several Baroque residences
between the Kügelgenhaus and Dreikönigskirche there are also delightful antique shops.

The Kügelgenhaus (Hauptstrasse 13) is one of three classical houses   ◀ Museum
and was the home of painter and Akademie professor Gerhard von   der Dresdner
Kügelgen, where leading figures of the German Romantic movement   Frühromantik
used to meet. Today, as the Museum der Dresdner Frühromantik
(Museum of Early Romantic Art in Dresden), it is devoted to the
period between classical and Romantic art, between Biedermeier and
the industrial revolution (hours: Wed–Sun 10am–6pm). Beyond it   ⏱
are three Baroque houses; Benjamin Thomae and Gottfried Knöffler
lived in the middle one (no. 17). In the rear courtyard of no. 19 the   ◀ Societätstheater
Societätstheater, founded in 1750, has been performing since re-

building was completed in 1999; it is the oldest citizens' theatre in Germany. Thanks to its small Baroque garden and the café L'Art de Vie it is more than just a cultural attraction.

Neustädter Markthalle
Opposite the ► Dreikönigskirche church is the market hall of 1899 with the Schwarzmarktcafé (Black Market Café) on the ground floor. Behind the church is the beautifully restored Königstrasse, an elegant shopping street and the heart of the Art Quarter and Baroque district. Commercial art galleries have opened in the many of the buildings. At Rähnitzgasse 8 is the Städtische Galerie für Gegenwartskunst (City Gallery of Contemporary Art, hours: Tue–Fri 2pm–7pm; Sat, Sun, noon–8pm). Nieritzstrasse is an unusual example of a street built in the Biedermeier period. Looking towards the Elbe from Königstrasse, there is a view of the ►Japanisches Palais.

Art Quarter ►

✱
Double fountain
At the end of Königstrasse is the busy Albertplatz with two attractive fountains, *Stille Wasser* (Still Waters) and *Stürmische Wogen* (Stormy Waves) at its centre, made by Robert Diez in 1894.

Erich Kästner Museum
Villa Augustin (Antonstrasse 1) houses the interactive Erich Kästner museum (► Famous People), which engages with the author in a truly original manner (opening hours: Sun–Tue 10am–6pm, Wed until 8pm).

Äussere Neustadt

Trendy quarter
Between Königsbrücker Strasse, Bautzner Strasse and Bischofsweg lies the Outer New Town, the largest surviving quarter from the late 19th century in Germany. This is where Dresden hangs out, with trendy cafés and corner shops.

Stroll and shop
Trams no. 7 and 8 stop at Bischofsweg, where Café Europa offers refreshment to shoppers. On the right-hand side of Bischofsweg, Kalahari sells African wine, books and craftwork.

Again to the right is Alaunstrasse, the quarter's main artery; diagonally opposite is Café 100, where good wine is served in the vaulted cellar.

The Kunsthofpassage, between Alaunstrasse 70 and Görlitzer Strasse, is a good place to while away the time in cafés and shops; it combines old rear-courtyard architecture with modern flair. Crafts-

! *Baedeker* TIP

The art of calligraphy

At Blue Child in Kunsthofpassage you can not only buy gifts and beautiful stationery, but also take courses in calligraphy and bookbinding, learn to make collages and photo albums, or create boxes with paper you have made yourself (information and bookings: tel. 802 90 68).

people sell direct from their workshops and in the café-tavern El Perro Borracho tasty Spanish food is served. Trendy sportswear is sold in Harlem at Alaunstrasse 53. At the intersection of Alaunstrasse and Louisenstrasse is the popular Scheunecafé (Alaunstr. 36-40), with good, affordable Indian food, and a beer garden in summer. Nearby in Katharinenstrasse are the most handsome **art nouveau houses** in Äussere Neustadt. Go left from the intersection along Louisenstrasse, and browse to the accompaniment of good music in Büchers Best (no. 37). Pass the cult

! *Baedeker* TIP

Cafè with art and garden

Raskolnikoff at Böhmische Strasse 3 is a classic Dresden café-pub with a special atmosphere, an art gallery and reasonably priced accommodation. Customers walk over sand to hand-made chairs. In the garden, beneath a spreading vine, a fountain splashes by an old sandstone wall – a place that no-one wants to leave (tel. 804 57 06).

café Planwirtschaft (no. 20) and a bit further on is Blue Velvet (no. 3), which has a store of trendy gear, and sip aromatic tea across the road in the Dresdner Teekontor (tea company). There are wonderful cafés, too, in the part of Louisenstrasse beyond Alaunstrasse: relax at no. 66 in Combo, decorated in chic 1970s style. Just opposite is the tempting Blumenau, with a menu that changes every day and smart coffee concoctions; in hot weather the glass front is open. The attractions in Rothenburger Strasse are Depot 4 (no. 14), and Bassta (no. 43), and shoes at Calzadór (no. 32).

The Kunsthofpassage: a colourful oasis for bric-a-brac, art and bars

Pfund's Molkerei: an unusually decorated dairy

Martin-Luther-Kirche

Old Jewish Cemetery ▶

★

Pfund's Molkerei ▶

The neo-Romanesque Martin Luther church, built in the years 1883–87, stands on Martin-Luther-Platz. On Pulsnitzer Strasse is the Old Jewish Cemetery (▶ Cemeteries). Further along Pulsnitzer Strasse on the left, past Café Neustadt, is Pfund's Molkerei (dairy) (no. 79). According to the Guinness *Book of Records* the »most beautiful dairy in the world«, it was decorated by Villeroy & Boch in 1892 with majolica tiles in art nouveau style.

Kraszewski House

The Kraszewski House at Nordstrasse 28 commemorates the Polish author Józef Ignacy Kraszewski. He is said to be world literature's most productive author with regard to the number of his published books (more than 600). His novels are concerned with relations between Saxony and Poland in Augustus the Strong's time (*Countess Cosel*, *Brühl* and *The Seven Years' War*). In the house where he lived visitors can learn something of his life and work, and of the intellectual, cultural and political relations between Dresden and Poland in the 19th century (hours: Wed–Sun 10am–6pm).

Garnisonskirche

For the Garnisonskirche (Garrison Church) take a tram (nos. 7, 8) to Stauffenbergallee. William Lossow and Hermann Viehweger built the Garrison Church between 1896 and 1900; the tower is a linking architectural feature between the former Lutheran and Catholic parts of the church, which was used for services by both denominations.

Pillnitz (city district)

Location: on the eastern outskirts of the city

Tram: Kleinschachwitz (no. 1), then Elbe ferry; Schillerplatz (nos. 6, 12), then bus (no. 83) to Pillnitzer Platz

Pillnitz, too, is a must for visitors to the Dresden area. It has a wonderful moated palace and a park by the Elbe where a 200-year-old camellia grows.

✦ ✦ Schloss Pillnitz

Schloss Pillnitz and its park on the southeast outskirts of the city are enchanting in their light, elegant serenity. The old Renaissance palace and its extensive gardens were a gift from Augustus the Strong to his mistress, **Countess Cosel** (► Famous People). After he rejected her, Augustus had the palace turned into a summer residence.

In Pillnitz the rulers of Austria, Saxony and Prussia met with French émigrés to discuss what to do in the face of the spread of the French Revolution.

The palace buildings consist essentially of three parts: the Wasserpalais (Water Palace), Bergpalais (Hill Palace) and Neues Palais (New

Architectural history

Pillnitz Plan

Gothic Ruin — Vineyard Church

100 m
330 ft

N

Hausbergstraße

Lohmener Straße

Dresdner Straße

Chinesischer Pavillon

Chin. Teich

Chinesischer Garten

Bergweg

Schulweg

← Orangerie

Palmenhaus

Flora

Floragarten (Holländischer Garten)

Pillnitzer Platz

Englischer Pavillon

Orangerie

Camellia House

Conifers

Schlossgarten

Lohmener Straße

Pirna →

Teich

• **Head of Juno**

Englischer Garten

P

Bergpalais

Car ferry to Kleinschachwitz

Gondola

Paille-Maille Course

Hornbeam Groves

Lustgarten

Schloss-kapelle

Restaurant ①

Dampfschiffstraße

Neues Palais

Flieder-hof ①

Wasserpalais

• **Lion's Head**

Elbe Steps

Pier

Dresden

© Baedeker ← Elbe **Pillnitz Island Nature Reserve**

Where to eat
① Parkcafé Pillnitz

Where to stay
① Schloss Hotel Dresden-Pillnitz

Hotels see p. 72, Restaurants see p. 100

Palace) with its kitchen and chapel wings on the site of the Renaissance edifice.

The Wasserpalais and Bergpalais were designed to mirror one another in the layout planned by Matthäus Daniel Pöppelmann and Zacharias Longuelune in 1720–23 . The two-storey wings, designed by Johann Daniel Schade and Christian Traugott Weinling to link the two palaces, were added in 1789–92. After the old palace was destroyed by fire, the new palace was built between 1818 and 1826 to plans by Christian Friedrich Schuricht. The banqueting hall in this part was painted by Carl Christian von Vogelstein (1788–1868).

Chinese style

Augustus the Strong's partiality for the exotic and the first wave of chinoiserie account for the style of the palace. Chinese motifs such as concave curved roofs and the forms of Wasserpalais and Bergpalais were fantasy elements of late Saxon Baroque.

The harmony of architecture and landscape and the charm of the façade painting are particularly in evidence on the Elbe side of the Wasserpalais. Stone steps with sphinxes on either side lead down to the river, with a landing-stage for the elector's gondolas. A 19th-century replica of one of these gondolas – the **Rote Tritonengondel** (red Triton gondola) – is on display in one of the park's hornbeam groves.

Arts and Crafts Museum

In the Wasserpalais the Kunstgewerbemuseum (Arts and Crafts Museum) founded in 1876 displays 17th and 18th-century furniture, glass, majolica, leather, tapestry and metalwork.

The Bergpalais shows a colourful mix ranging from traditional arts and crafts, such as pewter and stoneware and faience work, to contemporary design.

20th-century art is well represented, with products by the Deutscher Werkbund, an extensive collection of furniture by Richard Riemerschmid from the Deutsche Werkstätten Hellerau (▶ Baedeker Special p.46). Also on display are interiors from Schloss Pillnitz: the Watteau Room of c1850 and the late 18th-century Weinling Room (hours: May–Oct, Bergpalais: Tue–Sun; Wasserpalais: Wed–Mon 10am–6pm).

❗ Baedeker TIP

Time for China tea

Visitors to the Chinese Pavilion can have a relaxing hour listening to music and trying various kinds of China tea. The event includes information on the history of the pavilion and the history of tea. Ginger, nuts and dried apricots are a light snack to go with the tea (information and bookings: tel. 261 32 60).

For eating in style: the Wasserpalais dining-room

✳ ✳ Schloss Pillnitz Park

The pleasure garden between Bergpalais and Wasserpalais was not laid out until the 19th century. To the west of it is the Baroque part of the garden from Countess Cosel's time, with labyrinthine hornbeam groves. In the first square beyond the Bergpalais is the aforementioned gondola. At the end of the hornbeams is the start of the 500m/550yd paille-maille course; this popular 18th-century game resembles golf. The starting-point is marked by a large sandstone vase of 1785 by Thaddeus Wiskotchill. The course was originally intended to be a chestnut avenue reaching all the way to Dresden.

From 1778 the park was extended under Augustus III in the English landscape style, with narrow paths, groups of trees and shrubs here and there, a pond with a little island and a large bronze head of the goddess Juno on it, and the **English Pavilion** by Weinling. In the English garden is another rarity: an 8.5m/28ft-tall Japanese camellia, its crown spreading to a width of 12m/40ft. The Pillnitz camellia is the only survivor of four brought to Europe in 1770, and is the oldest in Europe. Planted on this spot in 1801, it has up to 35,000 red carmine blossoms from late February to April, and attracts many visitors. In winter it is protected by a greenhouse that is rolled away in summer.

Pleasure garden

◀ Hornbeam groves

◀ Paille-maille course

English garden

✳

◀ Camellia

The English garden and the conifer grove laid out in 1874 with conifers from all over the world, together with the Chinese and Dutch garden, form the »**scientific side of the garden**«. The orangery of 1730 designed by **Zacharias Longuelune** and the palm house are open to visitors (hours: Schlosspark 5am until dusk; guided tours: Easter, weekends in April, May–Oct daily 11am–2pm on the hour).

> ! **Baedeker** TIP
>
> **Camellia – certified genuine**
> Once a year, in the first half of March, cuttings from the famous Pillnitz camellia, and other types of camellia which flower in the same lovely carmine red, are sold on the palace grounds. Potters from Saxony sell attractive pots to match the plants (information: tel. 261 32 60).

From the **landing stage** southeast of the Schloss the return trip by paddle-steamer past picturesque vineyards and the three Elbschlösser and under the Blaues Wunder bridge to Dresden's Terrassenufer takes just under one-and-a-half hours (timetable, tel. 866 09 40).

Pillnitz Village

Pillnitz vineyard church

Not far from Pillnitz park, among the vineyards, is the vineyard church built by **Matthäus Daniel Pöppelmann** in 1723–25. The altar with a relief of the Last Supper, an excellent work by Johann Georg Kretzschmar (1648), was moved here from the chapel of the Dresden Renaissance palace when it was abandoned in the Baroque era. The steps and portal sculpture are by Benjamin Thomae.

Around Pillnitz

Richard Wagner Museum, Graupa

Opening hours:
Tue–Sun
9am–4pm

Not far from Pillnitz to the southeast is Graupa, a place associated with Richard Wagner; take bus no. 83. Wagner (▶Famous People), from 1843 master of court music in Dresden, retreated to a Graupa farmstead in the summer of 1846 in order to work on *Lohengrin*.
In 1907 a small commemorative site called Lohengrin-Haus was set up at Richard-Wagner-Strasse 6, which reopened in 2007 after alterations with an exhibition on Wagner's life and work as a musical dramatist during his Dresden years. There are plans to convert Graupa hunting lodge to Saxony's Richard Wagner Centre in the coming years.

Lochmühlen-weg

By the museum is the start of Lochmühlenweg, along which Wagner liked to walk. Right at the beginning is a monumental bronze head of Wagner by Richard Guhr (1873–1956). It is a one-and-a-half hour walk through the Wesenitz valley and romantic Liebethaler valley to the Lochmühle, once a water mill and, for a long time now, an inn with garden. Richard Wagner liked this place and here, too, he worked on *Lohengrin*.

The charming Schloss Pillnitz was once the summer residence of the Wettin dynasty.

In 1933 a bronze monument to Wagner, Saxony's first, was erected close to the Lochmühle, to commemorate the 50th anniversary of the musician's death. Following the contemporary view of Wagner, Richard Guhr – who paid for the monument out of his own pocket – portrayed the composer as guardian of the grail, in mystical ecstasy.

◄ Richard Wagner Monument

Prager Strasse

Location: Altstadt centre
Plan of inner city: C / D 2 / 3

Tram: Hauptbahnhof (nos. 3, 7, 8, 10); Prager Strasse (nos. 3, 8, 11, 12)

Prager Strasse links the Hauptbahnhof (main rail station) and ►Altmarkt. It was constructed after 1851, and until 1945 was the most elegant shopping street in Dresden with its shops, cafés and restaurants. There are plans for it to regain this status.

Promenade

It was enlarged into the main pedestrian axis in the years 1965–74, 700m/765yd long and 80m/87yd wide, which made it into one of the most profligate urban spaces in the GDR. The monotony is not relieved by any road intersections, but only by water basins with fountains placed across the street. In 1970–72 the projecting auditorium of the Rundkino (round cinema) was built, where there is now a puppet theatre. Directly adjoining it is the deconstructivist Kristall-

◀ Crystal Palace

palast of the UFA cinema by the Coop Himmelb(l)au group of architects, an outstanding work of modern architecture. The concrete nucleus with auditoriums is surrounded by a prismatic foyer of steel and glass.

Wiener Platz

Wiener Platz in front of the Hauptbahnhof was one large building site after 1994. Of the commercial buildings planned the most interesting is one reminiscent of the Dresden Kugelhaus (▶ Gläserne

Hauptbahnhof ▶

Manufaktur). The special feature of the main rail station built by Ernst Giese and Paul Weidner in 1892–95, with regard to both transport technology and architecture, is that it is simultaneously a terminus and through-transit station. The round extension on the north side was once the separate entrance for platform 16, reserved for the king. Conversion work by the British architect Sir Norman Foster, completed in 2006, replaced the old glass roof over the iron structure by a translucent Teflon covering.

Radebeul

Excursion

Location: downstream northwest, adjoining Dresden	**S-Bahn:** S 1 to Radebeul-Ost **Tram:** Schildenstr./Karl-May-Museum (no. 4)

Radebeul is inseparably linked with the name of Karl May, a writer of adventure stories who lived from 1896 until his death in 1912 in a house he called Villa Shatterhand.

Picturesque wine-growing town on the Elbe

Radebeul is bordered to the south by the Elbe, and to the north by the Lössnitz vineyards which go back to the 13th century. The disastrous phylloxera infestation of 1885–86 halted wine growing, and the slopes, soon known as »Saxony's Nice«, became favoured sites for spa and health-promoting ventures and villas for Dresden officials and manufacturers.

✶ Karl May Museum

The villa and log cabin Villa Bärenfett now house the Karl May Museum, one of the most impressive American Indian museums. The display in Villa Shatterhand focuses on the life and work of Karl

Meet real heroes with smoking guns at the Karl May Festival

May, whose books have often been filmed and are highly popular in Germany to this day. The exhibits include early Karl May editions, personal documents and furniture such as his desk, his library and other memorabilia.

In Villa Bärenfett there is a collection of Indian cultural items acquired on North American tours by Patty Frank, a famous performance artist at the time, and co-founder of the Karl May Museum.

Since 1992 Radebeul has organized an annual **Karl May Festival** on the weekend after Ascension Day, to which fans come from all over the world. It is a real experience to see Indian guests from Canada and the USA demonstrate traditional dances and ceremonies. Visitors can join the dance, accompanied by country and folk music, go out for a ride on mustangs and donkeys, or even join in a Wild West horse show. At the Wild West market lasso handlers and cowboys display their skills at stunt shows.

⊕
Opening hours:
March–Oct
Tue–Sun
9am–6pm
Nov–Feb
until 4pm

✱ Lössnitz

The Lössnitz vineyards are among the furthest northeast in Europe, and are situated in the warmest part of the Elbe valley; they extend via ►Meissen to Diesbar-Seusslitz and produce quality wines, especially from Müller-Thurgau, Traminer and Ruländer grapes.

Wine-growing

On the corner of Bennostrasse and Augustusweg is a grand mansion from a former winery named Sorgenfrei (carefree). Banker Freiherr von Gregory had the house built in 1783 amidst a park in French style. Today it is a top-class little restaurant with hotel.

Walk
◄ Haus Sorgenfrei

! **Baedeker** TIP

Wine festival

The autumn wine festival is held in Radebeul in September. It begins with the triumphal entrance of Bacchus in Radebeul-Altkötzschenbroda, the appearance of the wine queen, and the opening of the first barrel of Federweisser, a cloudy part-fermented wine. There are three days of entertainment and music, a firework display and a grand finale with a parade on the village green (www.weinfest-radebeul.de).

Benno-schlösschen ▶ The Bennoschlösschen at Bennostrasse 35 was built in 1600 and is the oldest surviving vineyard mansion in Lössnitz.

Schloss Hoflössnitz ▶ Continuing to the right along Hoflössnitzstrasse, note Schloss Hoflössnitz on the left (Knohllweg 37). It was commissioned by Elector Johann Georg I and built by Ezechiel Eckhardt in 1649. It has rich interior decoration, including 80 **ceiling paintings** by Albert Eyckhout depicting Brazilian birds. Inside the building the

Viticulture museum ▶ Weinbaumuseum, which is devoted to the history of viticulture, offers wine-tasting in its snuggery, and chamber music concerts (hours: Tue–Fri 2pm–6pm; Sat, Sun 10am–6pm; chamber music concerts: April–Oct on the last Sunday in the month, 5pm).

Spitzhaus ▶ A little to the north of Schloss Hoflössnitz, picturesque vineyard steps (Spitzhaustreppe) lead up to the Spitzhaus, built in 1622. Now an inn, it offers a charming view of Radebeul, Dresden and the whole spread of the Elbe valley.

Schloss Wackerbarth To reach Schloss Wackerbarth, go down Hoflössnitzstrasse, turn right along Augustusweg, and then take tram no. 4 from Weisses Ross to Radebeul-West. A ten-minute walk straight along Moritzburger Strasse and Am Bornberge leads to the two-storey palace which Count August Christoph von Wackerbarth, general supervisor of Saxon building works, commissioned Johann Christoph Knöffel to build on his vineyards in 1728–29. 19th-century alterations in historicist style on Renaissance models greatly changed the appearance of the Baroque building. The Schloss Wackerbarth vineyard is open for sales of fine wine and sparkling wine (»sekt«) daily

! **Baedeker** TIP

Wine in the palace

The state winery (Sächsisches Staatsweingut) in Schloss Wackerbarth offers tours with tastings: the wine tour to the vineyards and cellars, the sekt tour with explanations of how sparkling wine is made, a tour of the palace and its gardens, and a vineyard walk. Dates and prices: www.schloss-wackerbarth.de and tel. 03 51-89 75-50.

Schloss Wackerbarth hosts the state winery.

from 9.30am to 8pm, and the restaurant is excellent (Mon–Fri noon–10pm; Sat, Sun 10am–10pm). The terraced garden leads up on the main axis of the Schloss to a small octagonal pavilion, the Belvedere.

Rathaus

G 7

Location: Dr-Külz-Ring 19
Plan of inner city: C 3

Tram: Altmarkt (nos. 1, 2, 4); Pirnaischer Platz (nos. 1, 2, 3, 4, 7, 12)

One of the largest building projects in Dresden at the beginning of the 20th century was the new Rathaus (town hall). The enormous sandstone-clad building encloses five inner courtyards and mixes several styles of architecture, yet it still creates a harmonious overall impression.

Built between 1904 and 1910 to plans by Karl Roth and Edmund Bräter, it replaced the old Rathaus on ►Altmarkt.

The dominant element of the Rathaus and a landmark on the skyline of Dresden is the tower, precisely 100m/328ft high, surpassed only by the rebuiltHausmannturm at the ► Schloss, which is just 1m/3ft higher. The Rathaus tower rises from the east court and bears rich figural ornamentation displaying allegorized virtues. At the top is the Herculean figure of the 4.9m/16ft »golden Rathaus man«, crowned

★
Tower

by bastion and extending his right hand8 in blessing over the city, while his left hand empties a cornucopia. Richard Guhr created the Rathaus man, who survived the firestorm of 1945 unscathed and became a Dresden emblem.

The **stairwell** in the tower basement, painted in **art nouveau** style, is accessible only when special events are taking place.

Opening hours:
April–Oct
10am–6pm
(last ascent 5.30pm)

In front of the entrance to the Ratskeller is a sculpture of 1910 by Georg Wrba, *Bacchus Riding on an Ass*. In front of the east façade of the Rathaus a 1968 monument by Walther Reinhold commemorates the Trümmerfrauen, the women who cleared away rubble at the end of the war.

Sculptures

Sächsische Landesbibliothek

J 7

Location: Zellescher Weg 18   **Bus:** Staats- und Universitätsbibliothek (no. 61); Försterplatz (nos. 72, 76)

The Sächsische Landesbibliothek (Saxon State Library) originated as the private library of Elector Augustus of Saxony, established in 1556; it became one of the largest private libraries in Germany with the purchase of the libraries of Count Brühl and Count Bünau in the 18th century, and was open to the public as early as 1788.

Located from 1786 in the ► Japanisches Palais, it lost this home in 1945, and at the same time 400,000 books were either destroyed or seized. In 1996 the Sächsische Landesbibliothek and the library of the Dresden Technical University merged to become the Sächsische Landesbibliothek, Staats- und Universitätsbibliothek Dresden (SLUB). Since 2002 the libraries have been united under one roof: the SLUB building is a further addition to Dresden's stock of worthwhile modern architecture. Architects Ortner and Ortner arranged the library space partly above and partly below ground. In the lower part are book stores and the glass-roofed reading room; the travertine-clad »stone cubes« above ground house the administrative areas (dates and bookings for architectural tours, tel. 467 71 14).

The Buchmuseum (Book Museum) is not only a survey of 1150 years of the history of books, but also contains such treasures as a sketchbook of Albrecht Dürer, the score of Bach's Mass in B Minor and the best-preserved one of just three extant Maya manuscripts (hours: Mon–Fri 9am–4pm; tours Wed 4pm, Sat 2pm; special exhibition Mon–Sat 9am–4pm).

Book Museum

← *The dome in the town hall stairwell with its art nouveau decoration by Otto Gussmann*

Sächsischer Landtag (Saxon parliament building)

F 7

Location: Holländische Strasse 2
Plan of inner city: A 2

Tram: Theaterplatz (nos. 4, 8, 9)

The end of the GDR brought with it the re-establishment of the Free State of Saxony with Dresden as its capital, and a state parliament that needed a parliament building – a task to which there was no simple solution.

Parliament in modern dress
The historic parliament building, the Ständehaus on the ▶Brühlsche Terrasse,, was occupied by museums, so until 1994 the Saxon parliament met in the ▶Dreikönigskirche in Neustadt, which was temporarily adapted for the purpose. In the meantime, over the astonishingly short period of less than three years up to 1994, the first new parliament building in the former GDR was constructed at the end of the Elbe terraces, behind the Semper Opera. The Dresden-born architect **Peter Kulka** designed the L-shaped building, which has won international acclaim. The cool, clear and refreshingly simple architecture, transparent towards the Elbe and towards the city, fits without a break into the varied succession of buildings that stretches west from the Brühlsche Terrasse in the direction of the Marienbrücke (bridge) and represents a historic cultural axis. The parliamentarians meet in a round glass plenary hall which is separated from the foyer only by a screen-like curved wooden wall. An attraction for non-parliamentarians is the Chiaveri restaurant with a roof terrace overlooking the Elbe.

The regional parliament of Saxony in session

Erlweinspeicher
Behind the parliament building is the massive Erlweinspeicher warehouse; with its eleven storeys it is more than 40m/130ft high, and over 70m/230ft long. It was constructed in 1912 as one of the first self-supporting reinforced concrete buildings in Europe by Dresden chief architect **Hans Erlwein** (▶ Famous People). Its 20,000 sq m/ 215,000 sq ft of storage space have been filled over the years with raw tobacco for Dresden's cigarette industry, chemicals, raw materials for the baking industry, paper for newsprint production and much more – even schnapps for the Soviet army. It was already a

listed building in GDR times, and has now been converted into a
hotel for the congress centre behind it that opened in 2004. The as-
cending, ramp-like construction of the international congress centre
by architects Storch and Ehlers continues Dresden's moderate post-
modern phase, started by Kulka with the parliament building.

◄ International
congress centre

★ ★ Sächsische Schweiz (Saxon Switzerland)

Excursion

Location: approx. 35km/22mi upstream,
southeast of Dresden
Elbe river traffic: Landing-stages in
Pirna, Wehlen, Rathen, Königstein,
Bad Schandau

S-Bahn: S 1 to Pirna, Wehlen, Rathen,
Königstein, Bad Schandau

**Sächsische Schweiz (Saxon Switzerland) is the name given to a
highly popular area for hiking and climbing, the Saxon part of the
Elbe sandstone mountains that covers an area of 360 sq km/140 sq
mi and stretches as far as Bohemia.**

The »discovery« of the Sächsische Schweiz and its beautiful landscape
can be attributed in the main to two Swiss artists appointed to the

History

A golden autumn morning: Bastei bridge, and Lilienstein on the horizon

Dresden Kunstakademie in 1766: portrait painter Anton Graff and copper engraver Adrian Zingg began walking through the Elbsandsteingebirge (Elbe sandstone mountains) with their sketchbooks. They added »greetings from the Sächsische Schweiz« to their letters home, which aroused the curiosity of many of their artist friends. The name »Sächsische Schweiz« appeared in literature for the first time in about 1790 and was soon in general use, thanks to the German Romantic movement. Artists such as **Caspar David Friedrich** and Ludwig Richter wandered »back to nature« in Rousseau's sense along the so-called Painters' Path from Dresden via Pillnitz to Wehlen, Hohnstein and Bad Schandau. With his *Wanderer above a Sea of Mist* Friedrich created a well-nigh programmatic painting of Romantic enthusiasm for nature – inspired by the Sächsische Schweiz.

Tourists soon followed the artists and from the mid-19th century steamers and railway began to open up the area.

Today the Sächsische Schweiz is one of the most attractive tourist regions in Saxony; walkers find here the densest network of footpaths in Europe, extending over approx. 1200km/750mi.

Elbe sandstone mountains The Elbe sandstone mountains were formed by erosion: huge deposits of pure, block-shaped quartz sandstone measuring several hundred metres were thrown up from a Cretaceous sea; then the Elbe and its tributaries made deep cuts through it, creating bizarre and picturesque rock scenery.

In the course of time the present landscape arose amidst a 400m/1300ft-high mesa: the canyon-like Elbe valley and those of the short Elbe tributaries, farmed plateaus with their gravel and clay surface (100–120m above the Elbe valley), rocks like Lilienstein (415m/1360ft above sea level), Pfaffenstein (429m/1407ft above sea level), Königstein (361m/1184ft above sea level) and Grosser Zschirnstein (561m/1840ft above sea level) are remains of the once continuous blocks of sandstone with steep rock walls; and, towering aloft, cliffs such as the Bastei (305m/1000ft above sea level) and Schrammsteine (386–417m/1266–1368ft above sea level) are rock labyrinths with turrets and needles, gorges and flumes.

> ## ! Baedeker TIP
>
> ### The world's largest garden railway
>
> … operates in Kurort Rathen on 4.5km/3mi of track with 20 or 30 locomotives manufactured by the company LGB. It was constructed by a native of Dresden who was deported to the West after trying to flee the GDR in 1979, and since 2005 has been fulfilling his dream here. His track network near the ferry in Oberrathen even provides a first view of the Sächsische Schweiz, as the trains travel through replicas of the best-known rock formations and tourist destinations on a scale of 1:25 (Eisenbahnwelten Rathen; hours April–Oct daily 10am–6pm).

Nationalpark Sächsische Schweiz Shortly before the GDR joined the Federal Republic of Germany, on 12 September 1990, the Nationalpark Sächsische Schweiz was created. Since that time 93 sq km/34 sq mi of the Elbe sandstone mountains have been a conservation area. The national park consists of two geographically separate regions: the western part stretches from the town of Wehlen to Prossen and includes the Bastei; the eastern part stretches from the Schrammsteine to the German-Czech border. Information is available from the national park centre at ► Bad Schandau; guided tours with park rangers: tel. (03 50 22) 90 06 25).

✳ Pirna

✳
Gateway to Sächsische Schweiz

The old centre of the town of Pirna lies on the left bank of the Elbe. The name comes from the Sorbian language; »na pernem« means »on the hard stone« and refers to the sandstone which for centuries provided a good living for Pirna, and from which such famous buildings as the ► Frauenkirche in Dresden and the Brandenburger Tor in Berlin were made. The town's affluence allowed it to adorn itself with an impressive market place and streets of medieval, Renaissance and Baroque houses.

History

At the foot of the castle hill Frankish and Thuringian merchants established a settlement by the Elbe ford, first mentioned in 1233 in a

Pirna Plan

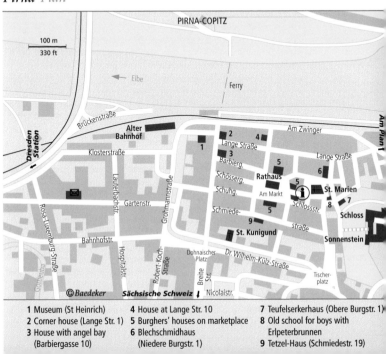

© Baedeker   **Sächsische Schweiz**

1 Museum (St Heinrich)
2 Corner house (Lange Str. 1)
3 House with angel bay (Barbiergasse 10)
4 House at Lange Str. 10
5 Burghers' houses on marketplace
6 Blechschmidhaus (Niedere Burgstr. 1)
7 Teufelserkerhaus (Obere Burgstr. 1)
8 Old school for boys with Erlpeterbrunnen
9 Tetzel-Haus (Schmiedestr. 19)

Meissen episcopal document, and designated a town in 1291. In the 14th century Pirna belonged to Bohemia and by 1639 it had developed into the most important town on the upper Elbe. In 1639, however, »Pirna's misery« began, when Swedish troops occupied the town; the Swedes came again in 1706, the Prussians in 1756 and the French in 1813.

Pirna prospered again in the industrial age after steam navigation began in 1837 and the railway arrived in 1848. Nazi domination brought with it the saddest chapter in the town's history: in the mental home and care home of Pirna-Sonnenstein more than 13,000 people were killed within the framework of the euthanasia programme. The end of the GDR turned out to be a blessing for the historic city centre, which was restored and renovated after the change. However, the »flood of the century« in 2002 affected the Sächsische Schweiz severely – large parts of the Elbe valley north of Pirna had to be evacuated. On 16 August the water level in Pirna's historic centre reached a height of three metres; today the damage has for the most part been made good.

✱
Marktplatz
Rathaus ▶

Pirna's picturesque centre is the market square painted by **Canaletto**, with the Rathaus (town hall) in the middle. It dates back to 1485, but was altered in 1555 by Wolf Blechschmidt and again after a fire in 1581, so that it has Gothic elements, such as the ground-floor doors, and Renaissance elements, such as the gable on the first floor. The tower was not added until 1718.

Burgher houses ▶

The market square is surrounded by remarkable burgher houses from different epochs. On the side closest to the Elbe, the town apothecary's shop Zum Löwen at no. 17–18 has an unusual portal with seat niches, and immediately next to it the former inn Weisser Schwan (no. 19), of which the house sign with date is still preserved. On the side closest to the Schloss the most striking house is the high-gabled one on the extreme right (no. 7; the tourist information office), which is first mentioned in a document of 1423. It is called the Canalettohaus because Canaletto immortalized it in one of his pictures of Pirna. On the south side of the market square two houses are worth noting: the merchant house (no. 9) with a late Gothic core, Baroque façade and mayor Volkamer's arms, and the town house at no. 12. The latter served from 1472 to 1686 as the iron exchange of Electoral Saxony, where iron ore was traded that had been mined in the eastern Erzgebirge and hammered and processed in foundries.

St Mary's church

Behind the Canalettohaus rise the church tower and roof of St Marien. In the main the church remains as it was built by Peter Ulrich of Pirna between 1502 and 1546. The interior is worth seeing for the reticulated vaulting in the nave and star vaulting in the aisles, ascribed to Jobst Dorndorf among others. Between 1544 and 1546 the vaulting was painted with motifs from Genesis and Exodus, and the

✱
Interior ▶

Christmas market on Pirna market place: Canaletto would have liked this view.

choir apse with pictures of the four Evangelists, whereby Luke and Mark have the features of Martin Luther and Philipp Melanchthon respectively. The ceiling paintings are among the few Protestant paintings of the 16th century to have escaped the destruction of the Thirty Years' War and 18th–19th century overpainting. The 10m/ 33ft-high Mannerist altar of Pirna sandstone was made by the brothers Schwencke in the early 17th century, and is a significant work of the late Renaissance. The base shows the Nativity, Last Supper and Crucifixion, the middle the Flood, and the top the Resurrection; at the sides are Elijah's ascent to heaven and Jacob's ladder. Goethe commended the font, which was probably made by Hans Walther II in 1561, for the lovely decoration round the base: 26 figures showing a day in the life of a child.

✱
◀ Altar

Opposite the northeast corner of St Marien is the 16th-century Blechschmidthaus, which has a striking portal with seat niches. As is shown by a portrait and stonemason's sign, this was the home of Wolf Blechschmidt, builder of the Rathaus. The first floor has a unique Renaissance beam ceiling.

Blechschmidt-haus

Teufelserker-Haus	It is not far from the southeast corner of St Marien to the 16th and 17th-century Teufelserker-Haus (Obere Burgstr. 1), which owes its name to the projecting bay adorned with a grimacing devil's face and a matching saying. Escobar on the ground floor serves Mediterranean cuisine and cocktails.
Erlpeterbrunnen ▶	Nearby next to the old boys' school is a fountain from 1583 named Erlpeterbrunnen with a rhyme encouraging the penniless to have a free drink there.
Tetzelhaus	At Schmiedestrasse no. 19 Johannes Tetzel, an adversary of Luther who preached indulgences, was born.
Lange Strasse 10	In this late Gothic burgher house Friedrich August II, son of Augustus the Strong, spent his first night in Saxony with his new bride Duchess Maria Josepha, the daughter of the Austrian emperor. The portal and splendidly painted wooden beam ceiling are wonderful architectural details.
St Heinrich monastery courtyard / Stadtmuseum ▶ ⏲	The chapter building of the former Dominican monastery of St Heinrich, built 1330–60 and dissolved in 1539, now houses the Stadtmuseum (town museum). On the first and second floors are exhibits relating to Pirna town history (opening hours: Tue–Sun 10am–5pm).
Schloss Sonnenstein	A steep ascent leads to Schloss Sonnenstein, of whose medieval origins little is left. The empty buildings belonged to the mental home and care home that were established in 1811 as one of the first institutions of this kind in Germany.
	A **memorial** recalls the Nazis' euthanasia programme that claimed the lives of more than 13,000 people at this place (opening hours: Mon–Thu 9am–3pm, Fri 9am–1pm; April–Oct every first Sat in the month 9am–3pm). On the hillside (Schlosshof 4) is a pleasant beer garden with a good view of the roofs of Pirna.

! Baedeker TIP

Artist's house

Paintings by the Dresden Impressionist Robert Sterl hang not only in the Galerie Neue Meister but also in the Robert-Sterl-Haus in Struppen-Naundorf, Robert-Sterl-Str. 30 (S-Bahn S 1 to Wehlen and a 30-minute walk). Views of the Sächsische Schweiz, portraits of musicians and landscapes inspired by his journey to Russia are on display (hour: May–Oct Thu–Sun 10am–5pm, tour on the last Sunday of the month at 3pm).

✶ Kurort Rathen

The small spa town of Rathen with its guesthouses, little hotels, eating-places and half-timbered houses is the tourist centre of the Sächsische Schweiz, situated at 115m/377ft above sea level at the foot of the Bastei. The castle of »Ratin«, mentioned in 1261, developed into a village of fishermen and boatmen. With the beginning of steamship navigation on the Elbe in 1836 and the opening of the Dresden–Schmilka railway in 1850, Rathen began to develop into a spa. It is divided into Oberrathen on the left bank of the Elbe and Niederrathen on the right bank, accessible via the Gierseil ferry. Rathen is a good base for hiking, especially up the Bastei and to the rock theatre.

Rathen's special attraction is the **Bastei** (305m/1000ft above sea level), a labyrinth of ravines above the Elbe near Niederrathen, where towering cliffs provide one of the most beautiful natural viewpoints in Europe. A travelogue of 1831 recommends the visitor to »put a few church towers one on top of another and then not feel giddy

Hikers cannot fail to love it!

when standing on the top«. The footpaths are marked and well secured. On the way to the viewpoint is the stone Basteibrücke (bridge); nearby is Neurathen's Felsenburg (rock castle).

A path leads from the Bastei down through the so-called Swedes' holes to the Amselgrund valley 160m/525ft below, with the Amselsee, an artificial lake made in 1934, and the Rathen Felsenbühne (rock theatre). The rock theatre was built in 1936. Its 2000 seats make it the largest **natural theatre** in Saxony, and one of the loveliest open-air stages anywhere. Towering cliff walls form the backdrop. The ensemble of the Landesbühnen Sachsen performs here from May to September. The Wehlgrund landscape impressed the painter Adrian Ludwig Richter and inspired the scene of the wolf ravine in Carl Maria von Weber's (▶ Famous People) *Freischütz*. This opera is always included in the Felsenbühne repertoire, which also

✶
Rathen Felsenbühne (rock theatre)

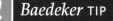

! *Baedeker* TIP

Boat trip on the Amselsee and Elbe
Pedaloes and rowing boats are for hire on the wooded lake called Amselsee, with a view of the rocks known as the Locomotive. Customers of the company Spasstours can paddle down the Elbe on the beautiful stretch from Bad Schandau (Mennickest. 29, Stadt Wehlen, tel. 03 50 24-7 10 84, www.elbe-erleben.de).

offers adaptations of world classics, operettas, children's theatre and Karl May dramatizations with trampling horses' hooves, wild shootouts and genuine cliff backdrop.

Königstein Town

From Königstein excursions are possible to Lilienstein on the opposite bank (by passenger ferry), to Pfaffenstein in the south and to

Excursions

From the Bastei there is an incomparable view of the Sächsische Schweiz.

notable sites of erosion such as the Barbarine. In the Bielatal valley running southwest, stark rock formations such as the bizarre pillars of Hercules are to be found.

✳ Königstein Fortress

🕐 Opening hours: April–Sept, daily 9am–8pm; Oct, daily 9am–6pm; Nov–March, daily 9am–5pm

Festung Königstein, one of Europe's most significant fortresses, dominates the Elbe valley from high above the town. A steep footpath goes straight up from the town, past the parish church; it is about one hour's walk and the path is marked with a blue bar or red dot. By car or bus the route goes east via the B 172, up to the fortress car park. From there it is still a good walk, or alternatively there is a tourist shuttle.

History The Bohemian Königsburg (royal castle), founded in 1200 and first documented in 1241, passed to the margraves of Meissen in 1459. In 1589 Elector Christian I began with extension work, which dragged on until the late 19th century. Militarily impregnable, the fortress has never been destroyed, and has therefore remained intact to the present day. Next to the main entrance is the **Georgenburg**, once Saxony's most feared state prison. The 152.5m/500ft-deep well was sunk from 1563 to 1569; the Garnisonhaus (old barracks), probably the earliest barracks in Germany, was built in 1589; the Altes Zeughaus (old arsenal) with cross vaulting in the ground floor hall was completed in 1594. The Kayserburg extension of the Georgenburg

Königstein Fortress Plan

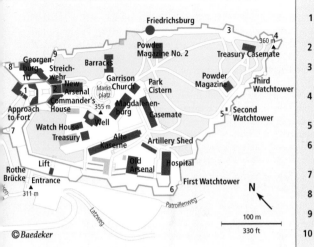

1 Entrance with ravelin and drawbridge

2 Gatehouse

3 Site of oak destroyed by lightning

4 East point of fortress (King's Nose)

5 Plague Casemate

6 South point of fortress (Zobel's Corner)

7 Horn with Seiger Tower

8 Georgenbastion

9 Tower of Hunger (Rösschen)

10 Descent from fortress

© Baedeker

was begun in 1359 and completed in 1619. The other buildings on the site include the Friedrichsburg (1589), the well house (1715 and 1736) for the aforementioned well, the Magdalenenburg (1622), the vat cellar (completed 1819), where the world's largest **wine vat** has a capacity of 250,000 litres, the new arsenal with Heldensaal (Hall of Heroes, 1631), the Georg battery (1679), the treasure store (1855), the garrison church (17th century) and finally the casemates (16th–18th centuries). The entire plateau is surrounded by a 1700m/ 1860yd-long fortress wall.

In times of crisis Königstein served as a refuge for the Dresden court, and also as a safe place for storing state treasures and art collections, as happened during the Seven Years' War. Yet the fortress was also the scene of court festivals, for which purpose Augustus the Strong had an enormous wine vat constructed by **Matthäus Daniel Pöppelmann**, with a capacity of one quarter of a million litres/ 55,000 gallons. On top of it a dance floor was built with room for 30 couples to tread graceful minuets. At the same time the fortress served to temper any opposition in the country: Johann Fried-

High culture refuge

> ### *Baedeker* TIP
>
> **Tours, concerts and markets**
> From April to October tours take place several times daily (audioguide at other times). Book tours on special themes or night tours at tel. 03 50 21-6 46 07. Organ concerts are held in the garrison church from May to October on the first and third Sunday in the month and at weekends in Advent. The atmospheric Christmas market on the weekends during Advent is not to be missed!

rich Böttger was confined in the Georgenburg state prison (1706–07; ► Famous People), as were such notable historical characters as Chancellor Krell (1591–1601), the anarchist Michail Alexandrovich Bakunin (1849–50), the Socialist August Bebel (1874), author Frank Wedekind (1899) and the painter and illustrator Thomas Theodor Heine (1899). Illustrious guests who came of their own free will included **Tsar Peter I** and Napoleon.

Military museum
In the two arsenals are **exhibitions** of the Dresden military history museum featuring fortress construction and Saxon **military history**. The gatehouse and Magdalenenburg house special exhibitions. In the Georgenbau the history of the state prison is documented, and in the commandant's house it is possible to view the fortress commandant's private rooms as they were around 1900.

✳ Bad Schandau

History
The town dates back to the mid-14th century; it is recorded as Schandau in 1430, and gained a town charter as early as 1445. The economy was founded on trade in wood, grain, wine and fruit, which were shipped down the Elbe as »Bohemian goods« and in tropical fruit, oil, petroleum, herrings and salt, which came upstream as »Hamburg goods«. The discovery of the »red rivulet«, a ferrous spring, led to the beginnings of a spa around 1730; in 1799 the first spa bath-house was built. Since 1920 the town has officially been known as Bad Schandau.

Brauhof
On the market square (no. 12) is the former Brauhof (brew yard), a 1680 Renaissance building with handsome portal and octagonal stair tower on the courtyard side.

St Johannis ►
The late Gothic church of St Johannis, altered in the 17th and 18th centuries, also stands on the market square; it has a sandstone pulpit supported by a figure of Moses, hewn from a single block of stone; the **altar** of 1572 was made originally by Hans Walther II for the ►Kreuzkirche in Dresden.

Lift to Ostrau ►
A 50m/164ft lift, built in 1904 by a hotel owner, goes up to the districts of Ostrau and Postelwitz, where there are pleasant walks between villas and traditional houses, both half-timbered and of the type known as Umgebindehaus, an eastern German type of dwelling that combines the features of a half-timbered house and a blockhouse.

Toskana-Therme in spa treatment house
The Toskana-Therme is a thermal bath which opened in October 2004 in the Kurmittelhaus (spa treatments building). It offers a range of therapies, and the liquid sound system is also an attraction for swimmers: sounds are perceptible underwater as well as above, and lighting effects make the water change colour. There are also special events that include the lighting effects in their programme.

Almost untouched: fresh greenery and cool waters in the Kirnitzsch valley

The permanent exhibition in the Nationalparkhaus Bad Schandau (Dresdner Str. 2b) explains »wilderness« as a process and a living environment. A multi-vision show demonstrates the beauties of the national park. There is a varied programme of events and it is also worth visiting the café (hours: April–Oct, daily 9am–6pm; Nov–March, Tue–Sun 9am–5pm; closed in Jan; www.nationalpark-saechsische-schweiz.de). **Nationalparkhaus**

Lichtenhain Waterfall

Take a tram ride along the romantic valley of the Kirnitzsch from Bad Schandau on the **Kirnitzschtalbahn**, an 8.3km/5.2mi stretch of tramline built in 1898. It takes about half-an-hour to reach the artificially formed Lichtenhain waterfall. This is a good starting-point for excursions, for instance a hike to the Kuhstall rock gate; a narrow cleft in the rock leads to the Wildenstein (336m/1100ft above sea level) – from both spots there is a magnificent view. The Nasse Schlucht and Fremdenweg lead from the Wildenstein to the summit of the Kleiner Winterberg, while in a southerly direction the Fremdenweg merges with the Reitstieg, which leads to the Grosser Winterberg (552m/1811ft above sea level), the highest peak in the Sächsische Schweiz east of the Elbe, where there is also an inn. **Kirnitzschtal**

✳ Schrammsteine

Around 3km/2mi upstream from Bad Schandau the Schrammsteine hiking and climbing regions begin; this is one of the most remark- **Rock climbing** able cliff areas in the Sächsische Schweiz. From the Kirnitzschtal tram stop Ostrauer Brücke a **footpath** leads into the Schrammsteine. There is a tradition of climbing here: what is celebrated today as free climbing was actually invented on the rocks of the Elbe sandstone mountains. Back in the 19th century climbers here already hit on the idea of hammering hooks into the rock only for safety purposes, to prevent a fall, and not in order to pull themselves up, so that the actual climbing relied on the strength of arms and fingers. A first manual appeared in 1913.

★ ★ Schloss

F 7

Location: Schlossplatz
Plan of inner city: B 3

Tram: Postplatz (nos. 1, 2, 4, 6, 8, 9, 11, 12, 47); Theaterplatz (nos. 4, 8, 9)

Next to the reconstruction of the ▶Frauenkirche, the rebuilding of the Schloss, the palace of the rulers of Saxony, is the most ambitious project of its kind in Dresden. The Schloss will be a home for the arts and sciences.

In the first half of the 13th century there was already a kind of citadel to protect the Elbe bridge on the site of the present Schloss. First documented in 1289 as a »castrum«, it was extended in the 15th and 16th centuries according to a plan whereby the Hausmannturm and parts of the north wing were erected in about 1400. In 1469–80 this was extended into a four-winged complex, and from 1485, after the Leipzig Partition, it served as residence for the Albertine Wettin dukes. In 1530–35 Duke Georg added the Georgenbau in early Ren-

Schloss and Stallhof Plan

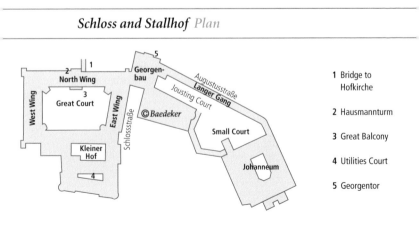

1 Bridge to Hofkirche

2 Hausmannturm

3 Great Balcony

4 Utilities Court

5 Georgentor

aissance style to the existing four-winged building. His successor Duke Moritz had the whole extended into a Schloss (palace), thereby creating one of the most significant Renaissance buildings on German soil. The chapel, the west wing and the Grosser Schlosshof (Great Court) were newly built during this epoch. In 1586–91 the Stallhof (stable yard), Langer Gang (Long Passage) and a stable building now known as the ► Johanneum were added. In 1701 a fire destroyed the Georgenbau and the east wing, which were rebuilt by 1719 in Baroque style. Within a space of six years from 1723, the Grünes Gewölbe was set up as museum of treasures in the west wing. In 1889, the Schloss was given uniform neo-Renaissance façades, a new south wing and a neo-Baroque bridge linking Schloss and Hofkirche to mark the 800th anniversary of the House of Wettin. After the Schloss lost its status as royal residence in 1918 with the abdication of Augustus III, the Schloss museum opened in 1922. In 1945 bombs razed it to the ground.

Although a start was made from 1962 on **rebuilding**, beginning with the Georgenbau, large parts of the Schloss remained as burnt-out ruins for almost 40 years. For the

The Georgentor links Schloss and Stallhof.

800th city jubilee, in 2006, the Schloss was resplendent once again, at least on the outside: the façades around the Grosser Schlosshof with gables and corner towers, the Kleiner Schlosshof and Wirtschaftshof have been rebuilt almost entirely in Renaissance style, the exterior façade in neo-Renaissance form. In 2008 the Georgenbau was finished. In 1991 the Hausmannturm reassumed its traditional place in Dresden's skyline.

Today the Schloss is a palace of **arts and sciences**: in 2002 the library and reading-room of the coin collection (►Albertinum) moved into the Georgenbau, followed in 2004 by the art library (opening hours:

Museums move in

SCHLOSS

✱ ✱ The Schloss, the palace of the rulers of Saxony, is the most venerable building on Schlossplatz, and parts of it are the oldest surviving remains in the entire city. The predominant style is Renaissance and neo-Renaissance. Today the restored Schloss is once more a seat of art and learning; it attracts art lovers and researchers in equal measure, especially since the restoration and reopening of the historic Grünes Gewölbe.

🕐 Opening hours:
Wed–Mon 10am–6pm

① Georgentor
The Georgentor followed two earlier gates. It was built in 1899–1902 and decorated with exuberant sculpture in neo-Renaissance style. The sculpture includes the 4m/13ft equestrian statue of Duke Georg the Bearded, after whom the gate is named, high up on the gable.

② Façades
The rebuilding of Dresden's Schloss involved a compromise between the historic Renaissance forms of the courtyards, neo-Renaissance façades, and contemporary requirements.

A breathtaking work: Johann Melchior Dinglinger's »The Court at Delhi on the Occasion of the Birthday of Grand Mogul Aureng-Zeb« (1701–08)

③ Hausmannturm
The Hausmannturm is accessible via the northeast stairway tower of the great courtyard. It has Dresden's highest viewing platform, looking out over the Elbe valley and Dresden's Altstadt.

④ Grünes Gewölbe (Green Vault)
The Grünes Gewölbe houses exquisite goldsmith work and jewellery. Thanks to its wonderful interior the vault itself is a gem, especially the historic Grünes Gewölbe, a late-Baroque total work of art restored to its original condition of 1733.

⑤ Kupferstichkabinett
The Kupferstichkabinett, a collection of engravings, drawings and graphic art, returned to the Schloss in 2004; this collection was established 450 years ago and is one of the oldest in the world.

⊙ Mon–Fri 10am–6pm) in the south wing and the Kupferstichkabinett (engravings and drawings) on the third floor of the west wing.
The Neues Grünes Gewölbe opened in autumn 2004 in the west
wing, and in September 2006 reconstruction of the historic Grünes
Gewölbe in its Baroque form of 1733 was finished. The
Planned
exhibition
spaces ►
Rüstkammer (armoury) from the ► Zwinger will not occupy the
east wing until about 2010; the so-called Türkische Cammer, however, will open in 2009. After that it is intended that visitors to the
Georgenbau will have a chance to see the Kunstkammer and Cranach Gallery, while visitors to the Langer Gang can see a gallery of
firearms, and also showpiece rooms from Augustus the Strong's
time and an exhibition on court pomp and ceremony.

✳
Georgenbau
The Georgenbau with Georgentor (1898–1901) links the Schloss to
the Stallhof. Of the first Georgentor, the Elbe-side portal (to the
west of the existing gate) has survived as has one of Dresden's most
important Renaissance monuments: the *Dresden Dance of Death*, a
frieze dating from 1534–36 which can now be admired in the ►
Dreikönigskirche.

Hausmannturm
Don't miss the view from the 68m/223ft-high platform of the
Hausmannturm, the city's highest tower at 101m/331ft. It got its
name from the tower guard, or »Hausmann«. It now has the form
given to it by Wolf Caspar von Klengel (1674–76), with a Baroque
roof and slender spire, but the basic structure of the tower is sub-
stantially earlier. In the tower the coin collection is displayed (►Al-
bertinum) with special exhibitions. Hours: April–Oct Wed–Mon
10am–6pm.

✳
Langer Gang
and Stallhof
The Langer Gang (Long Passage), built in 1586–88, links the Georgenbau to the former stable building, the ►Johanneum, today occupied by the transport museum. On the outside, along Augustusstrasse, runs the ►Fürstenzug (Procession of Princes). At the same
time it forms one side of the Stallhof (stable yard), which dates
back to the Renaissance with its round-arched Tuscan arcades. The
Stallhof was once the scene of knightly tournaments and games;
the ring jousting course with its two bronze pillars of 1601 still sur-
vives. In summer there are occasional re-enactments of tournaments.

✳
Schöne Pforte
The Schöne Pforte (Beautiful Gate) made in about 1555 for the
chapel by Giovanni Maria da Padua and Hans Walther II is considered **the finest German Renaissance gateway**, and following restoration has returned to its historic position at the entry to the
chapel. In the niches stand John the Baptist and John the Evangelist on the left, Moses and St Peter on the right. The relief in the
central section of the attica depicts the Resurrection, with Isaiah
and St Paul at the sides.

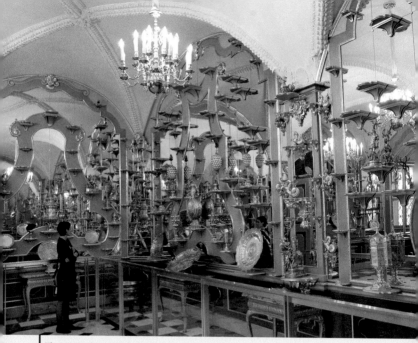

The Historisches Grünes Gewölbe is a total work of art.

★ ★ Grünes Gewölbe

The Grünes Gewölbe (Green Vault) is one of the most magnificent collection of jewels and treasures in the world. The collection owes its name to the electors' secret strongroom, a room with walls painted green in the west wing of the Schloss, where state documents, gold and jewels were kept, and which the inhabitants of the Schloss called »Grünes Gewölbe« from the 16th century. From these holdings, the Kunstkammer and the silver collection, Augustus the Strong assembled a new collection to which additions were constantly made; it was presented to the public for the first time in 1723–24 in this very vault, and from 1730 in a total of eight rooms. These rooms, designed by Matthäus Daniel Pöppelmann, were severely damaged in 1945. Although the collection had been put in storage in 1942, it fell into the hands of Soviet troops at the end of the war and did not return to Dresden until 1958.

Today the treasures are presented in newly renovated rooms in two sections: the Historisches Grünes Gewölbe is a restoration of the original appearance of the rooms which gives the visitor an impression of its full Baroque magnificence, while the Neues Grünes Gewölbe puts the spotlight on individual works of art, which can be examined thoroughly to reveal the love of detail that went into their making.

Historisches Grünes Gewölbe

🕐 Opening hours:
Wed–Mo
10am–7pm

In September 2006 the historic Grünes Gewölbe re-opened in its original location on the ground floor of the west wing: the Schatzkammer, which shows Wettin treasures, has been reconstructed according to Augustus the Strong's initial plan in the form designed by Matthäus Daniel Pöppelmann and realized in 1733 as a late Baroque **total work of art** with splendidly designed display walls and tables. The tour passes through nine rooms, showing the most exquisite items, starting in the Bernsteinkabinett (Amber Room) and passing through the Elfenbeinzimmer (Ivory Room), Weissgoldzimmer (White Gold Room) and Silbervergoldetes Zimmer (Silver Gilt Room) to the Pretiosensaal (Gem Room), which is almost completely covered in mirrors. Beyond that are the Wappenzimmer (Insignia Room) and then the highlight, the Juwelenzimmer (Jewel Room) with the Saxon-Polish crown jewels and electors' jewels. The *Moor with Emerald Slab* (photo p.263 be admired here. **Admission tickets must be pre-booked**: tel. 49 19 12 85 or www.skd-dresden.de!

Neues Grünes Gewölbe

🕐 Opening hours:
Wed–Mo
10am–6pm

There is an unbelievable array of ornamental vessels, drinking vessels, boxes, mirrors, clocks, figurines and diamond jewellery, including one setting with the largest green diamond in the world. Selected treasures are displayed in ten rooms: the southwest corner tower has micro-carvings in wood and ivory, centred on an item very popular with the public: a cherry pip carved in 1589 with 113 heads. A further highlight is the **Dinglinger Room**, which displays 18th-century treasures and collector's pieces, with important works of Augustan Baroque by Balthasar Permoser and **Johann Melchior Dinglinger**. The latter founded the famous Dresden jewellers' school in the late 17th century. Among the multitude of his works on display, special mention must be made of the golden coffee service for Augustus the Strong (1701) and the largest work, the ***Court at Delhi on the Occasion of the Birthday of the Grand Mogul Aureng-Zeb*** with 137 golden and brightly coloured, enamelled figures. Dinglinger, his brother and 14 assistants used 3,000 diamonds, rubies, emeralds and pearls in the seven years from 1701 to 1708 and Augustus the Strong had to meet costs of 58,485 talers, that is to say, 16,485 talers more than he paid for the building of Schloss ►Moritzburg.

A cook playing the griddle (before 1725)

✷ Kupferstichkabinett

🕐 Opening hours:
Wed–Mon
10am–6pm

The Kupferstichkabinett (literally: Copper Engraving Cabinet), is one of the oldest and most extensive collections of graphic art in the world; it was founded as an independent collection in 1720 from holdings of the Kunstkammer set up by Elector August c1560, and there was nothing like it anywhere else except in Paris. Since spring 2004 the Kupferstichkabinett has been located once more in the former rooms of the Kunstkammer on the third floor of the Schloss.

During World War II it was removed for safe keeping to Schloss ► Weesenstein, but after the end of the war it passed into Soviet hands and did not return to Dresden until 1958 – with the loss of approximately 15,000 leaves and the entire library. The spectrum of the Dresden Kupferstichkabinett with about 450,000 single leaves (drawings, prints, engravings, woodcuts, water colours and photographs) extends from the 15th century to the present day. The main emphases of the collection are early copper engravings of the German and Italian Renaissance, 18th-century graphics from England and France, works of the German Romantics and contemporary art from Germany and abroad. The collection of prints ranges from Van Eyck, Dürer and Rembrandt to Toulouse-Lautrec and Picasso; in addition, there are illustrated books and occasional exhibitions of Asian art, portraits and artists' posters.

◄ Graphics collection

> ## ! *Baedeker* TIP
>
> **Performers, musicians and craftworkers**
> The Stallhöfisches Adventsspektakel, held in the Langer Gang in the Schloss, brings the Middle Ages to life with performers, musicians and historic crafts. Mulled blueberry wine and freshly made delicacies are an essential part of the fun.

★ ★ Semper Opera (Sächsische Staatsoper Dresden)

F 7

Location: Theaterplatz
Plan of inner city: A 2

Tram: Theaterplatz (nos. 4, 8, 9)

On 13 February 1985 the world-famous Semper Opera re-opened on Theaterplatz, 40 years after the destruction of the city, with a performance of Weber's *Freischütz*, and a great tradition was resumed.

Reconstruction was based on Gottfried Semper's (►Famous People) second court theatre building of 1878; his first theatre of 1838–41 burnt down in 1869. Semper's involvement in the Dresden uprising of May 1849 forced him to flee, yet nonetheless the citizens of Dresden ensured that he was commissioned to build the second opera house. Semper worked on the plans in Vienna and put his son Manfred in charge of the building process. The second opera house was very different from the first. For the exterior Gottfried Semper used High Renaissance forms: the two-storey arch design of the front and the projecting entrance give the house a festive character. The third storey is set back and forms the transition to the high, unostentatious stage section. This theatre building incorporates Semper's ideal of the unity of form and purpose. The sculptural ornamentation on the roof of the stage section was done by Semper's son Emanuel, the bronze panther quadriga with Dionysos and Ariadne on the central front by Johannes Schilling. The sculptures of

First house on the square

◄ Exterior

◄ Sculptural ornamentation

The exterior merits attention during the day, but only in the evening does the Semper Opera reveal its true splendour

Goethe and Schiller on either side of the entrance, which survived from the first theatre, are by Ernst Rietschel. In the side niches of the façade are sculptures of the dramatists Shakespeare (bottom left), Sophocles (top left), Molière (bottom right) and Euripides (top right). The wings have sculptures of famous figures from theatre and opera. Semper also designed the entire interior and even left instructions for the painting work, which were utilized for the post-World War II reconstruction, so that auditorium, foyers and stairwells could be decorated in their original splendour and bright, festive colours. In the auditorium with royal box the original fifth balcony was sacrificed for the sake of improved viewing. The Semper Opera acoustics are still considered very good today.

Interior ▶

Guided tours take place several times a day; tickets are available only at the beginning of the tour, in the opera house. In order to see a **performance** it is advisable to get tickets in good time (▶ Practicalities, Music). Last-minute tickets are obtainable at the tourist information office (▶ Information); big hotels are also allotted a certain number of tickets.

Stadtmuseum

Location: Wilsdruffer Strasse 2
Plan of inner city: B 3

Tram: Pirnaischer Platz (nos. 1, 2, 3, 4, 7, 12)

The Stadtmuseum (City Museum) has an attractive home in the Landhaus, the only historic building still surviving on Wilsdruffer Strasse.

The Landhaus was built to designs by Friedrich August Krubsacius from 1770 to 1775. Up to 1907 the Saxon »Estates«, i.e. the provincial parliament, met there; then they moved to the Ständehaus (Estates House) on the ► Brühlsche Terrasse. The main front of the Landhaus faces Landhausstrasse rather than Wilsdruffer Strasse; it is classical in design, with six Doric pillars and a pediment. The Wilsdruffer Strasse façade is a more Baroque-looking garden front, with a central section containing the stairwell that extends over three storeys. The double curved Rococo stairs with wrought-iron railings are remarkably beautiful. The old outside portal by Johann Christian Feige the Younger is now the entrance to the Baroque garden in ► Großsedlitz.

✷ Landhaus
⊕ Opening hours:
Tue–Thu, Sat–Sun 10am–6pm, Fri noon–8pm

✷ ◄ Stairwell

The Landhaus has accommodated the city museum since 1965. At present two exhibitions can be seen: until 2010 a special exhibition on the ► Frauenkirche, and a new permanent exhibition devoted to the development of Dresden from its foundation up to the present day. The exhibits include 16th and 17th-century burial finds from the former Sophienkirche, and also stoneware by the firm of Villeroy & Boch. Items of outstanding interest are the oldest city seal (1309) and the wood panel painting *The Ten Commandments* by Hans der Maler (Hans the Painter) of 1528–29. On the first floor the Städtische Galerie Dresden displays its art collection.

Stadtmuseum

◄ Städtische Galerie

✷ Taschenberg Palais

Location: Sophienstrasse/Taschenberg
Plan of inner city: B 2

Tram: Postplatz (nos. 1, 2, 4, 6, 8, 9, 11, 12); Theaterplatz (nos. 4, 8, 9)

Augustus the Strong purchased a house on the Taschenberg in 1705, in order to replace it with a luxurious love nest for himself and his mistress, Countess Cosel.

He awarded the commission to Christoph Beyer, Johann Friedrich Karcher and Matthäus Daniel Pöppelmann; they built the Taschenberg Palais in the years 1705–08, one of the gems of Dresden Rococo

Dresden's grandest palais

The Taschenbergpalais is now a high-class hotel.

architecture. Over the following decades it was extended to include a west wing by Julius Heinrich Schwarze and an east wing by Friedrich Exner. Destroyed during World War II, it was restored and re-opened as a hotel in 1995; the exterior replicates the original, with reconstructed Baroque steps. The east court of honour wing is linked to the Schloss by a walkway.

By the entrance to the Sophienkeller on the Zwinger side of the Taschenberg Palais stands the **Cholerabrunnen**, a neo-Gothic fountain designed by Gottfried Semper and erected in 1843 in thanksgiving when the city was spared the cholera epidemic of 1840–41. Semper gave the fountain the form of an 18m/59ft-high Gothic tower or sacrament tabernacle, modelled on the Schöner Brunnen in Nuremberg.

Technische Sammlungen

G 11

Location: Junghansstrasse 1–3 **Tram:** Pohlandplatz (nos. 4, 10)

Opening hours:
Tue–Fri
9am–5pm,
Sat, Sun
10am–6pm

Science and technology have a long tradition in Dresden: the Technische Sammlungen, founded in 1966 as a technology museum, are located in the Ernemanngebäude, a building erected in 1923–24 by architects Högg and Müller for the Zeiss-Ikon works, and from 1945 headquarters of the Kamerawerke Pentacon.

There is much to be discovered in the museum: photography is a main theme, but there are also exhibits from the areas of electronics, micro-electronics, data processing, calculator, word-processing and entertainment technology, medicine and precision instrument construction, scientific equipment, musical boxes and gramophones. The permanent exhibition on Dresden's fire service history welcomes keen experimenters – in the fire laboratory visitors can try their hand at starting and extinguishing fires.

✶ ✶ Theaterplatz

Location: northern edge of Altstadt   **Tram:** Theaterplatz (nos. 4, 8, 9)
Plan of inner city: B 2

Although Gottfried Semper's plans of 1863 for an extension of the Zwinger as far as the Elbe were never implemented, the alternative solution that was indeed realized resulted in one of the most beautiful squares in Germany.

It is framed by magnificent buildings such as the Sempergalerie in the ►Zwinger, the ►Hofkirche, the ►Schloss, the ►Taschenberg Palais, the ►Semper Opera, the Altstädter Wache (guardhouse) and the Italian Village.

The Altstädter Wache was built in 1830–32 to designs by Karl Friedrich Schinkel. It is his only work in Dresden and one of the few instances of neo-classical architecture in the city. The pediment figure of Saxonia is by Joseph Herrmann, that of Mars by Franz Pettrich. The building was burnt down in 1945 and rebuilt by 1956, and now houses the tourist information office (►Information) and the advance booking office of the Sächsische Staatsoper (►Theatre, Music, Concerts).

Altstädter Wache (guardhouse)

Towards the Elbe, the square is completed by the »Italienisches Dörfchen« (Italian Village), which **Hans Erlwein** built in 1911–13.

Italienisches Dörfchen

This square has everything: tranquil grandeur and brilliantly illuminated opulence.

Although the name suggests a considerable number of houses, there is actually only one building. It gets its name from the workshop and living quarters of Italian artists and craftsmen who were here in the 18th century to work on the Hofkirche. The task of completing the Theaterplatz architecturally on the side towards the Elbe while at the same time preserving the sight lines across the river from both sides, a true challenge for an urban planner, was solved by Erlwein in masterly fashion. There is a two-storey central building with the former beer hall and dining-room adjoining as a raised pavilion. The neoclassical façade with its three-bay central section fits harmoniously into the overall architecture of the square. Figures by Georg Wrba adorn the pediment; Wrba and his pupils were also responsible for the lively sculptural works all round the building. The exquisite and buoyant decoration of ceilings and walls by Dresden artists was destroyed in 1945, but restored in the present café and restaurant. The terraced garden, the steps down to the bank of the Elbe and the Basteischlösschen restaurant, created in 1913 by Karl Hirschmann, complete the square on the north side.

Equestrian statue of King Johann The equestrian statue of King Johann put up in the centre of the square in 1889,is the work of Johannes Schilling. King Johann reigned from 1854 to 1873; under the pseudonym »Philalethes« he published a three-volume translation of Dante's *Divine Comedy* between 1839 and 1849.

Carl Maria von Weber monument In the east corner of the square, between the Zwinger rampart and picture gallery, stands the monument to Carl Maria von Weber; he is portrayed leaning on a music stand. It is considered the best work of the Dresden sculptor Ernst Rietschel.

✳ **Schloss Weesenstein**

Location: 15km/9.5mi southeast of Dresden

S-Bahn: S 1 to Heidenau, then by regional rail in the direction of Altenberg

Schloss Weesenstein in the Müglitz valley was the favourite residence of King Johann, who reigned from 1854 to 1873.

🕐
Opening hours:
April–Oct daily
9am–6pm;
Nov–March daily
10am–5pm
Guided tours:
Sun 3pm

It developed out of a border castle founded *c*1200. The irregular complex of buildings with a round tower of 1300 is in part hewn into the rock and has eight storeys. From the 15th century it was enlarged by the counts of Bünau into a castle and residence; the imposing Schloss dates back to the 16th century, and was given its splendid Renaissance portal in 1575.

Schloss Weesenstein, banqueting hall with leather wall-covering →

The old chapel of 1504 was replaced in 1738–41 by an oval chapel designed by Johann Georg Schmidt, a pupil of George Bähr. It has an outstanding altar with figures by Benjamin Thomae. The beginnings of the park beside the Müglitz date back to 1600; in about 1780 it was re-shaped as a park in the French style. Severely damaged by the flood of 2002, it has been newly laid out.

! **Baedeker** TIP

Cheers!
Schloss Weesenstein has its own brewery, with a history going back to 1510. Here there is live music every Wednesday from 7pm, and on the first Sunday in the month wild boar is roasted on a spit (tel. 03 50 27-4 20 04).

On the lower floors there is an exhibition on the life and work of King Johann, which also features his translation of Dante's *Divine Comedy.* Schloss Weesenstein is well known for its unusual diversity of wall-coverings made of leather, textiles and paper, for its picture tapestries and painted wall-coverings. There are regular readings and children's events in the Schloss; in the chapel there is organ music on Sundays at noon.

★ Wall-coverings ▶

★ **Weisser Hirsch** (city district)

E 12 / 13

Location: northeast
Funicular: from Loschwitz

Tram: Plattleite (no. 11)

At Weisser Hirsch, high up above the Elbe, there are no spectacular sights to be visited, but it is worth just taking a walk to look at the lovely villas with their gardens, mostly with wonderful views.

High-class residences

The district takes its name from an inn called Weisser Hirsch (The White Stag), which was built in 1688. In the last 20 years of the 19th century this became a fashionable residential area with a spa house, so that it was first designated »Weisser Hirsch Climatic Health Resort«, to which the title »Bad« (spa) was added in 1931. It continued to be favoured by the affluent; after 1945 prominent Dresden citizens such as state and party officials, scientists and artists still lived here. The whole residential area, extending along the Elbe slopes from Weisser Hirsch to Loschwitz, with almost 200 listed buildings, may be regarded as a kind of open-air museum of bourgeois villa architecture. The buildings are in a great variety of architectural styles, from art nouveau to Swiss Alpine.

Villa walk

Former Lahmann Sanatorium ▶

Opposite the tram stop, in Stechgrundstrasse, the Park Hotel stands on the right, in front of the Waldpark; it was built in 1914 in art nouveau style, and its Blauer Salon is now a popular venue for parties. On the other side of the road is the crumbling central Kurhaus

View of the Elbe slopes from the Blaues Wunder, with Weisser Hirsch at the top

of the former sanatorium founded by Dr Heinrich Lahmann. The founding of this particularly elegant sanatorium in 1888 was a key factor in elevating Weisser Hirsch to the status of a spa, and made it one of the most sought-after in Europe. Villa Urvasi was built in 1912 as part of the Lahmann Sanatorium with an extensive balcony front in Swiss style.

Across Bautzner Strasse, straight along Plattleite and then immediately right into the elegant Lahmannring, the villa at Lahmannring no. 3, and others, tell of glamorous times. To the right on the corner of Wolfshügelstrasse and Hermann-Prell-Strasse is the prominent art nouveau Villa Elbblick. Further along Wolfshügelstrasse is the striking Villa Abendstern. Turning right across Plattleite and then left the whole length of the Bergbahnstrasse, leads to Villa San Remo (no. 12) with its extravagant tower. From the adjacent Luisenhof restaurant, the »balcony of Dresden«, there is a fabulous view of the city and its surroundings. The inn was named after the wife of the last king of Saxony, Luise of Tuscany, in 1895; she set tongues wagging when she ran away with the composer Enrico Toselli, who was also her children's piano teacher. From Luisenhof the funicular goes down to ►Loschwitz, where there is a choice between extending the walk, crossing over the ► Blaues Wunder, or returning by river to Dresden.

The surprising dome of Yenidze illuminated at night

★ Yenidze

F 6

Location: southeast bridgehead of
Marienbrücke (Weisseritzstr.3)

Tram: Haus der Presse
(nos. 6, 11)

The most unusual building in Dresden is the former »Yenidze Oriental Tobacco and Cigarette Factory« on the eastern edge of ►Friedrichstadt, whose name derives from the tobacco-growing area around the Turkish town of Yenidze.

The building, visible from afar, rises up like a mosque with its 18m/ 59ft coloured glass dome, which is illuminated from within, and minaret chimney. The Dresden cigarette manufacturer Hugo Zietz awarded the commission to architect Hermann Martin Hammitzsch, and between 1907 and 1912 Hammitzsch erected one of Germany's first reinforced concrete buildings for the Yenidze tobacco company. At the time the tobacco mosque caused heated controversy and even led to Hammitzsch's ex-

> ! **Baedeker TIP**
>
> **Tales of 1001 Nights**
>
> When young and old gather under the illuminated dome of Yenidze to listen to a story-teller, it is like a scene from the Orient – especially when a belly-dancer performs (tickets: Tue, Wed 10am–2pm, Thu 2pm–6pm, tel. 495 10 01).

clusion from the architects' association. From 1952 cigarette production no longer took place here, and Yenidze was used as a tobacco store until the building gradually fell into disrepair. One attraction of the present building, which was converted into an office complex in 1997, is the Yenidze dome with hall, restaurant and **Dresden's loftiest beer garden**.

✶ ✶ Zwinger

F / G 7

Location: between Theaterplatz and Ostra-Allee
Plan of inner city: B 2

Tram: Postplatz (nos. 1, 2, 4, 6, 8, 9, 11, 12, 47); Theaterplatz (nos. 4, 8)

The Zwinger, built from 1709 to 1732, is a masterpiece unparalleled anywhere in the world, an apogee of the Baroque style and one of the most famous and original architectural works of art in existence.

Two artists of genius, architect Matthäus Daniel Pöppelmann (▶Famous People) and sculptor Balthasar Permoser (▶Famous People), summarized the architectural vocabulary of their time in a total work of art, in which clarity and restraint in building blend with the magical abundance and playful excess of Baroque sculpture. The Zwinger is also inseparably linked with the name of its patron, Augustus the Strong.

Opening hours:
Tue–Sun
10am–6pm

Initially the site was intended for splendid open-air festivals; it was given a wooden backdrop on the occasion of the visit of the king of Denmark in 1709. A year later Pöppelmann began to replace the temporary wooden structures with stone buildings. First the galleries and pavilions on the rampart side were constructed. By 1719 the Langgalerie with Kronentor and the corner pavilions on the Schloss side had been added. For the marriage of Elector Friedrich August II to Maria Josepha of Habsburg in 1719 Pöppelmann had to close the open space towards the Schloss as well. Initially he put up temporary wooden buildings that anticipated the curved galleries with corner pavilions and the city-side pavilion, now the Glockenspiel pavilion; by 1728 they had been executed in stone. Until 1847 the Elbe side of the building complex was enclosed by a high wall; then the present picture gallery was constructed on this spot to plans by Gottfried Semper. In the bombing of February 1945 the Zwinger was so badly

Architectural history

❓ DID YOU KNOW …?

■ … where the name Zwinger comes from? The German word »zwingen« means to constrain and the courtyard inside fortifications was called the Zwingerhof because enemy troops could be trapped there.

damaged that it seemed to have been lost for ever. However, rebuilding began in the same year, and continued until 1963.

Kronentor and Langgalerien

The magnificent Kronentor (Crown Gate) facing the Ostra-Allee is actually the main entrance to the Zwingerhof (courtyard). Its curved onion-shaped cupola rises up from the Langgalerie (Long Gallery) on Zwingergraben. Four gilded Polish eagles and the royal crown complete it; perhaps they were meant to represent German imperial eagles, since for a short time Augustus had hopes of becoming emperor. The lower storey of the Kronentor has an angled entablature and broken pediments; the first floor is set back, with filigree open work, and the attica is richly adorned with figures. The Langgalerien link the Kronentor to the corner pavilions and Bogengalerien (curved galleries).

Nymphenbad

The Nymphenbad with its playful water displays and nymphs is one of Balthasar Permoser's chief works; further works by him in the Zwinger are the central groups on the Wallpavillon and the Ceres, Vulcan and Venus of the Kronentor. The Nymphenbad is behind the

Zwinger Plan

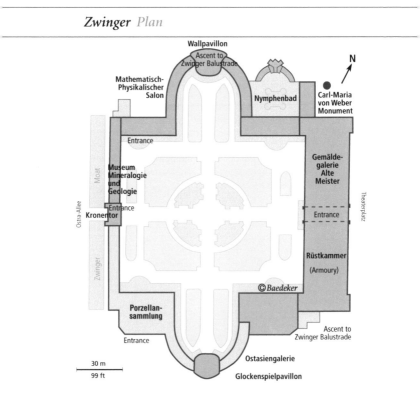

French pavilion and can be reached via the Wallpavillon; it is an intimate spot within the Zwinger grounds. In the centre is a subdivided square pond, into which water cascades from pool to pool from the height of the Zwinger rampart. The stalactite-like ornamentation, the grotto, water-spouting dolphins and Tritons enliven the fantasy design, into which the nymphs in the niches fit harmoniously. The nymphs on the southwest side are for the most part copies made in the 1920s, while those on the northwest side are mostly 18th-century statues by Permoser, Kirchner, Thomae and Egell. The nymph with the shell, the one going to the bath and the one leaving the bath, all on the left-hand side towards the cascade, were made by Balthasar Permoser himself. While restoration work is being undertaken in the ►Albertinum, a selection of its excellent sculptures is on display on the ground floor of the French Pavilion (Nymphenbad passage; opening hours: Tue–Sun 10am–6pm; entrance in Zwingerhof).

◄ Sculpture collection ◷

The Wallpavillon (rampart pavilion) of 1716 is the truly perfect part of the Zwinger, and at the same time the most significant of Pöppelmann's works. Consummate mastery of the principles of architecture and sculpture allows the building to dissolve, as it were, into a living sculpture. It is crowned by Permoser's 6m/20ft Hercules Saxonicus bearing the globe. Permoser carved the satyr herms straight from the stone, without preparatory models. The Saxon-Polish arms on the gable are surrounded by trumpeting sprites. On one side the youthful Augustus the Strong as Paris, with a royal orb instead of an apple in his hand, turns to Aphrodite while the »scorned« goddesses stand on the other side. The four winds announce the fame of the elector and king to the world. Throughout the Zwinger wonderfully designed flights of steps contribute to the overall architectural impression.

Wallpavillon

Later, whren the Glockenspiel Pavilion opposite came to be built, it was simply not possible to surpass the Wallpavillon. In 1924–36 a glockenspiel of Meissen porcelain was installed, as Pöppelmann had originally planned, giving the pavilion its special feature.

Glockenspiel Pavilion

It required an architect of Gottfried Semper's genius to create a building that simultaneously fitted into the whole ensemble and yet had its own individuality. Since 1855 the neo-Renaissance Sempergalerie has filled what had been an opening between Zwinger and Theaterplatz; with its triple portico it takes up the Kronentor axis, while at the same time creating a balanced contrast. The façade on the Zwinger side differs in design from that on the ►Theaterplatz side, in keeping with the surroundings. The sculptures of the gallery building (►Gemäldegalerie Alte Meister) are the work of Ernst Rietschel, Ernst Julius Hähnel and Johannes Schilling.

Sempergalerie

On several occasions between mid-May and early September the Zwingerhof is used as a wonderful location for open-air concerts.

Zwingerhof concerts

ZWINGER

★ ★ This palace is a world-famous masterpiece of Baroque architecture and was once August the Strong's symbol of power and glory: Here he celebrated great open-air festivals and gave extravagant balls. Nowadays the Zwinger's summer serenades give some idea of what it must have been like. The Zwinger displays the most exquisite art treasures, such as the famous gallery of Old Masters (Gemäldegalerie Alte Meister), the valuable porcelain collection and the impressive armoury.

🕐 Opening hours:
Tue–Sun 10am–6pm

① Wallpavillon (Rampart Pavilion)
The pavilion, dating from 1716, is the most significant work of Matthäus Daniel Pöppelmann. It is crowned by the 6m/20ft figure of Hercules Saxonicus, a work of the sculptor Balthasar Permoser, who adorned large sections of the Zwinger palace and grounds with exuberant sculptural ornamentation.

② Kronentor (Crown Gate)
The main entrance Kronentor rises above the Langgalerie on the Zwingergraben with its curved onion-shaped roof. The copper roof is partially gilded: Originally all the Zwinger roofs were blue and the walls were painted white, which, together with the gilding, represented the House of Wettin colours of blue, gold and white.

③ Sempergalerie
Since 1855 the Sempergalerie in the style of the High Renaissance has occupied the side of the Zwinger facing Theaterplatz, which until that time had been open. Semper said of his building: »The buildings are all united by a gallery which goes right round them … many residents of the city would like to take a walk and enjoy the sights that they can see there«.

④ Mathematisch-Physikalischer Salon
The northwest part of the Zwinger dates back to the first building phase and consists of two corner pavilions, both with two floors, which were originally linked by a single-storey curved gallery. This gallery served in August the Strong's day as an orangery. The middle of the gallery was subsequently rebuilt as the Wallpavillon.

⑤ Zwingerhof
The courtyard measures 116 x 204m/380 x 670ft on the inside, 170 x 240m/558 x 787ft on the outside.

⑥ Nymphenbad
The Nymphenbad, between the Wallpavillon and Sempergalerie, unites architecture, sculpture and fountains in a small space. Two curving stairs connect the lower floor with the elevated Wall-plateau.

⑦ Glockenspielpavillon
The glockenspiel of Meissner porcelain on the courtyard side was planned by Pöppelmann but not executed until the Zwinger was restored (1924–36).

An example of the lively and expressiveness power of Baroque sculpture.

✷ ✷ Porcelain Collection

Opening hours:
Tue–Sun
10am–6pm
Guided tour:
Thu 4pm

The Zwinger entrance through the Glockenspiel Pavilion leads to one of the most important porcelain collections in the world, which was established by Augustus the Strong in 1711 and is displayed today in the southwest pavilion and Bogengalerie. Augustus the Strong's passion for collecting embraced both products from his own factory and older pieces from the Far East; the result was a collection which can be rivalled only by those in the Istanbul seraglio and in Taipeh. At the entrance stand two of the 18 famous, or notorious, **dragoon vases**, which were obtained by Augustus the Strong from Friedrich Wilhelm I of Prussia in exchange for 600 of his cavalrymen, the Saxon dragoons – which works out at approximately 33 dragoons per vase. The exhibition displays Chinese ceramics from the 3rd century BC to the 17th-century Ming dynasty, burial goods from the Tang era, and early Japanese and Korean ceramics of the 16th–18th centuries, together with Japanese Imari porcelain of c1700. The museum has Meissen porcelain of the early and most brilliant era (1730–60) with large figures by Johann Joachim Kaendler and Johann Christian Kirchner, and also items from the Marcolini era (1768–1814).

East Asian Gallery

In 2006 the Ostasien-Galerie in the curved gallery to the east of the Glockenspielpavillon was added to the porcelain collection. Exquisite pieces of Far Eastern porcelain are on display here, including the so-called Vogelbauer Vase from Japan, the Chinese Qianlong Vase from the emperor's personal collection and Japanese Imari porcelain from the period around 1700.

✷ Mathematisch-Physikalischer Salon

Opening hours:
Tue–Sun
10am–6pm

The entrance in the northwest pavilion leads to the Mathematisch-Physikalischer Salon, which displays marvellous pre-industrial scientific instruments and timepieces from a period of 500 years.

This is one of the oldest and most important collections of scientific and technical instruments, and the largest German collection of terrestrial and celestial globes. The collections originated in a special selection of the treasures in the Kunstkammer and Naturalienkammer, which were merged in 1730 to form the basis of the Mathematisch-Physikalischer Salon.

The exhibits include instruments, apparatus and tools used in mathematics, physics, astronomy, chronometry, geodesy, geography, meteorology and calculation, including the oldest calculating machine in the world (1642) by Blaise Pascal, and also world maps and atlases. Among the greatest treasures are an Arab celestial globe of 1279, a globe clock of 1586 and a clock collection with a number of unique pieces, including a model of the Semper Opera's 5-minute clock of 1896.

✸ ✸ Rüstkammer (Armoury)

From the 16th to the 18th century the Saxon electors acquired show-piece arms, chain mail, hunting and equestrian equipment for their armoury, and in this way created one of the largest and most valuable collections of such items. More than 1300 exhibits from the whole of Europe and the Orient convey a sense of court festivities, knightly tournaments and the hunt. The best pieces are displayed in the armoury in the east wing of the Sempergalerie, which gives an overview of the skills of weapon smiths and craftsmen in past centuries. The exhibits include hunting weapons and gear, swords and daggers, jousting weapons, combination guns, oriental weapons and splendid garments. They give ample testimony to the cultural, military and political standing of Saxony during the Renaissance and Baroque eras. Among the most handsome pieces are the parade armour of the Swedish king Erik XIV for horse and rider (1562–64), children's armour belonging to the Saxon electors, the tournament equipment of Elector Augustus (1550–60), the elector's sword of Moritz of Saxony (1547) and blades fashioned by Spanish sword makers as well as fantasy helmets and shields for Baroque court festivals. The armoury is currently still in the Sempergalerie of the Zwinger; when the Schloss is fully restored the collection will return to its original home, as the »Türkische Cammer« already has.

Opening hours:
Tue–Sun
10am–6pm

Museum of Mineralogy and Geology

This museum too has its origins in the Kunstkammer of 1560; the first mention of exhibits in 1587 makes it one of the world's oldest museums of geology. The present-day collections include 400,000 mineral, fossil and stone items; most of them, however, are in store and only available to researchers. There are special collections of meteorites, tertiary plant fossils, and stones used for building and ornamentation. Further rarities are the precious silver steps from the historic Erzgebirge silver mine, the 21 eggs laid by a duck-billed dinosaur, and the female fish dinosaur with embryo.

Opening hours:
Tue–Sun
10am–6pm

INDEX

LIST OF MAPS AND ILLUSTRATIONS

PHOTO CREDITS

PUBLISHER'S INFORMATION

Illustrations etc: 175 illustrations, 30 maps and diagrams, one large city plan
Text: Dr. E.-G. Bauer, Rainer Eisenschmid, Margit Grünewald, Dr. Manfred Heirler, Dorothee Kaltenbacher, Helmut Linde, Christoph Münch, Hans Rösner
Editing: Baedeker editorial team (John Sykes)
Translation: Charity Scott-Stokes
Cartography: Franz Huber, Munich; MAIRDUMONT/Falk Verlag, Ostfildern (city plan)
3D illustrations: jangled nerves, Stuttgart
Design: independent Medien-Design, Munich; Kathrin Schemel

Editor-in-chief: Rainer Eisenschmid, Baedeker Ostfildern

1st edition 2009
Based on Baedeker Allianz Reiseführer
»Dresden«, 12. Auflage 2009

BAEDEKER GUIDE BOOKS AT A GLANCE
Guiding the World since 1827

DEAR READER,

We would like to thank you for choosing this Baedeker travel guide. It will be a reliable companion on your travels and will not disappoint you.
This book describes the major sights, of course, but it also recommends the best pubs, as well as hotels in the luxury and budget categories, and includes tips about where to eat or go shopping and much more, helping to make your trip an enjoyable experience. Our author Margit Grünewald ensures the quality of this information by making regular journeys to Dresden and putting all her know-how into this book.

Nevertheless, experience shows us that it is impossible to rule out errors and changes made after the book goes to press, for which Baedeker accepts no liability. Please send us your criticisms, corrections and suggestions for improvement: we appreciate your contribution. Contact us by post or e-mail, or phone us:

▶ **Verlag Karl Baedeker GmbH**
Editorial department
Postfach 3162
73751 Ostfildern
Germany
Tel. 49-711-4502-262, fax -343
www.baedeker.com
www.baedeker.co.uk
E-Mail: baedeker@mairdumont.com